Some of It Was Fun

C.1

Nicholas deB. Katzenbach

Some of It Was Fun

Working with RFK and LBJ

W.W. Norton & Company | *New York* | *London*

For information about permission to reproduce selections from this
book, write to Permissions, W. W. Norton & Company, Inc.,
500 Fifth Avenue, New York, NY 10110

For information about special discounts for bulk purchases, please
contact W. W. Norton Special Sales at specialsales@wwnorton.com
or 800-233-4830

Manufacturing by Courier / Westford
Book design by Judith Stagnitto Abbate / Abbate Design
Production manager: Andrew Marasia

Library of Congress Cataloging-in-Publication Data

Katzenbach, Nicholas deB. (Nicholas deBelleville), 1922–
Some of it was fun : working with RFK and LBJ /
Nicholas deB. Katzenbach. — 1st ed.
p. cm.
Includes index.
ISBN 978-0-393-06725-5 (hardcover)
1. Katzenbach, Nicholas deB. (Nicholas deBelleville), 1922–
2. Kennedy, Robert F., 1925–1968—Friends and associates.
3. Johnson, Lyndon B. (Lyndon Baines), 1908–1973—Friends and
associates. 4. United States. Dept. of Justice—Officials and employees
—Biography. 5. Attorneys general—United States—Biography.
6. United States. Dept. of State—Officials and employees
—Biography. 7. United States—Politics and government—
1961–1963. 8. United States—Social conditions—1960–1980.
9. Civil rights movements—United States—History—20th century.
10. Vietnam War, 1961–1975—United States. I. Title.
E840.8.K285A3 2008
973.922—dc22
2008017688

W. W. Norton & Company, Inc.
500 Fifth Avenue, New York, N.Y. 10110
www.wwnorton.com

W. W. Norton & Company Ltd.
Castle House, 75/76 Wells Street, London W1T 3QT

1 2 3 4 5 6 7 8 9 0

For Lydia, of course

Preface

I HAVE HAD GREAT LUCK IN MY LIFE: IN LOVE AND FAMILY AND FRIENDS and colleagues, in opportunities and responsibilities that have come my way. What follows are some random reflections on that good fortune.

This book contains recollections of eight years working for Bobby Kennedy in the Department of Justice and for President Lyndon Johnson as attorney general and undersecretary of state. It is not intended to be a historical work of scholarship, and it contains no significant new facts about the Kennedy and Johnson administrations. Nor is it by any means a complete account of what went on; it is simply what I remember and what, often arbitrarily, I have chosen to write about.

The book covers the period from 1961 to 1969—a time of collective optimism, full of energy and determination on the part of many of us, mostly World War II veterans, who gathered in Washington in 1961. There were successes and there were failures, and one could learn from both.

The bulk of what I have written is from memory, occasionally refreshed by newspaper clippings, oral histories, or books describing these events. I often had to go to such sources for dates, since after all these years, events sometimes seem to merge or get out of sequence. The conversations I have quoted, including those involving Presidents Kennedy and Johnson, are as I remember them—not accurate transcriptions but rather condensations of what I believe was said. While I vouch for the substance with confidence, I cannot do the same for the precise words.

Some of the conversations were transcribed, and in those cases scholars can check my representation that the condensations are substantively correct. I hope they are and I have tried hard to make them so, but I am aware that the mind is a very creative organ.

In my description of events I have tried to be factual and objective. But I know from experience that other actors would include different facts in their accounts. Where there are many participants—as in the legislative process—no one (including the best historians) ever has the complete picture, and each participant has a slightly different view arising from a somewhat different perspective. In most such cases, no actor has a monopoly on truth.

I had not met any of the Kennedys or Lyndon Johnson before I entered the administration in 1961, and much of the book describes getting to know them as I worked with them and struggled to understand our government. I grew to admire both Bobby Kennedy and Lyndon Johnson, though they certainly did not like each other. Both men had great strengths and, like all humans, flaws as well. Johnson's were perhaps more obvious to the world, and I think today the fact that Bobby was seen then by many as ruthless tends to be forgotten. Bobby was sometimes immature (although he matured rapidly), brash, and blunt. But for the tragedy of Vietnam, Johnson might well have gone down in history as a great president.

I think there are lessons from this period that are applicable today, and I try to set out some of them for the reader to judge. We certainly have not learned the lessons of Vietnam, and I am not particularly optimistic that we ever will. It will be obvious to the reader that the political system was very different in the sixties than it is today and that I am not happy with the direction in which we have traveled. Our most important legislation then depended on bipartisan support, and of the hundreds of calls I made on members of both houses of Congress, I can recall very few that were not discussions centered on the merits of the legislation, whether it dealt with civil rights, immigration, prison reform, or federal criminal law. Money was less important, and so was a member of Congress's dependence on those who could contribute it. I do not mean they did not consider politics. They did, but it was largely local—how the people of their state or district felt, not fear of alienating a large national interest group or major donors.

The president today has far more power than did either President Kennedy or President Johnson. That too is largely a function of the president's extraordinary fund-raising capabilities and the effects of mass communications. There is an obvious temptation to move further right or left because that is where the money is, even if the votes may still be closer to the center.

How much of the experience I had in the sixties is relevant today is obviously for the reader to decide. I think it is worth contemplating the many changes that have occurred and weighing which are of benefit to the people, which are not, and what can be done about the latter.

I hope young people will have the passion for government I had many years ago (and still have). It is, after all, their future that is at stake.

NICHOLAS deB. KATZENBACH
Princeton, New Jersey

Some of It Was Fun

I

I FOLLOWED THE 1960 PRESIDENTIAL CAMPAIGN FROM GENEVA, Switzerland, where I was on leave from the faculty of the University of Chicago Law School on a Ford Foundation fellowship. Earlier that year I had watched the Democratic convention on television before leaving for a tour of France and England with my two young sons. John F. Kennedy was an attractive candidate, with his youth, good looks, and a distinguished war record that particularly appealed to those of us who, like him, had been junior officers in World War II. President Eisenhower, despite his distinction and patented smile, was scarcely one of us. No general officer really was; they were too far removed from our experience.

We wanted to change the world and, in a sense, felt we had earned the right to try. Eight years of Ike had been mostly business as usual—or so it seemed.

Kennedy's choice of Senator Lyndon Johnson as his running mate was a little worrisome. Part of Kennedy's appeal was that he did not look or act like a politician, and Johnson's reputation was in strong contrast—the consummate political leader of the Senate, the wheeler-dealer, the great compromiser. It was hard to know what, if anything, he stood for, despite rhetoric reminiscent of the New Deal. One could understand the politics underlying his selection, but his candidacy contributed nothing to the excitement that JFK would ignite. That Bobby Kennedy was said to have opposed his brother's choice for a vice president made Bobby all the more appealing to me.

I had never met Senator Kennedy or any of his family. Had I remained in Chicago, I might have volunteered to help in the campaign, as many of my friends had done. But we had our family plans for a year in Switzerland, and that prospect too was exciting. Once I was off with my sons, Chris and John, for our European tour, I followed the campaign in the *International Herald Tribune* as best as I could, and scoured French newspapers for tidbits of news when I could not find the *Trib.* When my wife, Lydia, arrived in Geneva in September with our two very young daughters, she brought with her American newspapers, at my request. The election was obviously going to be close. It captured my interest and excitement far more than my research in international law.

After Kennedy was elected by a hair in November, I began to fret that while Washington would be home to an administration I could identify with, I was stuck in Switzerland with no part in it. As the names of possible appointees became public, I felt more and more left out. Adam Yarmolinsky, who had succeeded me as editor in chief of the *Yale Law Journal*, was helping Sargent Shriver put together lists of potential appointees. Abram Chayes, a Harvard Law professor and friend who, like me, taught international law, was being considered for appointment as legal adviser to the new secretary of state—a post I would have killed for. And to top it off, Byron White, a friend from my student days at Yale Law, was named deputy attorney general to help young Bobby Kennedy in the Justice Department. I wanted desperately to be a part of what would be going on in Washington.

"Well," said Lydia, "why don't you call Byron and ask him if there are any possibilities?" So I did.

Byron had graduated a year ahead of me at law school, and we had shared some seminars. I do not think I had spoken to him in the thirteen years since then, but he was as warm on the phone as though we had been together often. He had a dry sense of humor and seldom spoke more words than were necessary to make his point.

"I don't know of anything in Geneva," he said, "but if you are serious, you'd better get to Washington in a hurry."

I took a plane the following day.

I met with Adam Yarmolinsky, who sent me on to talk to others. Because I was teaching international law courses at Chicago, my interest was primarily in the State Department. But I had no country or regional expertise, and the principal law job, legal adviser, was clearly going to Abe Chayes. Somewhat discouraged by what seemed like a succession of closed doors, I turned again to Byron. Byron said he was putting together a team to help Bobby Kennedy in the Justice Department. Would I be interested? He had already recruited Louis Oberdorfer, another Yale Law star, for the Tax Division and was trying to persuade Burke Marshall, a close friend of mine since high school and another successor as editor in chief of the *Law Journal* at Yale, to head the Antitrust Division. Though I had not yet met the young attorney general designate, I began to feel that Justice was where I belonged. I told Byron that of course I would be interested, and he said he would take it up with Bobby.

Byron also discussed with me some of the others who were being considered for appointment to top department positions and asked me for suggestions. I think I may have made my greatest contribution to the Justice Department, and for that matter to the Kennedy administration, when I told Byron that I doubted Burke would accept the antitrust post. He had just been made a partner in the prestigious law firm of Covington and Burling and badly needed the extra income. (At that time assistant attorneys general were paid $15,000 annually.) But I thought he might be persuaded to take the civil rights post because of the strong convictions on racial equality he shared with his wife, Violet. He did in fact accept that position, where he became the architect of the government's civil rights policy and one of the great public servants of our time.

The job Byron suggested as a possibility for me was to head the Office of Legal Counsel. At the time I had never heard of it and had little idea of what it did or how important it was. He arranged an appointment with Bobby, and I had my interview at the appointed time. I have no clear recollection of the meeting. Bobby seemed to me very young, and I got the impression he did not know any more than I did what the legal counsel did. Mostly we talked about my teaching— he called me Professor Katzenbach, and I wasn't sure there wasn't an edge to the "Professor"—and academic interests, my young family in Geneva, why I wanted to join the Kennedy administration, and how I knew Byron. He told me about other appointments in the department. Herbert J. (Jack) Miller, an able young Republican lawyer whom he had worked with on the Hoffa investigation while on the staff of the Senate Labor Committee, would head the Criminal Division. William Orrick, another capable lawyer, from San Francisco, who had worked in the campaign, would head the Civil Division. He asked about Burke Marshall, I think, because he knew the importance of civil rights to the Kennedy administration and was uncertain about the modest and laconic Burke. In truth, there was no civil rights policy at the time, and I believe Bobby was concerned that the appointment of an identified civil rights activist such as Harris Wofford, who had worked hard in the campaign and wanted and deserved the job, might encourage civil rights leaders to expect more than the Kennedys could deliver. Fortunately, Harris and Burke were close friends, notwithstanding very different personalities, and Harris got a job in the White House, where he worked closely with Burke on race.

I could not help liking Bobby, although he scarcely fit my concept of an attorney general. I was excited by his obvious enthusiasm and by the quite extraordinary young people he was bringing into the department. More than any other person I met in Washington those two or three days in late December, Bobby confirmed my conviction that this was *our* administration, that my generation was taking charge. I was thirty-eight at the time.

The very next day, somewhat to my surprise, Byron told me that Bobby had decided to ask the president to appoint me assistant attorney general heading the Office of Legal Counsel but that I was not to tell anyone outside my family until it was announced. I returned to Geneva to make arrangements for my family to remain there so the children could finish the school year while I went to Washington.

The current head of the Office of Legal Counsel, Professor Keller of Georgetown, decided that he wished to remain in office until the end of January, when a new term started at the law school. While his refusal to resign with the change in administration was a little awkward for me, it was easy to understand why a new, young attorney general did not want to make a fuss. What impressed me, however, was Bobby's candor in talking to me about the situation, his finding me an office for the week or so I needed it, and most of all the respect he showed for my predicament. He said he wanted to see nothing from the Legal Counsel's Office that had not been approved by me, and he included me, not Keller, in all staff meetings. It was not much, but it certainly meant a great deal to me at the time. It is simply an early example of Bobby's empathy—one reason that the people around Bobby were so loyal to him.

Despite the minor embarrassment of being excluded from my office and ensconced in a temporary one in the law library, the first few days in the Justice Department were heady ones. For one thing, I learned about the responsibilities and duties of the Office of Legal Counsel. It had its origins as a spin-off from the Solicitor General's Office and was originally called the Office of the Assistant Solicitor General. Its most important duty was to give legal advice to the attorney general, and my position was sometimes referred to as "the attorney general's lawyer"—a description I later used in my confirmation hearing. The office reviewed important constitutional questions and legislative problems for the AG and, when requested, for other divisions, including the FBI, Prisons, and Immigration. Most important, at that time the attorney general gave the White House its legal advice; there was no competing White House counsel, though that title was used. Thus the Office of Legal Counsel served in effect as White House legal adviser (subject, of course, to the attorney general), and it had important files on past advice given. This role had occasionally been a source of tension between the AG and the head of Legal Counsel, because the head tended to establish a close relationship with the White House, to the annoyance of a jealous attorney general. In the Kennedy administration this problem never arose; it would scarcely have been possible to establish a relationship closer than that of the president's brother.

Like the Office of the Solicitor General from which it evolved, Legal Counsel has tended to be headed by lawyers with strong academic rather than political credentials. Many have gone on to important judgeships on courts of appeals, and three (Rehnquist, Scalia, and Alito) to the Supreme Court. In 1961 it had a small staff (roughly twenty lawyers) with a strong tradition of objective legal analysis, historical precedent from its own opinions handed to to presidents and attorneys general of both political parties, and a genuine pride of scholarship in its work. Today, with the practice (begun in the Carter administration) of the White House counsel's actually giving legal advice, the role of Legal Counsel (like that of the attorney general) has been diminished. Presidents of all persuasions like the powers of office and are more likely to get a green light from political appointees in the White House than from an office headed by an academic and staffed by civil servants. Thus Legal Counsel has, almost inevitably, evolved too far toward becoming an apologist for presidential power after the fact (it would be difficult for the attorney general to take public issue with White House counsel) rather than being a nonpolitical professional legal adviser.

I was confirmed in this view recently as I read Jack Goldsmith's *The Terror Presidency.* Professor Goldsmith, who headed the Office of Legal Counsel in 2003–2004, vividly describes the pressure put on him to conform his legal opinions and those of his predecessors with the desires of the White House and the vice president and the extent to which that pressure succeeded. Opinions by Legal Counsel are still, he affirms, the gold standard within the administration, reflecting its long history of scholarship and objective legal analysis, and, I believe, the extent to which the views of lawyers in the White House would be tainted by politics in fact and certainly in the public mind. True, the AG and his principal aides are also political appointees, who presumably share the president's political views and serve at his pleasure, but they can be more easily held accountable for their views by Congress than White House counsel. It is natural for them also to think of the president as their client and to seek to find ways for him to do what he wants to do. But what works for a private lawyer does not work for the attorney general or his aides. Under the Constitution, the president carries out the policies enacted into law by Congress, and the rule of law—the concept that we are a government of laws, not men—requires that he do so scrupulously, even when he would prefer a different outcome. All attorneys general have wrestled with the problem of political pressure to interpret the law as the president would like it to be, and a few have succumbed on occasion to that pressure. But if trying to please the president is substituted for one's honest professional opinion, I think both the president and the country are ill served. Public trust in the president and the Department of Justice is far more important than clever argument on behalf of a client or a search for loopholes or ambiguities in a statute. It sounds strange today and perhaps a little naive, but I think objective and honest legal advice in the interpretation of the laws is good politics and constitutionally necessary.

In 1961, Legal Counsel was an ideal post for an academic who loved government, and Bobby Kennedy was the ideal attorney general to advise. The appointment of the president's younger brother was, quite understandably, the subject of criticism, because of both his inexperience and fear of his political motivation. What Bobby, with Byron White's help, had quite shrewdly done was to staff the department largely with appointees with strong professional rather than political qualifications. The last thing he wanted was conduct that could be seen as politically motivated, and his staff was designed in both appearance and fact to give him that protection. Bobby wanted to go after Jimmy Hoffa and organized crime, but he appointed a Republican to head the Criminal Division, albeit in Jack Miller a person who had the same goals as he did. He knew civil rights would be a big issue for him and the department, so he avoided appointing Harris Wofford, a known advocate of the black cause, in favor of Burke Marshall, an exceptional antitrust lawyer—also one who he knew shared his own values. My absence in Switzerland during the campaign and my lack of any connection with the Kennedys, as well as my academic qualifications, became political assets.

A few days after the inauguration, President Kennedy held a White House reception for all the presidential appointees. Although not yet formally nominated, since the office was technically not vacant, I was invited. It was the first time I had ever met a president, and I was excited as I went through the receiving line. I was even more excited when, shaking my hand, the president said to me, "Nick, I'm so glad you'll be helping Bobby in the Justice Department." How on earth, I wondered, did he know that?

Byron took me down to the Senate Office Building to meet the chairman of the Judiciary Committee, Senator James Eastland of Mississippi, and two or three other members of the committee. The meetings were perfunctory but a necessary courtesy. Very soon thereafter my confirmation hearing was scheduled, and I appeared before the committee. Since I had been teaching at the University of Chicago, I was presented to the Senate Judiciary Committee by Senator Paul Douglas of Illinois, who, as it happened, I knew as the father of one of my close friends and college roommates as well as a fellow Rhodes Scholar at Oxford, John Douglas. John, a former Supreme Court clerk, was a Washington lawyer who later headed the Civil Division under Bobby. The hearing lasted only a few minutes. It was here that I described my position as "the attorney general's lawyer."

I returned to my office, and after spending perhaps half an hour on paperwork, I heard the attorney general's direct line buzz. When I picked up the phone, Bobby said, "Congratulations."

"On what?" I asked.

"The Senate just confirmed you." Pause. "I guess they thought I needed a lawyer pretty badly."

I had just had my first experience with Bobby's sardonic sense of humor.

One of the great benefits of working for the brother of the president was the fact that Bobby's power flowed down into the department. Nobody in other departments wanted to tangle with the young AG, and as a result the legal views of every lawyer in the Justice Department increased in value. Even the youngest recruits quickly acquired a swagger from working for Bobby. Our views on the law became golden. What may have begun as a question about what this very young, very political AG would be like to work for was quickly transformed into an enormous morale boost for all of us, except perhaps J. Edgar Hoover and his FBI. Hoover had been close to presidents for years, and now, in addition to his ideological differences with the new administration, he felt personally isolated.

While the ripple effects of Bobby's power quickly became obvious to all, there was another facet of his relationship to the president that benefited senior officials in the department tremendously. That was the fact that Bobby had no need to prove himself to his brother. I first became conscious of this early on, when I was reviewing an executive order on equal opportunity in government contracts that President Kennedy had put in the hands of Vice President Johnson. During the campaign, much had been made of the power of the executive to deal with racial discrimination through executive action, "with the stroke of a pen." Whatever his motivation, the vice president was determined to push executive power to the limits—perhaps to prove his own lack of bias, perhaps because more than anyone he knew the difficulty of getting meaningful legislation passed in this area.

In any event, Johnson turned, as he so often did, to Abe Fortas for help. Fortas was a brilliant lawyer and an ingenious one. Together with a young colleague in his Washington firm, William Rodgers, Fortas drafted a proposed executive order that pushed executive power to the limits and, in my judgment, somewhat beyond. We redrafted the order in my office, retaining many of the innovative ideas that Fortas, through the vice president, had proposed. Bill Moyers, Johnson's special assistant, and Hobart Taylor, a talented black lawyer from Texas on Johnson's staff, worked with us. Although Moyers was not a lawyer, he was intelligent, sensitive to the problems, and a pleasure to work with. The major area where Fortas would have gone further and we cut back was what could be required of unions. I had no problem requiring government contractors to hire without racial discrimination, but I did not believe we could reach their unions on matters of union membership. Johnson and Fortas essentially wanted to treat unions the same way employers were treated. Eventually Johnson's people agreed, and we put it all in proper form. In many ways it was far more like a statute than a typical executive order. It was long and complicated, and more explicit and comprehensive than any of its predecessors.

On a Saturday, Bill Moyers and I were working on what we hoped was a final draft—the lawyer in my office who was the expert on the form of such orders was making all the technical changes in spelling, capitalization, punctuation, and so forth—and late in the afternoon we came to agreement. The president was scheduled to review and sign the order on Monday. I called Bobby at his home at Hickory Hill and asked him if he wanted to review it over the weekend.

"Sure," he said, "why don't you bring it out to the house now?"

That was my first visit to the beautiful home in McLean, Virginia, where Bobby and Ethel and their large family lived. When I arrived, Bobby greeted me at the door, and as I handed him the order and the letter transmitting it to the president, I told him, "You've got to sign this letter and give it to the president."

"Well, what is it?"

I explained in general terms.

"Come in and tell me about it."

No sooner had he closed the door behind me than President Kennedy appeared and began asking me questions about the order, demonstrating a surprising—to me, at least—knowledge of its terms and its problems. Knowing that the attorney general had not yet reviewed the paper, I was embarrassed for him, as I had to take the lead in answering the president's questions.

"Did you get section 305, I think it is, worked out with the vice president? Is that satisfactory to him now?"

"Yes, we worked that out."

"Well, how about that question with the unions? Have you talked with Arthur Goldberg [then secretary of labor] about that? Have you worked that out all right?"

"Well, Mr. President, I think we've worked that out, yes, along these lines . . ." And I explained.

Then, to my continuing amazement, he went through four or five other sections by number, asking me how they had come out, and with Bobby looking on, I explained, to my embarrassment, "Yes, here is what we concluded. It's satisfactory to all concerned."

"Well," said Bobby to his brother, "I don't know why the hell I sign this thing and give it to you. Why don't you sign it and give it to me?"

He wasn't embarrassed. In fact, I think he was rather pleased that someone in his department whom he had known only a month could answer the president's questions.

In the months and years to come I was to see this side of Bobby repeatedly. He wanted the president to get the facts and the law from the person closest to the problem, and, unlike some other cabinet officers, he did not have to be that person. All of us experienced Bobby asking us questions about a problem and then saying, "Come over to the White House with me and explain it to the president." His pride was in the department he ran, the people who surrounded him, and service to his brother.

II

APPOINTING HIS BROTHER AS ATTORNEY GENERAL MAY HAVE PLEASED his father, but President Kennedy's choice was widely criticized by virtually everyone else. Clearly Bobby was not qualified by any traditional standards. He was too young, too inexperienced, too political, too brash, too immature in every way. All of these shortcomings were obvious to everyone, including Bobby. What was not obvious was Bobby's determination to do the job well and his capacity to lead, which had been overshadowed by his devotion to his brother.

The prospect of his appointment and the appointment itself were criticized by many academics and pundits. Bobby was not academically distinguished; he had graduated from the University of Virginia Law School in the middle of his class. He had worked briefly after graduation in the Justice Department, first in the Internal Security Division, charged with finding Soviet agents among actual or alleged American Communists, then in the Criminal Division, investigating political corruption in New York City. He left the department, somewhat reluctantly, to manage his brother's Senate campaign in Massachusetts against Henry Cabot Lodge, a strong incumbent in what promised to be a close race. Bobby's reluctance was based on his lack of knowledge of Massachusetts politics, concern about fundamental policy differences between his father and his brother, and fear that his own inexperience and youth would prove a devastating handicap.

John Kennedy won in a close election in which Kennedy money was freely spent and in which Bobby gained a reputation as a tough and often abrasive manager. While in the years I worked with Bobby in the department I never found him abrasive and never saw him as tougher on others than he was on himself, in retrospect the reputation is understandable, whether justified or not. Bobby was always straightforward, often blunt, and he expressed his views accordingly. A very young, very inexperienced, very wealthy, and very determined political amateur was bound to offend older politicians—and Bobby did. He lacked the suavity and the patience of his older brother, and it was bound to show. He did, by all accounts, handle his father well and earned paternal approbation for his management of the campaign, which meant a lot to a man whose older brothers were the family stars. It also contributed to criticism from the left, given his father's reputation as a conservative Democrat and a tough (to say the least) businessman. Critics cast Bobby as a young Joseph Kennedy.

After JFK was elected to the Senate, their father helped Bobby get appointed counsel to Senator Joseph McCarthy's red-baiting Senate Permanent Subcommittee on Investigations. There he worked for a short period with Roy Cohn, ferreting out alleged subversives in the State Department and the Voice of America. Bobby could not stand Cohn and resigned when Cohn was made chief of staff, only to be reappointed as minority counsel for the Democrats a few months later. Any connection with that committee was anathema to liberals, and Bobby probably made it worse by his fondness for Senator McCarthy, despite his voiced disapproval of what the senator, at Cohn's direction, did.

When the Democrats took over the Senate in 1954, Senator John McClellan became chair of the subcommittee and Bobby was counsel to the Democratic majority. While on the surface, largely for political reasons, the subcommittee continued to be concerned about Communist infiltration of government, Bobby found little in McCarthy's files worth pursuing. Gradually the investigations returned to the more traditional work of investigating fraud, bribery, influence, and incompetence in government contracts.

As a result of these investigations, the committee and its counsel gradually turned to a new field, labor racketeering (normally the responsibility of the Labor Committee), and in August 1956 Bobby persuaded McClellan to authorize an investigation. Thus began the Hoffa investigations, which occupied Bobby from 1956 until he became attorney general, and which he carried with him to the Department of Justice. Going after union corruption was not particularly politically rewarding and it was difficult, but Bobby persisted. Once he made up his mind, he was as dogged and fearless in pursuit of his objective as anyone I have ever known. When the Senate Labor Committee objected to the investigation on jurisdictional grounds, the Senate in 1957 voted to establish a new committee with members from both committees, the Select Committee on Improper Activities in the Labor or Management Field. Senator McClellan was the chairman and Bobby was chief counsel. The membership, except for Senators Patrick McNamara (a former trade unionist) and John Kennedy, was extremely conservative, and it was not difficult for liberals to see its mission as antilabor.

Bobby was genuinely concerned with decent unions and government and not interested, as many liberals viewed it, in a vendetta against organized labor—something his father might have approved of. The reality of organized crime and its significant power to corrupt through a combination of money, threats, and violence were not widely recognized. Bobby's perceived vendetta against Jimmy Hoffa was fueled by the perception that the committee was against labor, and given the record of the Investigation Subcommittee under McCarthy (who was a member of the Select Committee), many saw the committee, and Bobby in particular, as insensitive to civil liberties. Part of this perception came from not seeing the problem of organized crime as a reality before such a view was generally accepted. Part of it too came from the way congressional committees used the Fifth Amendment guarantee against self-incrimination. At the time it was not at all clear when a witness might, by answering a question, be found to have waived his right to remain silent. This uncertainty encouraged committees and their counsel to ask a long string of questions to which the privilege against self-incrimination was invoked. It was a favorite technique of Joe McCarthy's, and it was freely used by Bobby and by the committee. Justified by the claim that the innocent had nothing to fear, it was not a technique meant to uncover important facts so much as it was designed to smear witnesses, fairly or unfairly. Most academics, whatever their political views, strongly disapproved of this method of questioning witnesses, and to many it seemed a violation of the constitutional protection against self-incrimination by unfairly holding those who invoked the Fifth Amendment up to public ridicule.

While I was aware of the excesses of congressional investigations, especially those of Senator McCarthy, I had little knowledge of Bobby's role with respect to Hoffa and organized crime. The question raised by many liberals and given credibility by scholars such as Professor Alexander Bickel of Yale was whether or not the young attorney general would abuse his powerful position in his zeal to bring those he thought evil to justice. On that score, only time would tell.

There was never any question that Bobby saw Jimmy Hoffa and organized crime as evil threats to decent and honest government. His time with the McClellan Committee had convinced him that the danger was real, and there is no question that he was prepared to use the resources of government to prove his case. When he became attorney general, it was clearly his highest priority. His choice of Jack Miller, who was a court-appointed monitor of the Teamsters, to head the Criminal Division was a clear indication of where Bobby wanted the action to be. Miller shared Bobby's views of Hoffa.

What was significant was not what the press and commentators saw as a "Get Hoffa" motivation, but the simpler explanation that Bobby was a leader and an activist, not an ideologue. The department, apart from the FBI, is largely reactive. Crimes are committed, investigated, and prosecuted. The Civil Division supervises the defense of claims brought against the United States. The Lands Division looks to violation of environmental laws and so forth. The Antitrust Division acts, or refuses to act, mostly on complaints by business, although it may initiate cases on its own.

When he took the reins at the Justice Department, however, Bobby, unlike most attorneys general, was simply unwilling to wait for J. Edgar Hoover's FBI to dig up evidence and present it to U.S. attorneys around the country for prosecution. He perceived organized crime and corrupt labor unions as threats to decent government and saw it as his duty to organize the forces of Justice to prevent this evil. What he really wanted, and argued for vigorously in his book, *The Enemy Within*, was a National Crime Commission, but that was anathema to Hoover, who saw it, probably correctly, as both a threat to and a criticism of the FBI.

The FBI had in fact been incredibly slow to appreciate the existence, let alone the dangers, of organized crime. But given Hoover's stature and power, the young attorney general was not about to take him on in a public fashion. Nor was he willing to abandon his fight against organized crime or turn it over to the Bureau. Bobby had spent four long and difficult years investigating the Teamsters and its connections to organized crime. It was the subject he knew best, and he was not about to waste the knowledge gained working for the Select Committee or turn the resolution of that problem over to others. He was determined to be a part of it and bring it to a successful conclusion.

What he did was, in a sense, create his own mini crime commission, of which he was the chairman and leader. Not only did he make Jack Miller head of the Criminal Division, but he formed a small but important organized crime unit in the division and persuaded Ed Silberling, a formidable prosecutor from Frank Hogan's Manhattan District Attorney's Office, to head it. He then used his power as the president's brother to persuade the Labor Department under Arthur Goldberg and the Treasury Department under Douglas Dillon, with its huge Internal Revenue Service and Narcotics Bureau (then a part of Treasury), to assign agents to investigate organized crime and its links with organized labor and local and state government officials. He directed U.S. attorneys in those cities where organized crime flourished to assign attorneys full-time to investigations and involved the FBI in a major way. To coordinate and supervise the related anti-Hoffa activities, he appointed Walter Sheridan, a friend and a brilliant investigator, and Carmine Bellino, a talented investigative accountant, both of whom had worked with him in his role with the Congress. He also persuaded his old boss, Senator John McClellan, to sponsor and get Congress to enact laws that made it a federal crime to conspire across state lines to promote criminal activities.

One result of this legislation, along with the efforts to coordinate the intelligence and activities of a number of federal agencies, was simply to make organized crime a federal offense—a step that gave the FBI clear jurisdiction and promoted Hoover's cooperation. The FBI was not used to sharing intelligence with other agencies, but Bobby was persistent in seeing that all who needed to be involved *were* involved. He had monthly meetings in his office with all the principal lawyers and investigators, and he pressed for results. Bobby himself was exceedingly knowledgeable about organized crime and about Jimmy Hoffa, and the participants grew to respect that knowledge as well as the AG's determination to destroy the corruption and crime he was sure existed. Meetings of this kind were totally unheard of in the department, especially with a knowledgeable AG himself running the show. Bureau agents were accustomed to working within their own organization until they were satisfied a case could be made, and totally unaccustomed to sharing raw intelligence with the AG except through formal channels, let alone with investigators from other departments and agencies.

In my first year as legal counsel, I attended few of these sessions. I knew nothing about either organized crime or Jimmy Hoffa, and whatever legal expertise I had was unlikely to be called upon. But I was curious, probably because of the press attention to the "Get Hoffa" effort and the concern for civil liberties that was frequently expressed by the press. And Bobby was always welcoming. It was a characteristic of his department that nobody owned bureaucratic turf and all were encouraged to participate.

The all-day sessions were fascinating to observe. Bobby was clearly the leader, and not simply because he was attorney general. He impressed the group with his factual knowledge, and he encouraged free-flowing discussion and differing views. He was quick to appreciate suggestions, to praise efforts, to push for more without being critical. You could sense that this varied group was prepared to follow him and wanted desperately to please him, to find the facts that were needed, however difficult the task might be. I began to realize then, if I had not already seen it, that Bobby had the capacity to become an exceptional leader.

Of course, it did not hurt to be the president's brother. But it would be wrong to attribute his leadership ability solely to that relationship. What Bobby was able to do was to communicate his own enthusiasm and energy to others, to make them feel that they were members of a team and that what they were doing was important. His was not a collection of bureaucrats; far from it. His was a team of doers, people who could work together toward a shared objective and take pride in their membership on his team. He led in a way that was open and aboveboard, with shared intelligence, no secrets, no favorites. And his success was by no means confined to organized crime or Jimmy Hoffa. A positive spirit—the desire to do a good job—permeated the whole department.

An early example of the encouragement he gave to all occurred on Washington's Birthday. When Bobby came to work on the holiday, he noticed a number of cars parked in the department garage. Wishing to reward this dedication to the job, he got an assistant to take down license numbers and then wrote a personal note of appreciation to each employee. What had not occurred to him was the proximity of the department to shopping in downtown Washington. My assistant, Harold Reis, wrote to Bobby that on Washington's Birthday he could not tell a lie. He had parked in the garage while attending a performance at the National Theater. But despite the amusing aspect of Bobby's letters, they had an impact on the work ethic of department attorneys.

Throughout Bobby's tenure as attorney general, morale in the Justice Department was in the stratosphere. Part of this was sharing the power and prestige of working for the president's brother. But a much more important reason was Bobby himself. If there were fears among career employees that Bobby would sacrifice law to political aspirations, they quickly disappeared. Not only would that have been bad politics, which his many critics would have joyfully exploited, but he, with Byron White, had gone to considerable lengths to insure that his assistants were respected lawyers with far more professional than political credentials. Beyond that, it was never Bobby's desire or inclination to distort the law, to seek to exploit executive power through biased reading of legislation or legal precedent.

Early in his administration, the Criminal Division developed a corruption case against George Chacheris, the mayor of Gary, Indiana, and an early supporter of JFK for president, and took it to Bobby for his approval. The career lawyers waited skeptically while Bobby reviewed the case, thinking he would find a way to kill it. When, after careful review, RFK said Go!, he won their loyalty in a flash.

He saw law for what it is—a tool to implement policy, a part of the political system through which hopes and aspirations can be realized. What he did want to do was make the department matter, not simply by reacting to events but by leading in the right direction. He felt an excitement about law, about its capacity to help people achieve a fairer and more just society. He almost always tended to identify with the underdog, with the poor, the weak, the disenfranchised, and in a sense he saw law as the road to justice. I had thought of Bobby as a tough political pragmatist—and indeed he could be. But more and more I saw a young idealist struggling with the realities of a difficult world.

III

MUCH OF MY TIME DURING THE FIRST FEW WEEKS AS HEAD OF THE Office of Legal Counsel was spent trying to understand my responsibilities, organizing my office, and getting to know colleagues both in my own office and elsewhere in the department. It became clear quite quickly that Bobby saw the department as a group of teammates working to carry out the responsibilities of public servants, not as a bureaucracy composed of principalities over which he ruled. The team was not simply the presidential appointees that he had brought into the department. It included civil servants as well, and he went to great lengths to get to know as many people in the huge department as he could. He wanted everybody on his team, and he made that desire clear and believable to everyone.

There was virtually no formality in his leadership. In shirtsleeves, with a loosened tie, he roamed the halls of the department, dropping in on lawyers unannounced, asking civil servants what they were working on, showing an interest in what they said and speaking words of encouragement. He brought the young lawyers, most of whom were assigned to the Civil Rights Division, to his enormous office, where he engaged them in informal discussions about their work—and his. He never lectured anyone, and he treated everyone as an equal. It was obvious that this was not a calculated performance. It was simply the way Bobby was. And lawyers in the department, who had always envisioned the attorney general as a remote senior government official riding over to the White House in his limousine and far removed from the ordinary people, loved him for it.

Bobby was not a bad lawyer, but he did not hold himself out as superior, the way most attorneys general have done. Most attorneys generals are from Wall Street (or equivalent) firms, with little experience or interest in criminal law, which can be safely left to experts in the FBI and civil servants in the Criminal Division. Their interest tends to run along the lines of their experience—tax law, antitrust policy, large civil cases— and in these areas they want to see high-quality work that will impress their legal peers. These are the areas that interested Bobby the least. He was interested in the quality of investigations that led to results, not the quality of legal analysis in briefs or opinions designed to impress leading practitioners. To the extent that quality was important—for example, in the solicitor general's briefs to the Supreme Court or the department's position on constitutional issues—Bobby left the writing to his associates. He was interested in using law as a tool to implement policy and cared more about the bottom line than the reasoning that got one there.

The senior staff at the department was largely a mixture of Ivy League lawyers like myself, recruited by Byron, and those who had worked with Bobby in the Senate. In the former group were Louis Oberdorfer (Tax Division), Burke Marshall (Civil Rights), and William Orrick (Civil Division). Archibald Cox, the solicitor general, was in this group, although he was the choice of the president, whom he had worked for in the campaign while teaching at Harvard Law. Those who had worked with Bobby were Jack Miller (Criminal Division) and two prizewinning newspaper reporters, John Seigenthaler (executive assistant) and Edwin Guthman (public information). Because of Bobby's relationship to the president, the press was all over Guthman all the time. And there was not a better public information officer, or a more loyal one, in Washington.

Bobby also brought with him Walter Sheridan and Carmine Bellino to head up the Hoffa investigation, as well as his secretary, Angie Novello. Not in either group were Lee Loevinger, who left the Minnesota Supreme Court to head the Antitrust Division, and Ramsey Clark, the only senior appointee younger than Bobby, to head up the Lands Division. Working for Byron as his deputies were William Geoghegan and Joseph Dolan, both excellent lawyers who had worked with White in the campaign. Dolan had worked also in the office of Senator Kennedy and was familiar with the Congress, an important asset, since the deputy attorney general was responsible for the department's legislative program as well as judicial appointments. John Reilly, another campaign worker with political acumen, headed up the office dealing with U.S. attorneys' offices.

In retrospect, I think it would have been easy for the department to have split into cliques. But Bobby was determined to have us all working together as equals, and no one was allowed special claims to a particular turf because of title. There were exceptions. J. Edgar Hoover could not be a member of a team with such a young and inexperienced captain, although Bobby did make some inroads in the FBI's isolated bureaucracy on the organized crime front. And relatively little attention was paid to the Bureau of Prisons, run skillfully by James Bennett, or the Immigration Service, run accommodatingly (to Bobby and to the relevant congressional committees) by Ray Farrell.

What made it possible for Bobby to mold this group into a single team was the fact that all of us quite quickly came to appreciate the very talented people who were on the team and, even more important, Bobby's ability to engage the loyalty of each of us, both to him and to each other. We all participated in the making of policy, and he treated each of us as a valued colleague, not as the head of a division or someone with turf to protect. He encouraged the opposite—sharing problems and concerns and seeking the opinion of colleagues. The members of the group were sufficiently talented and self-confident to welcome a suggestion and to offer advice when it was sought.

It certainly helped that Bobby was a wealthy young man with a wife who, I sometimes thought, must be a caterer's dream of heaven on earth. Two or three times a week Bobby would call Ethel at noon and inform her that he was bringing six or seven of us home for lunch. When the weather was warm, we would sit by the pool at Hickory Hill, and Bobby would seek our views on many issues, often matters of policy far from the responsibility of the department but not, of course, this attorney general. More often he would use these informal occasions to get advice on matters within the department as well. I can recall vividly the approach: "Look, you guys, I've got a problem. You are all better lawyers than I am, but I'm the attorney general, so it has to be my decision. But that doesn't mean it has to be uninformed, so let's hear what you think."

And he would. The subject matter could be anything—organized crime, Hoffa, civil rights, legislation. The discussion was often vigorous, sometimes argumentative, but more often than not common ground was discovered. I found the comments informed, intellectually invigorating, and fun. It was of course heady to feel so close to the seat of power—a feeling often enhanced by the appearance of Jackie Kennedy enjoying a swim in the pool.

In the early days we were all trying to get a feel for our jobs and our responsibilities as well as each other. For this we depended on the career staff, who, in the case of the Office of Legal Counsel, I found talented and dedicated.

My first assistant, Harold Reis, was a career attorney who was a former editor of the *Columbia Law Review* and married to the sister of Morris Abram, a Rhodes Scholar classmate of mine at Oxford and a leader in the Jewish community. Harold was bright and energetic, and I would have been lost without him. There were some twenty lawyers in the office, and six or seven of them, like Harold, were of a quality any law firm would have been proud to hire. Of the utmost importance were files going back many years of the legal advice given by the office to the attorney general and to the White House directly. That advice was of high professional quality and free of political taint. I was determined to keep it that way, and Bobby totally supported that view.

There were good lawyers in the White House performing various political tasks but, despite the title of "counsel," rarely giving legal advice. I encouraged Bobby to make sure they came to the department for such advice and thus avoid the embarrassment of prior differing views. Further, not all the laws that apply within the executive branch are easy for lawyers coming from private practice to find. My credibility with the White House staff went up when they were on the verge of giving General Maxwell Taylor a title similar to one given to Admiral Leahy by FDR and specifically forbidden by statute. Ted Sorensen, who had been President Kennedy's principal aide in the Senate, and his two associate counsels appreciated the need to be sure the department agreed in advance, and used my office for advice. In addition, at Bobby's direction, they quickly refrained from meeting with lawyers whose clients had problems with the government, referring them to the proper division in the department. It was important to Bobby's public image as well as his personal integrity that politics not influence legal decisions, and being the brother of the president helped to insure that others did as he wished.

One problem that came up early in JFK's administration was the appointment of Joseph C. Swidler as chairman of the Federal Power Commission, an office the president had apparently promised him. This would necessarily involve the removal of the sitting chairman, Jerome Kuykendall, who had a year remaining in his term. Initially the problem of the president's power to remove the chairman did not come to me through channels. I read about it in the *Wall Street Journal* and thought we had better research the matter, because I had a clear recollection that the Supreme Court had ruled that presidents cannot remove members of independent commissions. I was concerned that JFK was about to make a mistake, and I alerted Bobby to the problem.

My recollection was correct. The Court's decision in the landmark case of *Humphrey's Executor* was still the law, and I got a memo from my staff saying so. I very nearly gave this advice to the White House, but when I discussed it further with Harold Reis, he said he wasn't satisfied that removing a person as chairman was the same as removing him from the commission, and only the latter was specifically forbidden. It was a distinction worth pursuing, and we did. There was no precedent one way or the other, but both of us became convinced that while the president's executive power did not extend to removing Kuykendall from the policy-making function of a commissioner, it might well extend to removing him from the administrative functions of chairman. Harold wrote a quite persuasive memo to that effect, and I signed it.

At the suggestion of the White House, we provided Kuykendall, Swidler, and the chairman of the House Commerce Committee, Oren Harris, with a copy of that memo. Kuykendall had been prepared to fight his removal from the commission, but he became more hesitant over his removal as chairman. Such a fight would be embarrassing to all. He would be locked out of his office and become the center of public attention in a cause he might well lose in court. Chairman Harris negotiated a compromise: his resignation in sixty days. Kuykendall agreed, but Swidler insisted that thirty days was all he would agree to.

Ralph Dungan, a White House political appointee who was following the appointment for the president, asked me to come to his office and talk to Swidler. I did, but he remained adamant, and the matter was obviously going to the president for a decision. I knew Bobby was with the president; I had not had the opportunity to brief him on the latest developments, and I had no idea what Dungan, whom I did not know very well, would recommend. I left Dungan's office and sent a note to Bobby saying that I had to see him. I got a note back: "Come on in." So into the Oval Office I went.

I told the president and Bobby, "If the issue of Kuykendall goes to court, I think we will win, but it will be a mess for everyone. He'll take sixty days and resign. Swidler insists on no more than thirty. I'd take sixty and be thankful."

President Kennedy said, "So would I."

At that point Dungan came into the office from the other door and said essentially what I had said, concluding, "Swidler wants to contest this, but I'd take Kuykendall's offer."

Without knowing each other and without discussing it privately, Dungan and I had arrived at the same conclusion. It was the kind of event that increased mutual confidence and respect.

In general the White House sought and followed the advice of my office directly and through the attorney general. But occasionally politics trumped law, though not in the way one would expect. In the major example I can recall, Ted Sorensen's advice on federal aid to parochial schools may have been more conservative than the advice he or I would have given to a non-Catholic president.

At a press conference, President Kennedy was asked about aid to religious schools and gave an answer that was quite knowledgeable and quite conservative. It had, after all, been a subject which, as a Catholic presidential candidate, he knew had been a hot button for many Protestants and Jews. He had been well briefed on the subject by Sorensen, who in turn had consulted a leading Protestant conservative author, Paul Blanshard. Given the importance of the subject during the campaign and the position taken by the candidate, the president's response was hardly surprising. Nor was the fact that my office had not been consulted.

Nonetheless, late that afternoon Bobby asked me to prepare a memorandum for the president on the constitutional limits of federal aid to religious schools and colleges. It was for an early morning meeting, and I am not sure that Bobby, who was not noted for scholarship or research, realized what a tough deadline he had imposed. With three or four of my most senior staff, I went to work, prepared for an all-night session. A little before midnight we completed our research and spent some time discussing our conclusions. Obviously, for our first Catholic president and his brother, this was a sensitive subject. Further, the president had already opined on the subject of school aid at the press conference and more generally during his campaign.

It would be wrong to say that the Constitution as interpreted by the Court was clear on the subject, and it was not easy to make a coherent rule from its decisions. My staff and I were inclined to think that the president's stated view was pretty close to the mark as far as elementary schools were concerned but that there might be more leeway if the recipient was a university.

My secretary had stayed on, and I began dictating our conclusions and reasoning, with help from Harold Reis and Leon Ullman, another able career attorney. I finished some two hours later and waited for the typewritten version. When none was forthcoming, Harold went to investigate. My secretary—who, incidentally, was excellent—was bent over her desk in tears. She couldn't read a word of her shorthand notes.

Harold and Leon got on the phone and located another secretary, who came to the office at about three in the morning. We began again, although this time it was a little easier than the first time. The memo was edited, completed, and sent to Bobby and the White House by seven a.m., and we were pretty proud of our work. It concluded—I think correctly—that the Constitution was quite strict on aid to elementary and even high schools but far more permissive in the case of higher education.

I went over to the White House with Bobby, and we stopped first in Sorensen's office, where we talked about the problem for a few minutes, and then proceeded to the president's office. Abraham Ribicoff, the secretary of what was then health, education, and welfare (HEW), was there. Understandably, he wanted as much leeway as he could to improve education in the United States. He was attempting to persuade the president to a more lenient view.

"Well, Mr. President," said Ribicoff, who was a very good constitutional lawyer and had clearly done his homework, "I think this is an issue under the Supreme Court's decisions on which you can go either way."

Bobby looked at me and I interrupted. "That may have been true yesterday, Mr. Secretary, but since the president has gone one way on it, it's somewhat less true today than it was before. There are areas of some flexibility here—for example, the whole field of higher education—but not much with respect to schools."

The president ignored me and said to Ribicoff, "What do you mean, Abe, I can go either way on it?"

Ribicoff replied, "I think you can either aid parochial schools or not, just as you please. Under the decisions, I think you are free on this subject."

While the decisions were not as clear as one would have wanted, I thought this view somewhat extreme, at least in the case of schools, as distinguished from higher education.

The president turned to Ted Sorensen. "How does Blanshard feel about that?"

Ted replied, "Why don't I call him and see if there is any leeway at all?"

Blanshard, of course, was a dedicated opponent of any aid whatsoever. When Ted called him, he expressed the view—not surprisingly—that in his opinion there was no distinction and no leeway at all.

President Kennedy commented, with some feeling, "Eisenhower could have dealt with this whole problem, but I can't."

And there it remained for the moment.

Aid to religious schools was probably the only subject on which it was a handicap to the president to have his Catholic brother as attorney general. It is hard today to understand the religious suspicion that underlay the feelings about having a Catholic president—the fear that religion would be politicized. Today the shoe is almost on the other foot, as God is invoked to justify political decisions. But the fear of many then was that the pope would be running the United States from the Vatican, and the Kennedys were forced to lean over backward to demonstrate that their religious beliefs did not control their political judgments.

We did eventually find a little more leeway than Blanshard would have approved. Later HEW published my memo as its own, and Bobby endorsed it. The press (aside, perhaps, from two or three reporters close to Bobby and the department) did not associate it with Bobby, and HEW was able to use it to aid higher education in some ways in religious universities and colleges.

My office dealt with a hodgepodge of other problems, some important, some far less so. A number of problems came up in connection with Jackie Kennedy's desire to redo the White House with gifts to make it into a more authentic museum reflecting its history. These problems brought me in contact with that lovely lady and led to a friendship that continued until her death. She sometimes treated me as her lawyer and sought advice on unrelated matters. But I was not always as accommodating as she (or, for that matter, the president) would have liked.

Some of the problems were as much political as legal. I advised Jackie that she should not accept a large gift from Jules Stein, head of Music Corporation of America, because we were about to sue MCA for alleged antitrust violations. That counsel was not well received by her and resulted in a very long phone conversation with the president, who was being the good husband. I suspect he talked to Bobby, and Bobby simply told him to talk to me. Probably both of them agreed with me but preferred to let me take the blame from Jackie. Shortly thereafter, at a White House reception, the president brought it up with me as Jackie stood alongside him in the receiving line.

"Nick, isn't there something we can do to help Jackie get that quarter of a million dollars? Perhaps later, when it's all over?"

I played along. "Maybe sometime in the future, but it would be a bad idea to do it right now."

The MCA case was in fact settled. I have no idea if Jackie ever got the gift.

In the days of the cold war we had problems created by a Congress which, in McCarthy-like fashion, wanted to stamp out the Communist threat within the United States. Both Bobby and the president were skeptical about the threat within this country as some saw it. Bobby, for example, left the Internal Security Division, which was charged with prosecuting such threats, in the hands of Walter Yeagley, which could be viewed as a sop to Hoover or, as I saw it, a way of minimizing its importance. Bobby required all matters to be reported directly to him, and he succeeded, with help from the rest of us, in mooting virtually every prosecution proposed by Yeagley and his staff.

One example was a program run by the post office to inhibit the entry of foreign political propaganda of a subversive nature as a danger to our national security. I discovered that the Eisenhower administration had appointed a committee of the National Security Council (NSC) to look at the program. The committee had unanimously concluded, after thorough study, that the program should be dropped because it had no significance at all in terms of national security. But with the election coming up, the Eisenhower administration had chosen to do nothing and leave it alone. I raised it with Bobby, who took up the issue with his brother on the phone.

The president thought the study by his predecessor provided a good basis to drop the program: "I don't like it. Let's get rid of it."

So we did, first getting the secretary of state, Dean Rusk, and the secretary of the treasury, Douglas Dillon, to join Bobby in endorsing the NSC committee's findings. All to no avail. As soon as our intentions became known, Congressman Glenn Cunningham introduced legislation to restore the program, which easily passed both houses. Then, as now, national security could be invoked successfully to justify all kinds of idiocy. Clearly there can be times during a war when such a program might be justified, at least in theory. We did not believe a court would uphold the prohibition on the present facts, but we wanted to preserve the theoretical option, so we went back to mooting the cases before they were brought. Corliss Lamont nonetheless brought a case seeking an injunction, and in 1965 the Supreme Court found the statute in violation of the First Amendment.

During the time I worked with Bobby, he was always sensitive to civil liberties and often courageous, as in this instance, in the positions he took. Given the team he had chosen, he would have to have been. But it went beyond that. Even in matters of organized crime and Jimmy Hoffa, where the temptation to cut corners would have been greatest, he never did. Yet during his lifetime he never succeeded in persuading liberals that he took seriously all the guaranties of the Constitution, even though every act he took—or refused to take—supported that position.

IV

THE KENNEDY-JOHNSON YEARS WILL BE REMEMBERED IN HISTORY FOR what was done with respect to race. But no one would have predicted that back in 1961. Civil rights was not at the top of the Kennedy agenda, perhaps because it was hard to envision a solution to the caste system of the South. This was true despite the fact that arguably Kennedy was elected because of the action he took when Martin Luther King was arrested in early October 1960 for sitting in at the restaurant in Rich's Department Store in Atlanta. Then-Senator Kennedy telephoned Mrs. King, and Bobby persuaded the judge to let Dr. King out of jail on bail. Those acts may have turned out the black vote in Illinois in sufficient numbers to give JFK the close election there, which decided the presidency.

It is difficult today to visualize the extent of racial divisions in our country and to recognize how overtly prejudiced most white Americans were against black citizens. While there is far more prejudice today than we are comfortable acknowledging, and it still plays a regrettable role in politics and economic opportunity, it has to a large extent gone underground. In 1961 the South was a formally segregated society. Racial discrimination also existed in the North, although not supported by law and for the most part less overtly. The North took pride in its occasional acts of tolerance toward black athletes or musicians; blacks could vote, but they were employed almost exclusively in menial capacities; housing was segregated, and as a result, so were schools. In the South the segregation was overt, essentially a caste system in which the far more numerous blacks were denied the right to vote through literacy tests, barred from places of public accommodation, educated (if that is the right word) in segregated schools. Especially since World War II there had been efforts by a minority of liberal whites to change this racial system, and groups such as the NAACP and the Urban League, composed of blacks and whites, had litigated successfully for recognition of rights for all. President Truman had integrated the armed forces—a major step—and in 1954 the Supreme Court in *Brown v. Board of Education* had ordered school desegregation.

There is an obvious irony in the fact that almost a century after fighting a bloody war over slavery and enacting three constitutional amendments designed to guarantee equality of the races, we still lived in a racially segregated society. The formal basis for this situation—and the constitutional justification for the South's Jim Crow laws—was the 1896 decision of the Supreme Court in *Plessy v. Ferguson*. With only a single justice dissenting, the Court held that a black railroad passenger could be forced to use separate accommodations as long as the separate accommodations were in fact equal. That separation could be required without "implying the inferiority of one race to the other." The Court explicitly used public education in segregated schools to demonstrate the reasonableness of its conclusion.

Even in 1896 it should have been obvious that segregation *did* imply inferiority—there was no other plausible reason to require separation of races—and what the Court saw as a legitimate use of police power was simply the white majority making certain that prejudice prevailed. It seems astounding today that only Justice Harlan dissented. Yet even in 1954, at the time of *Brown*, there were still justices who associated separation of the races with social preference, not racial inferiority. That in itself is a measure of the depth of racial bias in our society at the time—bias accepted as a matter of course by the Court itself.

When *Brown* was first argued in 1953, John W. Davis, one of the great Supreme Court advocates who in these cases represented South Carolina, believed he had prevailed in a Court divided 5–4 or even 6–3 and that *Plessy* would not be overruled. He may well have been right had it been decided at that time. What turned out to be crucial and unexpected was the death of Chief Justice Fred Vinson and the appointment by President Eisenhower of Governor Earl Warren of California to lead the Court. Warren was doggedly determined both to lead and to achieve a unanimous decision overruling *Plessy*. Remarkably, he did so. The Court ordered all schools desegregated "with all deliberate speed."

The depth of feeling in the South and the strength of its resistance to the Court was dramatically demonstrated in 1957 when Arkansas governor Orville Faubus, a racial moderate by contemporary southern standards, called out the State Guard to defy a court order admitting black students to the public school in Little Rock. That went beyond all expectations and had nothing to do with "all deliberate speed." Attempts at a negotiated solution failed, and President Eisenhower felt compelled to use federal troops to enforce the order and insure admission of the students. But that was not an end to the revolt by any means. The troops had to remain the entire time the students were in school, escorting them to class to protect them from angry white citizens. That was pretty much the end of school desegregation in the fifties.

What is of crucial importance is that these efforts to desegregate schools were not the only results of *Brown*. In holding that enforced separation of races in public schools violated the equal protection clause as "inherently unequal," the Court rejected the rationale of *Plessy* that separation did not denote inferiority. It was that rationale which had legitimized the Jim Crow laws and given constitutional, and therefore public, respectability to segregation. While the Court's holding in *Brown* was confined to schools, its rationale rejecting *Plessy* made it quite obvious that any state-ordered racial segregation would likely be held a violation of the clause.

Until *Brown*, efforts to attain racial equality in the South had been largely confined to the efforts of the Legal Defense Fund (LDF) in the courts under Thurgood Marshall's leadership. *Brown*, although not strictly relevant, created new expectations and thus opened up an entirely new political route. Rosa Parks was inspired to refuse to sit in the back of the bus, an act that joined blacks together in the Montgomery bus strike. Martin Luther King and the southern church leaders began to demand rights far in excess of anything the Court had decided but consistent with its spirit. Sit-ins in restaurants and at lunch counters that refused to serve blacks began taking place, and huge numbers of arrests for trespass followed.

When John Kennedy became president and I joined Bobby Kennedy's Justice Department, the LDF was bringing some of its school cases to fruition and Martin Luther King was leading marches and organizing sit-ins. With Byron White, Louis Oberdorfer, Burke Marshall, and I in positions of responsibility, the situation offered a pretty good test of a Yale legal education, but we found that none of us had taken courses in how to manage a peaceful revolution while preserving a government of laws. Burke, in his quietly persuasive way, took the lead.

We were faced with a nearly insoluble problem. In our federal system, both state and federal officials must comply with the federal constitution.

If they do not, the technical remedy is to secure a court order compelling performance. If such an order does not work and is forcibly resisted, what then?

The only practical means for law enforcement resisted by state peace officers, as at Little Rock, is the army. The federal government has a relatively small number of law enforcement officials in addition to federal marshals: the FBI, the IRS, the Immigration Border Patrol, the Alcohol and Tax Unit, and federal prison guards—all engaged in enforcing federal laws, but none with formal training in maintaining law and order. These officials could be given some training and sworn in as federal marshals, but given their other duties, it would be virtually impossible to put together a force of more than a few hundred. Further, there was a huge risk of making matters even more dangerous and violent if that force were put in confrontation with a similar force of state police.

Put differently, we were faced with civil rights groups seeking to exercise federally guaranteed constitutional rights but being forcibly opposed by local and state law enforcement. We had an obligation to see those rights vindicated. But the fact remained that most whites thought blacks inferior and used this excuse as justification for what was in fact racial discrimination and the denial of equal opportunity to blacks. I think this deep-seated bias made it hard for many whites—even those who supported blacks in their efforts to obtain equal rights—to identify with blacks in that struggle.

It was not because the Kennedys did not understand and sympathize with the efforts of Negroes (as African Americans were then called) to attain equal rights. Their understanding, like that of most white Americans, was far from perfect, but there is no question that they believed blacks were entitled under our Constitution to the same rights and privileges as other citizens, and they clearly understood that this was not being observed. Their conviction no doubt lacked the emotional fire that black leaders felt and which perhaps comes much more easily to the victim than to the observer.

The problem was not knowing what was right but knowing how to get there in our federal governmental system. The Congress was not willing or able to act decisively to insure equal rights. The civil rights laws passed after *Brown* in 1957 and 1959 helped lawsuits but did little to solve the underlying problem, despite substantial efforts by civil rights advocates. The filibuster, which required 67 votes to terminate debate in the Senate, could not be defeated when the issue was civil rights, but could tie up the Senate for weeks and then produce, with enormous effort, compromise legislation of very little substance. The Supreme Court had spoken decisively in 1954 in *Brown v. Board of Education*, but the southern states simply refused to comply. Eisenhower had used troops to enforce court-ordered desegregation in Little Rock—troops that continued to escort black students on a daily basis—but however courageous and correct, this was scarcely a model to be followed in several hundred school districts.

It would be comforting to think the Kennedys had a plan. They simply did not. There were ideas, but the sum total of them did not add up to much—certainly not nearly enough to satisfy the growing demands of black leaders like Martin Luther King. The tools readily available to the president, absent meaningful civil rights legislation, consisted of lawsuits and government contracts and, in limited situations, the use of troops to enforce court orders or maintain law if the state was unwilling or unable to do so.

The selection of Burke Marshall rather than Harris Wofford, who had worked with civil rights leaders during the campaign and was their clear favorite, was an effort to signal that while the administration was committed to civil rights, miracles should not be expected. I think the Kennedys believed that if blacks were permitted to vote and did in fact vote, the political impact of their vote would make problems more soluble, even though the vote had not solved problems of discrimination in the North. Still, breaking down the South's overt caste system was the goal of civil rights leaders and liberal politicians alike, and clearly necessary as a first step. But getting blacks registered to vote in the face of poll taxes and discriminatory literacy tests took time, which the administration did not have.

Bobby added some two hundred young and dedicated lawyers to the Civil Rights Division, and they concentrated on voter registration. Every case was difficult: the FBI (never an enthusiastic participant) had to investigate; witnesses who could not be intimidated had to be found; cases had to be tried, appealed, and so forth, requiring a matter of months or even years to make real progress.

In addition, the Legal Defense Fund was bringing school cases under *Brown*, clearly destined to produce further Little Rocks. Dr. King was continuing his sit-ins in restaurants and other places of public accommodation, and other groups were finding ways of testing both southern resolve to discriminate and Kennedy resolve to achieve equal treatment. Bobby was convinced that Eisenhower's use of troops at Little Rock had been a mistake and was particularly offensive to the South. He had the imaginative idea of creating a "marshal" force especially trained for such an assignment. He named Jim McShane, a much-decorated New York police officer, as chief marshal, and Jim put together a training program for U.S. marshals, supplemented by Border Patrol officers, prison guards, and alcohol and tax personnel. The legal basis was interesting. Under the law, a marshal in any state may swear in volunteers to help him enforce the law. All of us have seen this take place in western movies, and Bobby determined to use it to create a nonmilitary law enforcement unit under federal control. Jim was able to train some five hundred marshals, who could be called upon if necessary, although given their other full-time duties, the training was not extensive and their availability was limited to crises. The FBI was exempted from such service.

Not only was Burke Marshall a close friend of mine, but his first assistant, John Doar, had been one of my college roommates. John was usually somewhere in the South, building cases for trial or trying them. Burke would frequently drop by my office, which was close to Bobby's, on his way to or from seeing the attorney general. I kept in touch with civil rights issues, though in the early stages my involvement was quite minimal after working on the executive order with respect to federal contracts. Civil rights groups wanted even more extensive use of executive power, more than I thought could be constitutionally justified. The department's focus was on building voting rights cases.

The first serious crisis took place in May 1961, with the Freedom Riders. The Congress of Racial Equality (CORE), led by James Farmer, organized several busloads of integrated passengers to travel from the District of Columbia to New Orleans for the specific purpose of testing and challenging segregation in southern bus terminals. The Supreme Court in 1960 had determined that all such segregation was unlawful, but that determination had been ignored in the Deep South. Riders included many well-known civil rights activists, such as William Coffin, the chaplain of Yale. While the Riders traveled through Virginia, the Carolinas, and even Georgia without serious incident beyond a few arrests, it was increasingly clear that as they progressed into the Deep South, they were in real danger from segregationist groups such as the Ku Klux Klan and that they were courting violent reactions. That occurred first in Birmingham, Alabama, where the Riders were clubbed and beaten. Bobby sent his executive assistant, John Seigenthaler, to Birmingham as a presidential representative to see what could be done. John was able to get that group on a plane to relative safety.

But more Riders kept coming. The question was whether or not local law enforcement would maintain law and order or would look the other way and tolerate the violent acts of segregationists. If that happened, when was federal intervention justified? What did one have to know? And how would intervention and its timing be managed? Those kinds of problems involved my office, and under Bobby, crises involved everyone.

In this kind of potential crisis, intelligence is everything. The department simply did not have any. Depending on the FBI was essentially useless, for two reasons. First, the Bureau's intelligence was obtained from local law enforcement, with all the bias and distortion in racial matters that source implied; second, Hoover ran a bureaucracy—agents reported to the special agent in charge, who reported to an assistant director in Washington, who reported to Hoover, who would send a memo to or occasionally telephone the attorney general. Agents were forbidden to talk directly with the AG or his staff. The result was that the Associated Press ticker was almost always at least half an hour ahead of the Bureau in getting the facts.

We met in Byron White's office and tried to determine what to do. Byron gave a very objective presentation to Bobby, pointing out that we had no real intelligence on what local law enforcement would do, but that if they failed to act again, as they had done in Birmingham, we had a very serious problem in getting marshals to Alabama in any timely fashion.

One obvious course was to seek assurances from Alabama's governor, John Patterson. Seigenthaler met with him and had an unsatisfactory talk. Bobby tried to get him on the telephone. Patterson had been a very strong supporter of Kennedy at the 1960 convention, but the governor was not taking his call. Bobby said he would get the president to call him, which worried me, because I feared he would not take the president's call either. That turned out to be the case. I thought the governor's refusal to take the calls was sufficient evidence that he was "unwilling or unable"— in the words of the statute—to maintain law and order. But both the president and Bobby remained reluctant to commit the marshals. Both were more cautious than either Byron or I was. Both the president and Bobby would have liked the civil rights groups to have called the whole thing off, at least for a time. But there was no chance of that, and quite some resentment at the suggestion.

I find it hard to believe that some of this reluctance on the part of the Kennedys was not political, in the sense that several southern governors, Patterson in particular, had been for Kennedy as the Democratic candidate and surely would help a little with his current problems. One could hope, with some reason, that the solidly Democratic South would give the Democratic president they supported some leeway. The fact was they would not. But it may have taken a little time for the Kennedys to understand that fact. The Democratic Party had been schizophrenic about race for at least two decades. Nobody said that compromise was now at an end and the South would defect. Members of both the Senate and the House from the Deep South tended to vote with Republicans on most issues, but their power—their committee chairmanships—had been gained through seniority as Democrats. The party was still of importance to them. As Strom Thurmond, then a Democrat, once said to me in frustration, "I am a Democrat. I have always voted with the Democrats to organize the Senate." But that was about as far as it went.

Still, in retrospect, I find it hard to fault Bobby and the president. Their jerry-built marshal force of five to six hundred was conceivably useful as an emergency force. But it could not replace local law enforcement in several places at once or for any length of time. The alternative was the army, a second Reconstruction with consequences of enormous importance to our federal governmental system. Nor could one fault the civil rights groups and their supporters, who were seeking only to exercise rights guaranteed them by the Constitution—rights which, in the final analysis, were the responsibility of the federal government to enforce if the states did not. The objective was to get the South to abandon its caste system and accept its obligations under our Constitution. Undoubtedly the Kennedys were right in seeing voting rights as the best path to that end. But the timing was simply impossible if it had to be done through lawsuits on a voting-district-by-voting-district basis. And legislation at that time was clearly not an alternative.

Seigenthaler and Bill Orrick, the Civil Division head, who had accompanied him to Birmingham, met with Floyd Mann, the head of the Alabama Highway Patrol and a professional police officer of integrity. He promised protection on Alabama state highways, and a bus of Freedom Riders left Birmingham for Montgomery, with a police escort as far as the city limits. But when the bus arrived at the Montgomery bus terminal, a mob with bats and clubs attacked, undisturbed by the Montgomery police force. Seigenthaler, attempting to assist one of the Riders, was viciously attacked and badly beaten—all of which was carefully photographed by an FBI agent who did not see fit to interfere. Seigenthaler lay in the gutter for quite some time before being taken to a local hospital. The delay was caused by a massive "breakdown" of the white ambulance corps, which was thus unavailable to assist victims of the mob.

Bobby was furious and dispatched the five hundred previously assembled marshals under Byron White to the scene. There could be no serious question about the failure to maintain order by local police. Dr.

King headed by plane for Montgomery to preach that day—Sunday, May 21—and Governor Patterson told Bobby that he and General Graham, commanding the Alabama National Guard, could not guarantee King's safety. That seemed unbelievable, and was probably a ploy to get Bobby to call off Dr. King's sermon—as if he could, even if he tried. Fifty marshals escorted Dr. King through town to his church, and fifteen hundred blacks showed up at the church to hear King preach. An angry mob surrounded the church, burned a car in front of it, and gave every indication of preparing to burn down the church itself. Bobby assured King that marshals were on their way to protect him and his flock—but there was a problem of transportation. Byron solved it imaginatively by commandeering post office trucks, and the marshals were indeed on their way. But there was a serious question whether the marshals, armed with tear gas, could in fact hold off the mob. Eventually they were reinforced by the Highway Patrol under Floyd Mann and a few National Guardsmen under General Graham, and a standoff resulted, which lasted through the long night. Paratroopers at Fort Bragg were put on alert, despite the Kennedy reluctance to use federal troops. At dawn, Bill Orrick negotiated a truce with Graham and persuaded him to allow the blacks safe passage out of the First Baptist Church and back to their homes.

But the Freedom Riders were not done. Bobby wanted them to call off the rides, saying that they had made their point. That did not sit well with the civil rights activists, who were determined to push on to Mississippi. Former governor James Coleman, a racial moderate by southern standards, told Burke Marshall that when they arrived in Jackson they would be arrested and that Governor Ross Barnett could not be trusted. Bobby turned to Senator James Eastland, chairman of the Judiciary Committee, who was fond of Bobby. Despite their strong differences on race and liberal legislation, Eastland was always a man of his word. He told Bobby that the Riders would be safe from violence but that they would all be arrested in Jackson. And that is what happened.

Bobby wanted a cooling-off period. The civil rights activists wanted to keep the pressure on. What, if anything, could be done to satisfy CORE and the Freedom Riders? One of the lawyers in my office, Robert Saloschin, had done a good deal of work with the administrative agencies and suggested that we petition the Interstate Commerce Commission (ICC) to require the desegregation of all buses and bus terminals. Saloschin and I met with Robert Ginnane, general counsel of the ICC, but without any success. Ginnane doubted the authority of the ICC to deal with more than economic regulation.

But Saloschin had the bit in his teeth. "Well, the attorney general can formally and publicly petition the commission to desegregate all buses and terminals if he wants to."

That seemed a dramatic and somewhat original way of supporting the Freedom Riders, and Bobby liked it. So did the president. It did not really satisfy the civil rights groups, but it helped.

The petition, which, unusually, included Bob Saloschin's name as a reward for his ingenuity, was a powerful document that we filed on May 29, just about a week after the Montgomery mob's attack on the First Baptist Church. At least here the FBI's pictures of the violence had an impact. Finally, in September, the ICC came out with a sweeping order abolishing all segregation in travel, vindicating the Freedom Riders' efforts. Even then, it took the Civil Rights Division two years actually to enforce the order throughout the South.

The Freedom Rides were the first of a series of civil rights crises, and there were lessons to be learned. I am not sure how well we learned them, but it was a beginning. Bobby was pleased that we had not had to use troops and that the marshals had behaved so decisively to save Dr. King and his congregation. He saw it as a vindication of his policy of using civilian law enforcement—which it probably was not, as later events at Ole Miss proved. In retrospect, I think it fair to say that the success of the marshals was enormously aided by the presence of Alabama law enforcement under Floyd Mann, but the importance of this support may not have been adequately appreciated at the time.

Bobby's continued urging of a cooling-off period on the Riders was very unpopular with civil rights advocates. Bobby's concern, which all of us shared, was that Riders would be killed and that the federal government really lacked the power to prevent this from happening, although civil rights groups did not accept that conclusion. We could, under the law, put marshals on buses, the way marshals now travel on airlines. But a marshal or two or three on a bus was not going to control a mob. We could send in federal troops if the state was unable or unwilling to preserve peace and order. The approach of southern law enforcement to the preservation of law and order was simply to arrest the demonstrators, as Mississippi had done—obviously unsatisfactory to us, but what was the alternative? Attempts to get southern law enforcement to preserve law and order in a constitutionally correct way meant court injunctions, more than occasional violence, lost time as court processes dragged on, and iffy results from some southern judges.

Bobby's aversion to using troops had its roots in the presidential campaign and the criticism of Eisenhower's use of troops to enforce a court order to integrate the public school in Little Rock. The imaginative creation of a force of marshals was an effort to find a better alternative. But the Freedom Rider problem demonstrated that if state and local law enforcement officers simply would not do their job, five hundred marshals were not going to be a viable answer in the South as a whole. Using marshals raised the possibility, avoided in Montgomery because of Floyd Mann's efforts, of confrontation between local law enforcement and federal marshals—a truly frightening scenario.

Civil rights groups understandably put their rights under the Constitution as their top priority and demanded protection by the government. If it required the army, fine—send in the army. But there were other constitutional issues, primarily preserving, if possible, a workable federal system. How to achieve both was the problem. Troops did not seem any kind of long-term solution. Once they were committed to doing the job of local law enforcement, there was the obvious difficulty of withdrawal. What would happen when they left?

We had to try to make the political system work. Bobby got some private foundation funds to help CORE with voter registration. We continued to litigate. We supported groups like the Legal Defense Fund in court. Where possible, as in Birmingham, Burke Marshall secured compromises between blacks and whites. Black leaders like King continued to demonstrate and get arrested. We sought injunctions. The clock continued to tick.

V

ONE DAY IN THE FALL OF 1961 BOBBY ASKED ME TO TAKE A LOOK AT
the Satellite Communications Act. At the time it was uncertain whether
satellites in space could be used for commercial communications, but
if they turned out to be successful, they could be a very economical
substitute for long-line cables under the ocean and to remote locations.
Newton Minow, the dynamic new head of the Federal Communications Commission (FCC), was sponsoring a law that created a private
corporation to be owned by the telephone companies, primarily AT&T.
There was opposition by some Democrats, led by Estes Kefauver of Tennessee in the Senate, who wanted a government-owned corporation,
in part because so much of the opportunity came as a result of government space programs and in part because they disliked AT&T's near-
monopoly position. Lee Loevinger, who headed the Antitrust Division,
and Emanuel Celler, chair of the House Judiciary Committee, were also
unhappy with AT&T's role.

Bobby said that the president, despite Minow's closeness to the White
House, had some concerns about the FCC proposal and wanted me to
take a look at it. I did.

I shared concerns about turning satellite communications over to
existing companies with AT&T so dominant. It was also clear that government ownership—which was not such a bad idea—did not have a
prayer of passage in either the House or the Senate, even with JFK's
support. I suggested a private corporation whose stock would be sold to
the public and which would sell its communications capacity (if space
satellites worked) to the telephone companies. But it was to be a unique

corporation, because the president would have the power to appoint a minority of directors charged with insuring that the public interest was served.

Bobby liked this public-private compromise, and so did President Kennedy. My office drafted the bill, and it was submitted with administration backing. Kefauver did not like it. Neither did Senator Robert Kerr of Oklahoma, the most powerful man in the Senate and the sponsor of the FCC proposal. It was attacked by both camps, and administration witnesses testifying before the Senate committee were not doing too well. Eventually it came my turn to testify.

I was not an experienced congressional witness, but I certainly got an education that day. Kerr was not only powerful but very intelligent and articulate, an experienced businessman with a southern sense of humor. From the beginning he went on the attack, and I defended the proposal as well as I could, getting in several digs to the effect that I saw no reason to increase AT&T's power through what amounted to government subsidy. I was no match for the senator, particularly in his clever use of funny stories to make his point. I was a witness all morning, and at lunch he asked me to resume in the afternoon. We did, and he continued to beat me up mercilessly.

"Mr. Katzenbach, this morning I thought we made some progress. But now you remind me of driving my family back to Oklahoma in that big old car of mine. That car is a fine car, but it doesn't seem to be able to pass a Coke stand or a gas station without stopping, and then we have to start all over again." And so forth.

When I finally got back to my office, I was feeling pretty depressed about my innovative proposal. My secretary buzzed me: "The president is on the phone."

"Yes, Mr. President," I said with dread.

"Nick, I've just been talking with Bob Kerr." I knew it. It was bound to happen. "Can you have lunch with Senator Kerr tomorrow?"

"Of course, Mr. President, but I doubt he'll want to have lunch with me after my testimony today."

"Why do you say that? He told me you were the first administration witness who knew what he was talking about. That's why he wants to have lunch with you. He has some suggestions he wants you to think about."

I called Senator Kerr's office and made arrangements for lunch in the Senate dining room the next day. When we met, the senator told me that he did not particularly like my proposal but that perhaps it could be made to work. He was concerned that AT&T, without an ownership stake, would not buy into the new service if it came to pass and that the result would be disaster for the investing public. His suggestion was that half the shares be purchased by the carriers, half by the public, and that the president continue to be able to appoint directors as in our proposal. It seemed to me a reasonable suggestion, in some respects superior to what we had initiated, and I told him I would transmit it to the president after careful consideration and make my recommendation to him.

Senator Kerr, who was chair of the Senate Finance Committee, had just been engaged in a long fight with the administration on its tax proposals and was eager, I think, to do something of political service to the president to make up for his prior opposition. I recommended his changes to the president, and we proceeded along those lines. That was not quite the end of the story. Kefauver continued to push for his bill and commenced a filibuster against the Kerr proposals. AT&T continued to oppose anything but the FCC proposal. Senator Kerr called me into his office along with Horace Moulton, AT&T's general counsel, and told us in no uncertain terms that we should come to agreement. The remarks were obviously aimed at Moulton, not me.

"I know you two fellows can agree because you are two of the smartest fellows I know," said the senator. "Why, if you were any smarter, I don't know what you'd be—maybe senator from Oklahoma."

Republicans had joined with Kerr and some fellow Democrats to end Kefauver's filibuster. To end debate in the Senate—to invoke cloture—required two thirds of the senators to vote affirmatively. Since southern Democrats, who used the filibuster to defeat civil rights legislation, and those from western states with small populations traditionally never voted for cloture, it was a Republican-led effort to attain the necessary 67 votes. They succeeded, and although I doubt it occurred to any at the time, that vote became a crucial factor in persuading some Republican senators to vote again for cloture ending the southern filibuster and securing passage of the 1964 Civil Rights Act.

The filibuster had always been the means by which southern Senators prevented a vote on the merits of meaningful civil rights legislation, and supporters of the legislation had never been able to muster the necessary 67 votes to end the debate. There was a move in the Senate in the fall of 1961 to renew efforts to change the vote required for cloture from 67 to 60 votes, the supermajority specified in Senate Rule XXII. The argument put forward by Senator Kenneth Keating, a liberal Republican from New York, was that Article I, Section 5 of the Constitution, which gives each house the power to determine its rules, requires only a majority vote to make or amend its rules and that requiring a two-thirds vote to amend Rule XXII is therefore unconstitutional. Since the Constitution explicitly states those situations where a supermajority is required (such as expelling a member or overriding a veto), it follows that to add supermajorities to other situations would be to deny rights guaranteed by the Constitution to a majority.

The Senate is presided over by the vice president, who, with the help of the parliamentarian, rules on such questions. In both 1957 and 1959, Vice President Nixon had ruled that any provision of the Senate rules adopted by a previous Congress that denied a majority of a new Congress the right to make its own rules was, in his opinion, unconstitutional.

In September 1961, I received a request from Vice President Johnson to inform him on this point. It did not seem to me an appropriate matter for the executive branch to espouse, because it was so obviously an internal Senate matter, whatever its impact outside the Senate. Obviously the change being sought by liberals such as Keating would make a world of difference with respect to civil rights legislation, but it was anathema to southern Democrats and most Republicans.

Uncertain what to do, I spoke to Bobby, but he told me simply to use my own judgment. He did not want to be involved, I think because it involved LBJ. I therefore did essentially nothing except try to be helpful. I sent the vice president summaries of the best arguments I could find on each side of the issue. Nixon had confined his ruling to adoption of a rule at the beginning of a new Congress. Keating wanted to extend this to any rule at any time. That extension was significant.

The argument that the constitutional specification of supermajorities excludes Congress from making additional limitations on its own powers is not particularly persuasive. To put those situations beyond the power of a majority scarcely suggests that Congress itself could not create others. In essence, Keating wanted Section 5 to be read as a prohibition of any rule that prevented a majority from cutting off debate.

Senator Lyndon Johnson, then majority leader, had pointed out at the time the difficulty with the Nixon position. Unlike the House, whose entire membership is elected every two years, only a third of the Senate is elected biennially. The House adopts or readopts a complete set of rules every two years, but the Senate has from its very beginning seen itself as a continuing body whose rules remain in force until changed. This was a view accepted by constitutional scholars, including Edward Corwin, my favorite professor at Princeton, and one that the Nixon view simply ignored.

I took no position, but it was clear that Johnson had no reason to change his mind, and nothing I wrote would have given him reason to do so. Obviously civil rights groups liked the Keating view. But rejecting it did not really say anything about civil rights. At least I hoped it did not.

VI

IN THE DEPARTMENT OF JUSTICE AT THAT TIME, JUDICIAL NOMINA-
tions were primarily the responsibility of the deputy attorney general,
who also had responsibility for legislation and, generally, congressional
relations. That made sense, because most nominations to the district and
circuit courts were in fact made by the senator or senators from the state
involved who were members of the president's party. Where there were
no senators from the president's party, there was usually freedom for the
administration to choose.

Since federal judges are an important part of the federal governing
mechanism within a state, it makes good sense to give senators a voice
in their selection. At the same time, it is vitally important that judges are
politically independent and rigorously nonpartisan once they don their
robes. It is also important that they are competent lawyers. Politicians
want to use their power to recommend as a reward for loyal political
supporters who do not necessarily possess the other qualifications that
judges must have.

In an effort to insure the quality of nominations, Attorney General
Herbert Brownell, under President Eisenhower, got the American Bar
Association (ABA) to appoint a special committee with a member from
each judicial circuit to evaluate the professional qualifications of potential appointees when requested by the AG and rate them as "extremely
well qualified," "well qualified," "qualified," or "not qualified." Generally
the president was reluctant to nominate a candidate recommended by
the senator involved who was rated "not qualified." Reluctance did not
mean he might not oblige a powerful senator or that he could successfully

name someone else. It usually simply meant that the vacancy continued until the senator named a qualified candidate, and the continuing vacancy put some local pressure on the senator to do so.

The Senate enforced its power to name the candidate by dint of the practice of the chairman of the Judiciary Committee not to hold a hearing until he received a "green card" from the senators representing the state involved, indicating their assent to the nomination. In addition, as a matter of courtesy, other senators did not oppose persons thus deemed acceptable, so the hearings were almost always perfunctory love fests.

Where there were no Democratic senators to contend with, the administration had a relatively free hand to nominate candidates, though there could be some pressure from powerful congressmen or local political powers. In the Kennedy and Johnson administrations, we generally used those circumstances as opportunities to appoint Republicans who were not political and who were "exceptionally well qualified," thus improving our statistical record on both counts and making the local bar happy to have truly excellent appointments.

During my time in the Justice Department, I was entirely satisfied with the objectivity, thoroughness, and competence of the ABA committee, which was chaired by Bernard Segal, a Republican from Philadelphia (although, understandably, senators would have preferred less objective judgment). His committee never tried to influence a nomination, and since its investigation preceded any nomination, it was in a position to get unbiased and confidential opinions as to a candidate's competence from sitting judges and fellow lawyers. Because the trial bar has a major stake in trying cases before competent and apolitical judges, I felt then, and still feel, that the ABA committee performed an essential purpose.

There was little or no input on these appointments from the White House when a Democratic senator was involved. There were occasional efforts from those dealing with the Senate to urge us to go along with a particular senator's choice. Lawrence O'Brien and Michael Manatos, who worked from the White House on legislation in the Senate, did try to persuade us to recommend an unqualified candidate desired by a Democratic senator from time to time when a vote was needed, but Bobby, to his credit, resisted the pressure in almost all cases.

But there were some exceptions. Senator Kerr wanted a candidate whom the ABA committee found unqualified, but Kerr was so vital to the president's tax proposals and economic program that JFK succumbed. Indeed, I believe Kerr took pleasure in the finding, because when the president nonetheless sent the nomination to the Senate, it demonstrated Kerr's power. When, subsequently, there was another Oklahoma vacancy, the committee found the candidate to be not qualified, by a 6–5 vote. I called Bernie Segal and suggested that it was in everybody's interest to change one person's vote, since I was sure Kerr would once again get his way. Eventually Bernie must have seen my point, because the formal report to the Senate found the candidate qualified, 6–5. Actually, both judges turned out to be surprisingly good.

At the beginning of the Kennedy administration the Congress passed the Omnibus Judicial Vacancy Bill, creating some fifty new judgeships around the country. In the Office of Legal Counsel I had little or nothing to do with judicial appointments generally, but Bobby was concerned— rightly—about southern district court judges. Senator Eastland wanted the first appointment under the new act to be his, and he wanted his college roommate, William Harold Cox, to be the judge. The ABA rated him "extremely well qualified." But Bobby was concerned about how he would rule on civil rights cases and wanted to interview him. I had some reservations about the propriety of such an interview, because the department is the biggest litigant in the federal courts and because it seemed to me insulting to ask a distinguished lawyer whether or not, as a judge, he would follow the law. Bobby persisted, but was very narrow in his questioning. Cox assured him that he would follow the Constitution as interpreted by the Supreme Court. He was nominated, confirmed, and, as Bobby had feared, turned out to be impossibly racist in his rulings.

The system was not perfect. Perhaps no system can be. But Bobby's effort was to insure that judges respected and followed the law whether they liked it or not—which is a lot better than encouraging judges to follow their own social or political preferences, which I fear is where we have been heading in recent years. If we truly want competent judges to be politically independent, they will not be subjected to long interviews by political appointees in either the White House or the department.

While Legal Counsel was not involved in judicial nominations, I did get involved, more or less accidentally, in Kennedy's first appointment to the Supreme Court. Since it led to my promotion to deputy attorney general, I strongly emphasize the "accidentally." Nominations to the Supreme Court do involve the president personally. They are not only of great public importance and interest; they are the president's choice and are unlike other judicial nominations for that reason.

Justice Charles Evans Whittaker had informed the president of his intention to retire a week or two before it became public knowledge. Byron White became actively involved both because of his position and because of his familiarity with the Court through his clerkship there. He talked with me about possible candidates. He was particularly interested in Judge William H. Hastie of the Third Circuit, which sat in Philadelphia, who was black. While I did not then speak to Bobby directly, I assumed the interest was shared by him and perhaps even by the president. Byron also asked me for a list of the names of people I thought should be considered, and he shared the list he had composed with me. Our lists had a number of names in common. I dug out all of Judge Hastie's opinions and reviewed them.

The lists contained a number of obvious names of outstanding judges and scholars. From the State supreme courts there were Roger Traynor, chief justice of California, and Walter Schaefer, chief justice of Illinois. From the academic world came Paul Freund of Harvard, the leading Supreme Court scholar and historian, and (my addition) Edward H. Levi, provost of the University of Chicago and former dean of its law school (and later attorney general under President Ford). Arthur Goldberg, secretary of labor, was on the list, and I added an outstanding woman, Professor Soia Mentschikoff of Chicago (who prior to her appointment at Chicago was the first woman partner in a major New York law firm and the first female professor at Harvard). There were two or three others, but those I have named were the most serious candidates. As far as I could determine in conversations with Byron and later with Bobby and the president, there were no preconceptions as to whom to appoint or with respect to any particular political or social philosophy, except no racists need apply.

At the time I did not know if anyone on the Court was consulted. I thought it possible that Bobby had talked with his old friend and mentor William Douglas and perhaps even with the chief justice. If so, he did not share those conversations with me. I prepared a long memorandum on Hastie, in which I concluded that he wrote good, competent opinions, but I could not see the brilliance of a future Justice Black or Frankfurter or Douglas. That may have been unfair, because the Third Circuit, unlike the D.C. Circuit or the Second Circuits, tended to get fairly pedestrian issues. I think I also felt—as I know I did later, when Thurgood Marshall was appointed by Johnson—that the first black justice should be someone with whom blacks identified far more than they would with Hastie.

Byron and I prepared a list for the president to consider, with a brief description of various candidates. Byron had to leave town for some engagement in Denver, and I sent the list to Bobby. He said Paul Freund was a pretty obvious candidate, although I had reservations about President Kennedy's again turning to Harvard, this time for his first appointment to the Court. I think it may have been my Yale background talking, because Freund was certainly outstanding. Bobby's reservation was different. He told me that the president had offered Freund the post of solicitor general and Freund had turned it down in order to finish his Supreme Court history. He said he did not think a person who had turned down his brother should now be rewarded. I think where an outstanding candidate for the Court is involved, the fact that he turned down a lesser post to finish important academic work should not have been a factor and showed a certain immaturity on Bobby's part. We talked about some of the other candidates, and Bobby told me that the president had promised Arthur Goldberg that he would be considered, but he thought it was too early and that Goldberg was needed in the cabinet. At the time important wage negotiations in steel and other basic industries were taking place, and the president was trying hard to keep a lid on inflation. At the same time, he said that the idea of someone identified with JFK was appealing.

I asked Bobby if he had thought about Byron. He said he had, and that Byron ought to be considered. I told him he should think hard about it, because Byron's going on the Court would leave a huge hole in the department. I pointed out that John Seigenthaler had just left to become editor of the *Tennessean* and that he and Byron were the two closest advisers Bobby had. That annoyed him. He told me that he would not stand in Byron's way and that he was perfectly capable of running the department without him. I should see if Byron was interested.

I phoned Byron, and he was somewhat ambivalent about any desire to be a candidate. "The president can do much better than that," he said.

"The geography is good," I replied, meaning that a justice from Colorado would be preferable to adding a second from Massachusetts or California.

He repeated, "I think the president can do much better than that, and I would rather not be put on the list."

I said, "You are on the list. Do you really want me to scratch you off?"

"Well, I wouldn't be happy if you scratched me off entirely. But go ahead."

I thought the response ambiguous and did not push further. I reported the conversation to the attorney general and left Byron on the list that went to the president.

I met with the president and Bobby and expressed my views and, to the best of my ability, those of Byron. Appointing the first African American to the Supreme Court would have been quite sensational, but it was never discussed in my presence in those terms. When I gave the president my opinion that Judge Hastie was competent but not outstanding, he seemed to dismiss the idea of nominating him, although Bobby persisted. JFK was particularly interested in Justice Schaefer from Chicago—perhaps because Mayor Daley was interested too—but Schaefer had been born a Catholic and then raised a Protestant. That worried the president significantly. I also said that Justice Traynor, in my opinion, was intellectually superior. I thought Ed Levi, also from Chicago, was truly excellent, as was Freund, but that perhaps the president would not want to appoint a second Jew to the Court.

He blew up at that. "Why the hell shouldn't I?"

I explained the tradition of the "Jewish seat," then occupied by Felix Frankfurter, but the president was not impressed.

Then we got to Byron, and the president was quite enthusiastic about the idea. We also discussed Freund, who was obviously a strong candidate and one who would be well received by virtually everyone. I thought nominating Freund was like nominating a second Frankfurter and that nominating Traynor was like nominating a second Black. Both seemed to me extremely competent and extremely predictable. Strange as it sounds today, I thought predictability was a negative quality. It meant in a sense that the president was making the nomination because of the candidate's views, not simply his competence. And those views obviously had political consequences.

I left the meeting with the impression that it would probably be White, Hastie, or Freund. Bobby wanted Hastie and was still opposed to Freund because he had turned down the president. White had the advantage of being identified with the president and not with any particular set of views. The question with Hastie was whether he was the person to be the first black on the Supreme Court.

A day or two later I received a phone call from the president. "Byron really wouldn't be acceptable to the ABA, would he?"

I have no idea where he got this notion.

"He would be very acceptable to the bar. I have no doubt about that."

"What makes you think so? He's never been on the bench or written any scholarly articles or anything."

I said, "Mr. President, there isn't a practicing lawyer alive who wouldn't like to see someone like himself put on the Court, so not being a judge or a professor will be no handicap to Byron. If you want, I'll check it out with Bernie Segal."

"Do that," he said.

While I had talked to Bernie on previous occasions, I do not believe I had ever discussed the ABA's Committee on Judicial Appointments with him. I expressed some reservations about the need for an ABA opinion on the qualifications of a Supreme Court justice, since I could not imagine a president appointing anyone without a distinguished background. These would, I thought, always be people with national reputations, unlike candidates for the lower courts, whose qualifications could be impeccable but not well known outside their state. Bernie did not disagree. But he said the members of the committee worked very hard on trying to give a fair assessment of lower court candidates and that asking their opinion in advance on Supreme Court nominees was almost a reward for their hard work. I mentioned Byron, and Bernie told me he was confident that within a few hours he could get the committee to find Byron "exceptionally well qualified" if that was the president's selection. I also suggested to Bernie that four classifications were unnecessary in the case of the Supreme Court and made invidious distinctions between highly qualified people, and he agreed that that might be the case.

I told the president of our conversation, to which his reply was "No kidding." I also told both the president and Bobby that I was going to Williamsburg on a long-promised birthday trip for my oldest son and his friends. While there, I read in the newspaper that President Kennedy had nominated "Whizzer" White, the great All-American halfback and former Pittsburgh Steeler, to the Court. The nomination was extremely well received by Congress, the public, and the bar. There was also speculation that I would succeed Byron as deputy, which turned out to take place.

As I look back on that first nomination by JFK to the Court and compare it to what has been happening in recent years, I feel both sad that the process has become so politicized and somewhat naive to have thought that an obvious political institution would not be co-opted by ideological views, as it has been to a substantial extent.

Nominations to the lower federal courts have long had a political component, which is why, in effect, senators nominated and the president consented. In general these appointments were seen as a reward by a senator for an old friend and supporter, often a campaign manager or U.S. attorney, and frequently a person without much court experience. To raise the quality of the candidates without necessarily changing the political facts of life was the reason Brownell got the ABA involved. Trial lawyers have always believed that trial experience is an indispensable qualification for the district court, which is one explanation of why so many federal prosecutors have moved up the ladder to the bench.

Most trial lawyers will say that the political or ideological views of a trial judge are not very important. What is important is his experience with litigation, his demeanor on the bench, and the fairness of his rulings on evidence. He can be an excellent trial judge without being a brilliant scholar or an imaginative conceptualist. There can be problems, and we had them with the appointment of blatantly racist judges in the South. That is why Bobby decided to interview judges personally, to get their assurances that they would follow the Constitution as interpreted by the Supreme Court. Even that, of course, did not work, and I am not at all sure anything would have. But it may have led to the present practice of lengthy interviews of district court candidates by the department and, worse yet, of court of appeals candidates by lawyers in the White House. If so, it was an unfortunate precedent. There is no need for such interviews to determine the qualifications of a candidate, which can be determined by other means and interviews by other persons. When done by political appointees in an administration, it cannot help but influence the process in terms of what is expected of the nominee by the biggest and most powerful litigant, who also has the power of nomination and probably appointment. Worse, it suggests to the public that the process is political in the sense of assessing policy preferences rather than competence, independence, fairness, and objectivity. Of course, at least in regard to certain issues, that appears to be exactly its purpose today.

Arguably, on the court of appeals trial experience is less important and intellectual excellence is a legitimate objective. Here the very fact of appeal often indicates that there are open questions of interpretation to be determined. For that reason law professors, appellate lawyers, and government officials are frequent candidates, along with judges who might be promoted from the district court. But here too interviews by White House officials are not necessary to determine qualifications and once again suggest to both the candidates and the public what decisions are acceptable in certain areas of high political concern.

Our form of democracy, importantly, encompasses what we call the rule of law. What we mean by this concept is simply that government officials, both executive and judicial, will apply known, preexisting rules fairly and objectively and will change those rules or create new ones only in constitutionally prescribed ways, usually legislation. It is the accepted role of courts to insure that the rules are obeyed, by the political branches and by themselves. To promote this result, judges are expected to become nonpolitical and nonpartisan on assuming the bench and are given lifetime tenure.

Complete objectivity is certainly an unattainable goal, and concepts of fairness can vary. Legal realists are clearly right that words cannot completely control results and that when a judge dons his black robe he cannot completely shed a lifetime of experience in how he sees the world or become a robot without values, prejudices, and preferences. But this fact of life does not make the goal of objectivity and fairness a sham. We can ask judges to do their utmost to repress their own prejudices and bias and attempt to their utmost to achieve that objectivity without which the Constitution is at risk. If one assumes that this view is shared by judges and the bar generally (and I have no doubt that it is), both the supervisory and the collegial role of appellate courts, with the potential of different viewpoints articulated for consideration not only by litigants but by one's colleagues, helps.

The Supreme Court lacks such supervision as a practical matter, but it does have collegiality, which permits nine very intelligent people to share their views on a specific problem before them. It plays a political function, but that is largely as an umpire, maintaining the balance of power between the branches of government, the federal government and the states, and the people and governmental power—the limitations of the first ten amendments. In our federal democratic system, that role is crucial, because at bottom it is the mechanism for assuring the integrity of the political system. The judiciary is not the branch that establishes policy, but it does and should find policy in the Constitution itself—usually procedural policy, which insures that the political system works with all the freedoms and prohibitions against governmental overreaching that the founding fathers envisioned in very general terms.

Over the past century our political system has become infinitely more complex, and important shifts of power have taken place. As the population has grown and people have become increasingly interdependent, government at all levels has become more intrusive. The Great Depression brought federal and state governments into both economic management and social welfare. Two World Wars and several lesser ones greatly expanded executive power, already growing under the demands of the economy. The role of Congress as the policy-determining institution has given way to increasing delegation to the executive and substituting a supervisory role for itself. These fundamental changes have unavoidably brought the Court into more and more controversies of political consequence and made the integrity of the legal process even more important.

That the issues before it may appear to be more political than in the past can be a temptation to the Court to make more policy—to "legislate" more than is proper for its limited role. Obviously it cannot avoid making policy at the margins, however a case is decided. Perhaps it has gone further than necessary on some occasions and exceeded its proper role, though I think those occasions are rare, if indeed they exist. What is far more dangerous is the effort to politicize the Court by attempting to predict how a nominee will vote on particular issues of political moment without regard to the proper role of the Court. The danger is less that the predictions will be correct than the fact that these efforts themselves suggest to the public that the legal process is a sham and that all decisions are political. Politicizing the appointment process does affect the Court by casting doubt on the objectivity of its decisional process. The fact that complete objectivity is impossible does not lessen the value of the effort to play the judicial role as honestly as one can.

Byron White was nominated for the Court because he had the necessary intellectual credentials and because he was known to and identified with the president. He had graduated from Yale Law School with the highest grade average in twenty years, had clerked on the Supreme Court for Chief Justice Vinson, and was a partner in a leading Denver law firm. It could be predicted that he would be careful in his approach to a problem, that he understood the workings of the Court, and that he did not have strong preconceptions that would not yield to reason and facts. That I, at least, could not successfully predict his decisions is borne out by the fact that in the first case I argued before him, only a little more than a year later, his was the lone dissent.

Years later I asked Byron, quite improperly, why on earth he had dissented. He replied, in typical White fashion, "Nick, it was either because I did not understand your argument—or because I did."

The same, I think, could be said of Arthur Goldberg, whom Kennedy nominated as Frankfurter's replacement, although I think Goldberg's more widely known liberal convictions made him somewhat more predictable. But it was his excellence as a lawyer, his performance as labor secretary, and his loyalty to JFK, not his constitutional views, that got him nominated. Similarly, under LBJ, no one could have had more outstanding credentials than Abe Fortas, Johnson's first appointment, and LBJ's only reservation was that he might be criticized for appointing a crony. It was not Fortas's views but his friendship and his qualifications that got him nominated.

I do not suggest that the views of a potential Court nominee were irrelevant. None of the three would have been nominated if their views had been dramatically at odds with those of the president. But neither were their views necessarily very similar to one another's. And competing with White were two persons, Hastie and Freund, whose views were quite different. Political considerations have always been present in a general way. One would expect a liberal president to appoint a person with political views similar to his own, and the same could be said of a conservative president. But more important than those views is the dedication of the appointee to the legal process, to the constraints of the judicial role, and to the fact that determining policy within the limits of the Constitution is for the Congress, not the judiciary. Perhaps this limited role has been helped in the past by the fact that political views have not strayed far from the political center. Other considerations have also weighed importantly. Geography, for example, has been considered important, and so has sponsorship by powerful senators. What seems to me more important is that none of these candidates were being pushed on the president, or defended or attacked by special interest groups, *because* of their views, a common practice today. That, of course, is the unhappy product of the growing gap between the political parties and the fact that government has ceased to be from essentially the center.

Perhaps it is unfair, but clearly qualified candidates who have espoused what are thought of as extreme positions on the right or the left may not be acceptable candidates. It is not simply that their political views seem far out, but that there is a fear that the strength of those views might get in the way of reasoned judgments based solely on the evidence before them. That is rarely the case, but it may be a legitimate concern in some quite exceptional situations.

Today we go through what amounts to a charade that is harmful to the Court by suggesting that a candidate's views outweigh his or her qualifications. The effort is to find ideologically satisfactory candidates and then to seek to bolster their credentials. At the same time, preserving the image of independence and objectivity, both the president's staff and members of the Senate Judiciary Committee assert that it is improper to inquire how a candidate might rule while in fact making every possible effort to find out.

VII

THE JOB OF DEPUTY ATTORNEY GENERAL IS VERY DIFFERENT FROM THAT of legal counsel and in many ways less interesting for someone with my background, who loves law and problem-solving. For the first time in my life, I had a big administrative responsibility, was point man with Congress, and had absolutely no experience in how to do either job.

My duties were to serve as alter ego to the AG, so I often had the choice of deciding matters or discussing them further with the attorney general. In addition, the deputy was responsible for the legislative program and for judicial appointments. That meant a lot of time for me on the Hill. One aspect of being deputy, which was quite exciting at first, was attending cabinet meetings when Bobby was not available. Bobby regarded them as somewhat of a waste of time and often skipped them. It gave me the opportunity to meet the heads of departments and, for the first time face to face other than in a receiving line, Vice President Johnson. Bobby, of course, was right. Nothing of real importance was ever discussed.

I decided, after talking it over with Bobby, to take primary responsibility for the areas he cared least about and which, in fact, were the least important at the moment. I suggested that the Criminal Division and the Civil Rights Division report directly to Bobby and that the other divisions report first—and usually finally—to me. The solicitor general, Archibald Cox, was quite independent, and it was up to him to keep us both informed if he saw any problems. The same was fundamentally true of Prisons and Immigration. I got endless memos from the FBI but rarely dealt directly with Hoover. I recall Byron briefing me on my responsibilities and pointing to a stack of FBI memos. "I haven't had a chance to read those yet," he said. That same stack remained unread during my tenure, and I have often wondered if I missed something important. I doubt it.

My initial contribution, which at first was quite unpopular with my colleagues, was a written reporting system. Bobby had rather wistfully complained that he often did not know what was going on in the department. The memos I suggested, on a daily basis for the major divisions and weekly for the others, were designed to keep the attorney general (and me) informed of major problems in not more than two pages. I defined "major problems" as (1) what the assistant attorneys general thought most important, (2) something that might appear in the press, and (3) something the White House might inquire about. After bitter complaints about unnecessary paperwork, the system was begun and soon began to run smoothly. Before long the assistant attorneys general were happy, because it required their various sections to report to them in the same fashion, albeit in more detail, and they found this a convenient way to keep track of what was going on in their own divisions. The edited short reports went to Bobby, Ed Guthman in Public Information, and me. I felt I had the makings of a bureaucrat, though I could never hope to compete with J. Edgar Hoover. I think more than any other single act, those reports made both Bobby and me feel that we knew what was going on and served to bring us together with a better basis of mutual understanding. We could discuss problems on an even level. And it was a godsend to Guthman, who had to know what was going on, what progress was being made, and where the problems were to do his job effectively.

I was fortunate to have inherited from Byron two outstanding deputies in Joe Dolan and Bill Geoghegan. Both knew their jobs—and, for that matter, mine—far better than I did and pitched in to make the transition as smooth as possible. I spent time on the legislative program, modest as it was, by talking at length with members of Congress on the Judiciary Committees of the House and Senate, primarily with the chairmen. Joe and Bill did most of the work on judicial appointments, and I usually got involved only when a senator's candidate was clearly not qualified or when the ABA had found that to be the case. Vetting a candidate thoroughly can be a lot of work, and we were reluctant to ask the ABA to do this when the result was predictable. Sometimes a conversation on my part with Segal would suffice to convince a senator to find another candidate. We always tried to get two or three candidates from a senator so we could pick the best-qualified, but that ploy seldom succeeded.

As I've noted, the chairman of the Senate committee was James East-land of Mississippi, and Emanuel Celler of New York led the House Committee. Two people could not be more different. Celler was an aging liberal from Brooklyn who spent only the middle of the week in Washington. He came from a safe Democratic district where he got 90 percent of the vote, but he constantly worried about any position he espoused that he thought might offend some of his supporters. It was a constant problem to get him to schedule hearings or press his various subcommittees to do so. Apart from that, he was easy and pleasant to work with.

Senator Eastland was a conservative southern racist who liked Bobby, had liked Byron, and was prepared to like me. He ran his committee efficiently, and if you did not discuss civil rights, he was easy to work with. I could run down our legislative program and get definitive answers: yes or no, when, who had to be persuaded, and often a suggestion on how to do it or why it was not possible. He was always courteous and always available. Despite his views on race—which may have been as political as they were social—I respected him.

I remember one morning sitting in his conference room waiting to ask the senator about a bill when most of the committee came in, followed by the chairman. It was obviously an executive session, and I jumped up to leave.

"No need to leave, Nick," said Eastland. "This won't take long."

"I've called this meeting to discuss private immigration bills," he said to the others. "I suggest we vote out all bills proposed by senators on either side of the aisle who are up for election this year." Pause. "There being no discussion, the motion is passed."

And that was that. The senators filed out of the conference room.

Eastland made it clear to me that any discussion of civil rights legislation was out of bounds, and obviously he would be of no help. That included the nomination of black judges for confirmation, but he did indicate to Bobby that they would be confirmed after what he felt was appropriate delay. I don't think he really cared very much, but he had a race role to play for his constituents in Mississippi. One major instance was the nomination for the Second Circuit Court of Appeals of Thurgood Marshall, whose work as head of the Legal Defense Fund made him a target for white southerners. Eastland scheduled no hearing after his nomination in 1961, and President Kennedy took the unusual course of a recess appointment to the court—good for one year. Eastland had told Bobby in confidence that Thurgood would be confirmed before the end of the term, so neither Bobby nor Thurgood was particularly concerned. But the two Republican senators from New York, Kenneth Keating and

Jacob Javits, raised a fuss about the delay and forced Eastland's hand. The hearings went on for several days, with Eastland allowing all kinds of scurrilous testimony.

On about the third day of the hearings, I got a phone call from the president. "Did you see that picture on the front page of the *New York Times* of Keating and Marshall? Who the hell nominated him for the court, me or Keating? From now on I want you to pick up Thurgood in a car, take him to the hearing, and stick right with him."

So I did.

The next morning we arrived at the hearing and were seated side by side when Senator Keating came into the hearing room. Keating was a member of the Judiciary Committee, but before taking his place on the rostrum he came down to greet Thurgood and sat down on the other side of him. The photographers arrived, but I was alert. Fearing a picture of just the two of them and the president's wrath, I got behind them and leaned over in the middle—but not low enough. The next morning, there was the paper and a picture of Keating and Marshall—and no me. The president called, somewhat testy, as I had feared.

"Keating and Marshall are on the front page of the *New York Times*. Where the hell were you?"

"Well, Mr. President," I said, "that's my necktie hanging in between them."

A short silence was followed by a chuckle as he realized what had happened. "Nick, do better next time."

In general I think the transition from legal counsel to deputy went smoothly, largely because Bobby was tolerant and both Joe Dolan and Bill Geoghegan were now experienced enough to be enormously helpful. Bobby respected my legal judgment, as he had that of Byron and his other Ivy League team members. The fact that he did not value his own legal skills highly, unlike most attorneys general, but at the same time wanted to use the law correctly turned out to be a strength. We were a team and worked as a team under his leadership.

There were some problems, more awkward than serious. One was Lee Loevinger and the Antitrust Division. Lee had given up a seat on the Minnesota Supreme Court to take the antitrust job and had been strongly sponsored by Senator Hubert Humphrey and the secretary of agriculture, Orville Freeman. He was very bright, an excellent lawyer, and (at least in my opinion) a terrible administrator. Despite obvious qualifications, intellectual, political, and personal, he never became a member of the team. He traveled a good deal and enjoyed making speeches, which were uniformly excellent. But he could not run his division.

I was not an experienced antitrust lawyer and knew far less than Lee did about the law. I would read the memos he sent seeking authority to bring a case and find them almost incomprehensible. I would ask Burke to look at them, despite his being overworked, and he usually confirmed my judgment. You could not tell from the memo whether the case was a good one that should be brought or not. And since virtually every antitrust case gets close political scrutiny, it was pretty important to know.

I would talk to Lee when he was available and often got the same response. "I know it's not a good memo. My people simply can't write very well, and I don't have the time to edit everything they do. But I'm satisfied it's really a good case."

Since he had the time to write first-rate speeches, I found that annoying—the more so because I knew I would have to defend the case to some inquiry from Congress or the White House.

Bobby wanted a vigorous antitrust policy, but he also wanted a sound one. Loevinger's Republican predecessor, Robert Bicks, had filed a number of cases in the closing months of the Eisenhower administration and received praise for his courage from the liberal press, but he left us with a number of lemons, many of which Bobby had to dismiss. It is hard to think of anything Bobby disliked more than bringing a bad case which had to be dismissed and then being criticized by liberals for its dismissal. So running the Antitrust Division had been an important priority for Byron, and unfortunately, Lee Loevinger just was not the right man.

Apparently Byron had made similar complaints, so Bobby was prepared to do something about it. We both liked Lee, and he had powerful sponsors. Eventually Bobby found a place on the Federal Trade Commission that suited Lee's judicial abilities. It helps to be the president's brother. And we agreed after much discussion that Bill Orrick, who was the best administrator in the department, would be ideal for the job despite his lack of antitrust experience. Like a good soldier he took it, albeit reluctantly.

One of Bobby's strengths, which many have commented on, was his eagerness to learn. Late in 1961, before I was promoted, Bobby had persuaded Arthur Schlesinger, the great historian and White House liberal intellectual in residence, to set up a monthly seminar, usually held at Hickory Hill. Bobby's concept was simply that there were many ideas outside the Beltway to which it would be healthy to expose government officials operating in different fields, because we all tend to become too focused on the immediate problems of the areas we are responsible for. The guest list of "students" was, to say the least, eclectic. By and large the speakers were exceptional, everyone participated, discussions were lively, and attendance was always close to 100 percent. I was enormously flattered when Bobby included Lydia and me on his list—a list that included Jackie and occasionally the president, the Robert McNamaras, the Stewart Udalls, the Averell Harrimans, the Arthur Schlesingers, and a few others. What I found most interesting was spending time with government officials and their wives—people I usually saw either on business or socially—in a different and more intellectual setting. Discussion and questions added a dimension to one's knowledge of colleagues and, more important, helped one feel an intimate part of the administration.

I recall one session in which George Kennan, the great Soviet expert, talked about Eastern Europe, where he then held an ambassadorship, and the Soviet Union. For some reason I now cannot remember, he began discussing poverty in Europe and in the United States. After a few minutes, Averell Harriman, the multimillionaire statesman and FDR's ambassador to the Soviet Union, stood up and interrupted. "George," he said, "you know far more about Eastern Europe and the Soviet Union than anyone I can think of. But you know nothing about poverty, and I have been studying it all my life!"

It brought the house down, but I am not sure Averell understood why.

Lydia recalls a meeting with the well-known psychoanalyst Lawrence Kubie, from Baltimore, as guest speaker. Dr. Kubie spoke at length about his summer vacation on an isolated island in Puget Sound and having volunteers from the town show up to help with his daily fishing expedition. Dr. Kubie suggested that the tales of woe and trouble from the islanders were no different from those he heard every day in his private practice in Baltimore. At the question period after his speech, which emphasized that people from all levels of society shared the same human life issues, Ethel Kennedy asked, "Dr. Kubie, will you come to Hyannisport for next summer's vacation?"

A more poignant occasion—at least in retrospect—was a session held upstairs in the White House living quarters in which Professor Eric F. Goldman, a presidential historian, discussed what made presidents great. President Kennedy was fascinated and well informed, asking a number of good historical questions. Finally, almost in exasperation after a discussion of Lincoln and Franklin Roosevelt, he remarked, "It looks to me like you have to die in office to be classified as great by historians."

VIII

THE SPRING AND SUMMER OF 1962 I SPENT TRYING TO GET ON TOP OF my new job. Surprisingly, in some ways I had less contact with Bobby and the White House than I had had as legal counsel. In civil rights we went along from crisis to crisis, trying to concentrate on voter registration but with the constant need to deal with arrests of black demonstrators or sit-ins and with the constant threat of violence by white sheriffs or by racist mobs. The dangers were real. The country needed time to work out peaceful solutions—if, indeed, that could in fact be done. Blacks, understandably, were out of patience with any process that denied them rights that had been guaranteed them for a century.

The problem remained the same. The South wanted peace and was for the most part opposed to violence. Dr. King preached nonviolence despite enormous provocation—for which this country owes him a great debt—but it was not easy for him to control his more militant young followers. Maintaining law and order to southern police officials meant arresting black demonstrators and people at sit-ins. That meant maintaining peace at the price of constitutionally guaranteed rights—hardly a solution satisfactory to the department or its young attorney general.

The department was criticized on all sides. Civil rights leaders did not doubt the Kennedys' good intentions but were critical of what they considered too much caution. This view was shared by the Civil Rights Commission, which was openly critical. In the South, Bobby Kennedy was seen as a brash young man with no respect for southern customs. The country generally wanted peaceful solutions but was quite divided on who was responsible for what violence, threatened or actual.

Critics were quite right that from a legal point of view, we had the power to do more. The Legal Defense Fund, for example, brought a number of school desegregation cases. There was enough legislation to empower us to bring such cases, but it was a long and tedious process to desegregate schools district by district. We were more inclined to promote voting registration. But the problem was not whether we had legal power. It was always how to get compliance with the law. The best bet was litigation and a court order requiring certain specified conduct from state or local officials under pain of imprisonment for contempt. The Kennedys liked that approach, because it put much of the onus for an unpopular act on the courts, and more clearly than any other alternative it allowed what appeared to be a neutral law enforcement posture rather than a political objective. The department, after all, is meant to enforce the law, not its own policy preferences. The threat of imprisonment for contempt was fine if it worked. But if it had to be enforced against a prominent law enforcement or political figure, there were obvious problems of arrest and punishment—direct confrontation between federal and state authorities.

The approach of both Bobby and Burke Marshall was always, insofar as possible, to avoid confrontation and see if it was not possible to mediate differences and arrive at a compromise. This "half-a-loaf" approach where fundamental rights are concerned is not very satisfactory, but none of us was able to come up with anything better. It did give us the opportunity to engage more reasonable elements of the white community in seeking peaceful solutions and laying some groundwork for the future. But it was seen as unprincipled cowardice by many of the more liberal elements.

Burke Marshall prevented bloodshed in Birmingham by working out a compromise between Dr. King and the business community. John Nolan, another former Supreme Court clerk, who had succeeded Seigenthaler as Bobby's executive assistant, did a similar crisis management job in Gadsden, Alabama, and others worked quietly in Atlanta, Albany, and elsewhere with school boards and police chiefs—not really under the illusion that they were effectively solving civil rights problems but putting out fires and gaining time. A major initiative was mounted by Bobby using William vanden Heuvel to attempt to resolve the school crisis in Prince Edward County, Virginia, perhaps the nadir of intractability. Authorities there, rather than integrating public schools, simply closed them in 1959, and the white students for the most part attended private schools. A legal action to require the county to reopen the schools was stalled in the courts, and 1,700 black children were going uneducated.

Vanden Heuvel worked out an interim plan to lease the schools with funds that had been privately raised, and some exceptional teachers volunteered to teach. The program was so successful that a few white children attended the black schools. Five years later, all schools were finally ordered reopened by the court.

In September came the problem of James Meredith's admission to the University of Mississippi. The case had been brought successfully by the Legal Defense Fund, and the department joined as *amicus curiae* in the Supreme Court. Justice Hugo Black issued an order requiring the university to admit Meredith under pain of contempt for the board of trustees, including Governor Ross Barnett. Bobby had several telephone conversations with the governor, seeking his assurances that Meredith would be admitted and that the state would maintain law and order. As Governor Barnett weaved and evaded through several long conversations, it became increasingly evident that he was playing games and had never seriously intended to admit Meredith. For example, the local authorities trumped up criminal charges against Meredith—charges made out of whole cloth—and said he would be arrested if he tried to register. The governor responded that he was powerless. Justice Black was adamant, as was the whole of the Fifth Circuit Court of Appeals. But the governor would not make a clear commitment, and when he appeared to do so, he promptly withdrew it. Bobby was furious but quietly determined to prevail through rational persuasion, if that was possible. Our message to Barnett was that he could protest all he wanted, but he should be prepared to yield to superior federal law and be able to keep the peace.

As usual, maintaining law and order meant maintaining order at the expense of law. Barnett wanted Bobby to postpone Meredith's admission as the way to maintain order. Since Barnett did not want to be charged with criminal contempt, he wanted Bobby to back down. Bobby dispatched some six hundred federal marshals under Jim McShane to a naval base at nearby Memphis, this time with all the necessary transportation. He was prepared to allow the governor to save face by yielding to the superior federal force, but he needed to be confident that law and order would be maintained. He thought the governor had agreed, but with Barnett, one could not be sure. There was never a question in Bobby's mind that Meredith would register and attend the university and that the court order would be enforced. Not to have done so could have been a disaster leading to violence which none of the civil rights leaders could have controlled, destroying the credibility of the department he headed. At the same time he wanted to use reason and persuasion to accomplish what had to be accomplished, and that may have been a serious misreading of the strength of southern racism.

Near midnight on Saturday evening, September 29, President Kennedy signed an executive order putting the Mississippi National Guard in federal service—with the exception of the commanding officer, General Cameron, who was also Judge Cameron of the Fifth Circuit Court of Appeals. We felt we might need him more in his judicial capacity. Units of the regular army were also put on alert, but the hope was that neither they nor the guard would in fact be needed. Bobby's biggest fear, and indeed the president's, was that there would be a confrontation between the military and local law enforcement.

On Sunday, September 30, I was in my office at the department, as were Bobby, Burke, and others, still trying to hammer out a suitable plan for Meredith's admission to Ole Miss. Bobby rang me early to ask me to go on *Meet the Press* in his place, since he was still dealing with the Meredith matter. When I had finished that assignment, I returned to his office, about noon. He looked tired and haggard—more so than I had ever seen him. He looked up at me and said, "Nick, do you have anything important going on this afternoon?"

"No," I replied.

"Would you mind flying down to Oxford and taking charge of the marshals? I'd feel much better if you were there."

"Okay," I replied. "What do you want me to do?"

"Nothing much," said Bobby. "Just get Meredith registered and keep the peace." This with a smile.

"Any ideas?" I asked.

"The governor says that Colonel Birdsong and the state Highway Patrol will help. He says the campus is deserted today and it's a good time for Meredith to get ready to register. But obviously I don't trust him."

Just about then Harold Reis stuck his head in the door to say goodbye.

"Harold," said Bobby, "are you doing anything special this afternoon?"

"No," said Harold. "Why?"

"Well," said Bobby, "I wonder if you'd be free to go with Nick."

"Okay," said Harold. "Do I have time to pack a bag?"

"No," said Bobby. "You're leaving now." We picked up Ed Guthman and Norbert Schlei, who had succeeded me as legal counsel, and got a car to go to Andrews Air Force Base.

As we were leaving the office, Bobby looked up and said, "Nick, don't worry about anything. The president needs a moral issue."

For the first time I realized he was really worried about us. It was his way of saying to be careful.

As the four of us headed for Andrews, Harold innocently asked, "Where, may I ask, are we heading?"

"Oxford, Mississippi," said Guthman.

"Oh," said Harold, smiling. "Next time I'll ask first."

At Andrews we got on a JetStar and headed for Oxford. The pilot then informed me that the runway was 200 feet below the minimum length. I called Jeeb Halaby, who was head of the Federal Aviation Authority (FAA), for permission to use the short runway. He was reluctant to give it but finally consented, provided we jettisoned most of our fuel, which we did. As we arrived at Oxford, I looked out the window and saw several hundred white-helmeted marshals, along with a crowd of curious observers, awaiting our arrival. We landed at about six o'clock and rushed to the very end of the runway, where the pilot turned to me.

"Are you sure they are friendly?" he asked.

I told him they were, and we taxied back to where they were waiting by the terminal building.

We were met by John Doar, Jim McShane, and Joe Dolan, who arrived with Colonel Birdsong. John briefed us on the most recent developments. Lou Oberdorfer was in the basement of the Federal Building, manning a Border Patrol radio that could keep us in touch with one another throughout the Oxford area by walkie-talkies. I called Bobby collect to see if there had been any change in plans. There had not been. The plan, worked out with Colonel Birdsong, was for half the marshals to go on campus to the Lyceum building, which was the principal administrative building and the one where Meredith would register in the morning. John Doar would remain at the airport with the rest of the marshals to wait for Meredith to arrive and escort him to his dormitory room, where he would remain with a few hand-picked marshals to guard him.

Dolan and I proceeded the mile or so to the campus in a Highway Patrol car with the colonel. Half the marshals followed us in army trucks and were shouted at and jeered by a crowd as they proceeded. A large group of Mississippi Highway Patrol officers under Colonel Birdsong were in cars in front of the Lyceum. State Senator George Yarborough, the Speaker of the Mississippi House, was in the Lyceum building representing the governor and wished to talk to me.

I went with Joe Dolan and Norb Schlei to the office being occupied by the senator. Colonel Birdsong was with him. I told them I was delighted to see the Highway Patrol, that Governor Barnett had promised law and order, and that I thought in view of their presence it would be wise to put the marshals out of sight, in reserve. Could we perhaps use the gym for temporary housing?

Senator Yarborough was less than accommodating. Not only would he provide no temporary accommodations for the marshals, but since we had taken control of the campus, he was going to order the state Highway Patrol to leave. All he wanted was to avoid violence, and since we had enough people to control any violence, the Highway Patrol served no useful purpose. The gist of my argument was that if he removed the patrolmen, violence would occur. It was my understanding that the governor had promised they would remain to help maintain law and order. It was clear to me that the marshals were a red flag to students but that the Highway Patrol, composed of Mississippians, might be able to preserve order.

I put my case to Colonel Birdsong. "Colonel," I said, "this is a matter for a professional police officer and not something either Senator Yarborough or I can really judge. I would like your views as to which course would be more likely to lead to violence and which course would be more likely to avoid it."

The Colonel was not much help. "For God's sake, don't put me in the middle," he said.

I told the senator that I doubted he had the authority to remove the Highway Patrol without conferring with the governor. Joe Dolan called Bobby and told him our problem and suggested that the governor instruct Yarborough not to remove the patrolmen. Yarborough refused to call Barnett because he knew the governor's views, but while he was refusing to call Barnett, Barnett called him. After the call, he told me that neither he nor the governor wanted violence and that the Highway Patrol would be withdrawn in an orderly way. He tried to negotiate a time for withdrawal, and I argued that they should stay as long as necessary. He appeared to acquiesce.

While we were conferring with the senator, two things happened. John Doar had quietly escorted Meredith, unobserved, to his dormitory room and left him there with a small group of marshals. Outside the Lyceum, a crowd was gathering and getting more and more unruly. The line of marshals around the building was inside the ring of patrol cars, but the orange vests and white helmets of the marshals were clearly an incentive for attack by the crowd. The crowd, many of whom were students returning from a football weekend away from Oxford in Jackson, assumed that the marshals were protecting Meredith, who they thought must be in the building.

Senator Yarborough said he would go out and calm the crowd. Did we have any loudspeakers? We did, but discovered we had left them with the group at the airport. To his credit, the senator made an effort to disperse the crowd, but without loudspeakers it just did not work. The crowd got increasingly vicious, burning an army truck and throwing stones, rocks, and bricks at the marshals.

The Highway Patrol made little or no effort to break up the crowd. Perhaps it was so far out of control that the time to do so had passed. The patrolmen's presence had at first deterred the crowd, but they became increasingly less effective. Colonel Birdsong told me they had no crowd control equipment, no tear gas and no gas masks, and therefore he hoped we would not use tear gas. He did not suggest any alternative. I told him that tear gas was a last resort and that we would try to avoid its use. Could he perhaps move the crowd back? The patrolmen made a halfhearted effort and moved the protestors two or three feet. Maybe more was not possible.

As things got uglier and more violent, a number of the Highway Patrolmen got in their cars and left, over my protests, but a skeleton force remained. In addition to stones and bricks, people in the crowd began to throw an occasional Molotov cocktail (Coke bottles filled with gasoline). I authorized McShane to use tear gas when and if he found it necessary. The marshals put on masks and got their gas guns at the ready. It was already too late for tear gas to be effective as a dispersing force. There were too many rednecks in the crowd, in addition to the returning students, and they were too worked up. When we used the gas, the rest of the patrolmen disappeared. The senator had quietly disappeared earlier.

The crowd grew rapidly as more and more outsiders joined the students. They were convinced that Meredith was in the Lyceum building and began mounting ever more serious attacks. Before long gunshots rang out, and it was obvious that four hundred marshals with tear gas could not control a crowd that was building from two or three hundred to two or three thousand. The marshals were all armed but under strict orders not to use their handguns (except for the few guarding Meredith), and they did not, despite the extreme provocation of being shot at. I declined to give them permission, and they requested that I ask Bobby.

Shortly after arriving earlier in the evening at the Lyceum, I had found a pay phone and called the White House collect. We kept that line open all night, taking turns speaking to Bobby, the president, and Burke Marshall. In a very real sense it became our lifeline and Bobby's source of information. I relayed the marshals' request to Bobby, who declined permission for them to shoot, quite rightly. We were trying desperately to avoid any significant bloodshed, and using small arms would not help. What we needed was the military, and although using soldiers was what we had all tried to prevent, it soon became clear that nothing but a show of overwhelming force would suffice. Shortly after ten o'clock, when the president was on the air (although I did not know this at the time), I reluctantly told Bobby we needed the army.

Getting the army from Memphis to Oxford became a comedy of errors and made a long night even longer. President Kennedy, unaware that Colonel Birdsong had left the campus minutes earlier and that the crowd was beginning to get violent, had gone on television with a speech designed to praise the governor, the university, and local authorities for yielding to the Supreme Court order and admitting Meredith. Governor Barnett was denying any such yielding, and the result was that the speech had a negative impact on the crowd and on the increasing number of rednecks converging on Oxford.

Another result of the speech was that the troops on alert in Memphis went off alert and left the airport. If needed, they were to fly to Oxford rather than come by ground in a convoy, which would have taken a good deal more than an hour. In addition to dealing with the problem of recalling them, we needed to equip them with rifles for the rapidly escalating riot at Oxford, as they were prepared only for military police duty in an unarmed situation. The local contingent of the National Guard did arrive at the Lyceum—a company under the command of Captain Murry C. Falkner, a nephew of the famous writer, who arrived with a broken arm from missiles thrown by the crowd. Ironically, one of the soldiers was Governor Barnett's son. It said a good deal about the mood and the composition of the crowd that they would attack their own so viciously, and the guardsmen deserved a lot of credit for responding to the order to enter the campus.

We were running short of tear gas, the crowd was building, and there was no sign of the army. The president was on the phone to both Army Secretary Cyrus Vance and General Creighton Abrams, who had been assigned the responsibility for military support. Not only were the delays unfortunate in the circumstances, but army communications were less than perfect. Vance was depending on a planning schedule with estimated times to tell the president where the troops were and when they would arrive at the airport in Oxford. Several times Bobby told me on the phone that the troops were arriving at the airport. We knew they were not, because our people stationed there reported that they were not. And this infuriated the nervous president and attorney general sitting in the White House. We were nervous too, but somehow a Border Patrol marshal drove a truck with a fresh supply of tear gas from the airport through the campus, and the marshals, despite many injuries, continued to perform outstandingly in the face of attack and gunfire. They resisted the obvious temptation to shoot back, which a less disciplined and less courageous group would have done. That simple restraint showed enormous respect for Jim McShane and, in my view, for the attorney general. That night 2 civilians were shot and killed by rioters, 1 marshal was shot in the throat, 25 others had gunshot wounds, and 160 marshals in all were injured.

Eventually the army did arrive—some 25,000 troops under General Charles Billingslea—shortly after midnight and none too soon. We were in fact out of tear gas, and we had waited anxiously for almost an hour as the troops made their way the short distance from the airport to the campus. At my suggestion they secured the power station and the nearby chemistry building, two areas that I had been concerned about all evening. I also suggested putting roadblocks on all the roads going into Oxford and taking any guns. I told them to tag the guns and assure the owners that they could recover them when things quieted down. In rural Mississippi every pickup truck contains a gun for squirrel hunting, and there were an extraordinary number of squirrel hunters out that night.

I wasn't remotely sure what authority the army had to take this action, but it seemed like a good idea at the time. I got a telephone call from Judge Cameron.

"Has the President declared martial law?" he asked.

"No sir," I replied.

"What is your authority for establishing these roadblocks and confiscating all those guns, then?" he asked.

"We aren't confiscating them," I replied. "They will be returned as soon as things calm down, and no one is being arrested or charged simply for having a gun. I think it's essential to get things back to normal."

There was a short pause, in which I think General Cameron may have replaced Judge Cameron. "Good idea," he said.

The military quickly took over, the crowd dispersed, and the beautiful campus became an armed camp reeking of tear gas. At 8 a.m., James Meredith, escorted by John Doar, Jim McShane, a few marshals, and some soldiers, registered as a student at the University of Mississippi. He was taunted and cursed by his fellow students and needed protection by the army throughout his time there, but he tenaciously stuck it out—a brave man who received perhaps the most expensive public education in our history.

Shortly after Meredith was registered, I got a telephone call from the dean of the Mississippi Law School, Robert Farley, who like many of us in the department, was a graduate of Yale Law School.

"Nick," he said, "how would you feel about coming over to the law school and talking to the students about the Constitution and civil rights?

"Are you kidding?" I asked.

"No," he said. "Seriously, I think it would be a good idea. It's their Constitution too. And it's time the problem was discussed rationally, not politically."

"Okay," I said, and we arranged for me to go to the law school auditorium at eleven.

When I arrived, the auditorium was packed with students and faculty. I had washed up but must nevertheless have cut a pretty bedraggled figure, given the fact that I did not even have a toothbrush, thanks to Bobby's spontaneous decision-making. I said a few words about why we were there and the enforcement of court orders and the history of James Meredith's effort to be educated at Ole Miss and then offered to answer questions. My eight years of teaching law students paid off, and I actually enjoyed myself. Two things impressed me, one positively and the other negatively. First, the faculty often jumped into the discussion, invariably on my side. I remember one professor leaping up after a long question—in fact, more speech than question—and saying loudly and convincingly, "You never learned anything like that in my class!"

The second impression was the dislike, almost hatred, of Bobby. The students seemed prepared to believe that he enforced civil rights simply as the effort of a privileged northern brat to disturb the southern way of life, as if it were some sort of rich man's game. But it was encouraging as time went on to see how the atmosphere changed and the students became genuinely interested in the problems and the difficulties—a credit to Bob Farley and his faculty.

When I left the law school, I immediately encountered another problem. General Billingslea, apparently with the permission of Secretary Vance, had determined that roadblocks manned in part by black soldiers were offensive to local whites. He had removed blacks from that duty. This seemed to me the height of absurdity—to send the army to insure the admission of a black student and then remove black soldiers from their normal duties and confine them to tents. The press would—and in fact did—quite rightly indulge in an orgy of criticism. I tried to get in touch with Bob McNamara and with Vance, feeling certain that there had been some mistake, without success. Finally I called Bobby and the policy was quickly withdrawn, but not until serious damage had been done to the army's image and, inevitably, the Department of Justice's also.

The problem now, as I saw it, was to remove the bulk of the troops who were occupying the campus and to get back to something closer to normal as quickly as possible. That proved to be almost as slow a process as getting the troops there in the first place. General Billingslea was reluctant to leave before he had in his judgment completed the assignment, and he was not particularly interested in my judgment. He became somewhat more attentive when someone explained to him the distinction between deputy attorney general and deputy marshal, but he still saw it as a military show.

I received a phone call from Senator Eastland, who was at his Mississippi plantation and wanted to know if the campus was safe. I had not realized that his daughter was a student at Ole Miss. I told him it was the safest place in the United States unless he was worried about the presence of 22,000 soldiers, many of them black, on the campus. He laughed and invited me to visit him on his estate. I think to his surprise I accepted. I borrowed a Border Patrol car and drove down to see him. I was curious to get his assessment of what had happened.

When I arrived at the plantation, the first thing I noticed was a badly broken television set.

"What happened to your TV?" I asked.

"Well," he said, "I had some guests Sunday night and we turned on the set to hear President Kennedy's address. One of them got so mad he threw a chair through the screen."

He asked me a number of questions about the riot and seemed amused by the role we believed General Edwin Walker had played in rallying the rioters. General Walker, himself a racist and now retired, had commanded the troops that protected the black students desegregating the school in Little Rock during Eisenhower's presidency and apparently was trying to make up for this terrible sin. But the senator, unlike many of his colleagues, was never talkative. He did make it clear that he thought Barnett untrustworthy, and he was critical of Bobby for trying to negotiate with him. Beyond that I learned little, but unlike most of his southern colleagues, Eastland was moderate in his criticism of the Kennedys.

We had gotten the wounded marshals the medical attention they required and hospitalized a number, made arrangements for Meredith's protection, and returned the guns that were claimed (somewhat sheepishly), so I headed home. John Doar, who as always had been a courageous leader Sunday night, had made most of the arrangements and remained in charge.

There were a few things still to do in Washington. Academicians were furious at the university for its attitude toward Meredith's admission and wanted to punish it by removing its accreditation. I spent a good deal of time persuading them that this was a bad idea and pointing to the governor's dominant role. I thought, in fact, the university administration had done a terrible job, but I did not see how isolating the school and punishing the many innocent students would help. Was I influenced by the fact that the daughter of the chairman of the Senate Judiciary Committee attended the university? Probably.

Over the next few weeks I made a few trips to Ole Miss simply to satisfy myself that things were in order. Meredith would occasionally have emotional flights of fancy and ask that we remove both the marshals and the troops. He was right, of course, that they should not have been necessary. But, unhappily, they were.

On one of my return flights, a major-general from the Signal Corps rode back with me from Memphis. I asked him what he had been doing there, and he said that he had been doing a study of army communications during the Oxford riot. The army brass had been very upset because the Department of Justice communication system seemed to be far more effective, and he was trying to determine how this could have been the case.

"General," I said, "I'll let you in on the secret. What you do is put a dime in a pay phone and call the White House collect."

At first he did not believe me, but then he understood what had happened to embarrass the Pentagon with its state-of-the-art communication system. Later I saw the result of his study—and of the army's embarrassment—when the University of Alabama was integrated.

In the long run, the riot at Oxford and the willingness of the president to use significant military force to enforce the court order and prevent far more serious bloodshed was an essential foundation to the successful integration that eventually took place throughout the South. But at the time it seemed a failure in virtually every respect. It received accolades from African nations, who were surprised that the white power structure would actually go to such lengths. But civil rights leaders were unhappy. They saw the failed negotiations with Barnett, which had postponed Meredith's enrollment for several days, as an indication of lack of resolve on the part of the administration and of the white political leaders' willingness to use blacks as pawns. This was aggravated by President Kennedy's speech, which, on the mistaken assumption that Governor

Barnett was keeping his word and would keep order while Meredith enrolled, praised the university and its traditions, expressed confidence that the students would uphold its honor, and regretted the use of force (the marshals) to secure Meredith's admission. The Kennedys were the civil rights leaders' best hope, but those leaders were disappointed at what they viewed as political maneuvers and efforts to appease Dixiecrats.

Bobby was enormously unhappy at the use of troops but took full responsibility for what had happened. He never suggested in any way that I or others on the spot could or should have acted differently. One of his strengths was that you knew from the outset he would never second-guess your decisions—when he put you in charge, you were in charge, and his role was to back you up in every way he could.

In retrospect, I think neither Bobby nor the rest of us fully appreciated the lengths to which southern political leaders would go to try to preserve what they saw as traditional customs. I am sure Bobby thought that, as rational people, they would understand that in the final analysis the federal government had to prevail and that violent resistance would not be helpful to them or to the country. More than anything, he feared a confrontation between state and federal law enforcement, particularly if the federal law enforcement was military, arousing bitter memories of the Civil War. We expected opposition in courts to integration of schools, despite the Supreme Court's decision in *Brown*, and anticipated that southern officials would try to take full advantage of the provision to integrate "with all deliberate speed." We thought that the fact of a court order, rather than simply an executive decision, would be persuasive, and that it would not be forcibly opposed; that is, once politicians were convinced of our determination to enforce it, they would yield, however bitterly they denounced the action.

In one sense we were right. Fundamentally, most southerners did not want violence. The problem was, the whites did not want integration either. Since intimidation in one form or another—ranging from the violence of the Klan to the arrests for trespass and the refusal to register voters—had worked for decades, protesting the actions of the "central government" served to strengthen the hand of the more radical racists. Negotiation could achieve minor advances, but it could not break the back of a caste system. Southern moderates wanted law and order, but it was their law, not that set forth in the federal Constitution.

At Washington, protocol often seated me next to Justice Hugo Black, from Alabama, at social events. Justice Black saw the Constitution and equal rights as we did. Indeed, Lou Oberdorfer had been his law clerk.

But he frequently would say to me, shaking his head seriously, "Neither you nor Bobby understand the South."

It annoyed me at the time. In retrospect, I think he was right.

The riot at Ole Miss opened our eyes, but it also opened those of many southerners. Barnett was not popular for having let things get out of hand. If Bobby and the president had not persisted, or if Meredith had thrown in the towel, things might have been different. But that did not occur. What we learned was that once a decision was made, it had to be enforced, and one had to be careful not to encourage southern officials to think, mistakenly, that a compromise could be reached. In a way, despite our dislike for troops as a tool of civil law enforcement, it was probably easier for the South to accept the military because of its own honorable military tradition.

It took Ole Miss far longer to integrate in a meaningful way than it should have. I visited the university thirty years after the riot and finally saw a thoroughly integrated campus, with a university chancellor who welcomed blacks but was saddled with the past in his efforts to build the school's academic reputation. James Meredith was there, celebrating his son's receipt of a Ph.D. from the university. A building on campus was named for Bob Farley, and I had the pleasure of speaking from the steps of the Lyceum, looking out on the beautiful grove that had been the center of the riot that night.

Bobby would have been pleased with what I saw.

IX

IT WAS ON AN OCTOBER MORNING WHEN I WAS IN BOBBY'S OFFICE—I don't remember why—that he asked me what my reaction would be if we knew the Russians were sending nuclear missiles to Cuba. I said that was ridiculous—certainly the Russians knew better than to take about the most provocative act imaginable.

"Well," he said, "they are. Look, keep this absolutely to yourself and meet me in the State Department in half an hour. Find a plausible excuse for going there."

I did. Bobby met with one group weighing the pros and cons of a blockade, and he asked me to sit with the military action people, who were discussing a surgical strike to eliminate the missiles, and to let him know how plausible I thought that plan was. I attended those meetings and reported my thoughts to him. I confess I am a skeptic about surgical air strikes and probably wasn't a good choice to comment on the military plans. I had seen the target missed too many times from my airplane in World War II.

My connection with the Cuban missile crisis was peripheral and confined to meetings in the State Department, not the White House. Most of what I read in Bobby's account in *Thirteen Days* was news to me. I was never a member of the famous ExComm group of advisers. But there were two aspects I did observe, which are worth noting because they were so like Bobby Kennedy. First, a great deal of time was spent discussing the moral issue—how could we justify an all-out attack on Cuba in the eyes of the world and our own democratic values? It was the most powerful argument against a military solution. Second, Bobby ran the meetings as he ran those in the Justice Department. Everyone was equal and everyone's opinion was valued.

During discussions of the military option, the question of the fate of the Cubans captured in the Bay of Pigs fiasco came up. In April 1961, some 1,200 Cuban refugees who had been secretly trained in Latin America by the CIA in an exercise to overthrow Castro, beginning under President Eisenhower, were landed in Cuba with President Kennedy's approval. The mission was a total failure, with many of the refugee soldiers killed, a few rescued by American destroyers, and the remainder imprisoned. President Kennedy took full responsibility for the mission, although privately he was furious at the CIA and the joint chiefs, who had optimistically approved its feasibility.

The issue was not that anything could now be done about the Cuban prisoners; it was simply that if a military attack occurred, John McCone, the new head of the Central Intelligence Agency, expressed the view that we could probably write them off. While much more serious matters were at stake with the possibility of atomic war, it was nonetheless very worrisome, to say the least.

A day or two after the resolution of the missile crisis, probably on November 29, Bobby called me into his office and said that the president was very interested in getting the prisoners out of Cuba if that was at all possible. He said James Donovan, a New York lawyer who had been active in Germany in securing prisoner exchanges between East and West in Berlin and who had been assisting the Cuban Families Committee with respect to the prisoners, had an idea that perhaps the $53 million ransom Fidel Castro insisted upon might be accomplished by a combination of drugs and cash. The concept was that the drug companies would donate drugs to a private charitable organization, receiving a tax deduction for the contribution, and the private organization would, through Donovan, arrange an exchange of prisoners for the drugs.

Bobby asked me to "look into it"—the RFK management style.

My knowledge of tax law being what it is, I asked Lou Oberdorfer whether, just offhand, it sounded feasible. He said he had already talked to Bobby and on the basis of the tax law itself it might well be, but he had no idea about the attitude of the Internal Revenue Service. He said he would explore it with Stanley Surrey, the IRS commissioner. Surrey thought it might be feasible if handled absolutely aboveboard, with no favors to anyone.

As a result of that discussion, Lou Oberdorfer prepared a quite detailed plan of action, and we had a meeting in my office with Oberdorfer, Surrey, his counsel, Mitchell Rogovin, and one or two others. We concluded that we might be able to approach the problem in the way Lou proposed, and that it was important to deal with it as a private matter, with routine rulings strictly according to the regulations. We also felt that it was important to deal with it quickly, to keep the private parties in the public eye and any governmental role assisting the private parties in the deep background, and, if at all possible, to get the prisoners home for Christmas, just a little over three weeks away. Our major concern was Castro's reaction so soon after the missile crisis. We were, I think, just slightly crazy.

Following the Monday meeting, and again in accordance with Bobby's management style, I simply asked Lou to take charge and do it. I said I was available to help as needed.

Lou spoke to his former law partner, Lloyd Cutler, whose firm represented some big drug companies, and from there the operation moved forward at breakneck speed. The drug companies proposed the drugs they would be willing to donate—normally those they had difficulty moving in the marketplace. Donovan was responsible for getting Castro's okay to the proposals, and the IRS set up an operation to value the drugs for tax purposes. We were conscious of the political hazards, and the IRS, if anything, valued extremely conservatively. Since the products were not bestsellers, this conservative valuation was not a big problem for the companies. Indeed, none of them came close to realizing the maximum allowable deduction. While keeping our activity in the background, the president and the attorney general did make encouraging statements about the activities of the Cuban Families Committee and the drug companies' efforts to help the prisoners return to their families.

Lou suggested that it would be easier for both the drug companies and the IRS if the donations could be made to a well-known charity such as the Red Cross rather than to the committee. Given our self-imposed time restraints, we went directly to the American Red Cross and met with John Wilson, the executive vice president, and his counsel, Harold Starr, giving them a very general picture—which at that stage was about all we had. They thought it would be difficult but not impossible and that it would appear a far more customary operation if the Cuban Red Cross were involved, and perhaps if their own representatives could be present in Cuba to insure the integrity of the drug distribution. Back to Jim Donovan, who said that Castro was amenable to both conditions. The willingness of the Red Cross to participate and Donovan's ability to persuade Castro were essential to the operation.

The arrangement Donovan negotiated with Castro was for $50 million in drugs and $3 million in cash. For some reason, all of us, including

Donovan, were sure that the cash figure would be lost in the end and the deal would be drugs only. But since it was a private transaction between the Families Committee and the Cubans, we needed the legal niceties of such a transaction. This would require a $53 million letter of credit to insure delivery of the cash and all the drugs; we wanted the prisoners out by Christmas and were willing to send the first three plane cargos of drugs for them, but Castro had to be confident that the rest of the drugs—some forty shipments—would in fact be delivered. One problem was that no American bank was permitted to deal directly with Cuba, so the letter would have to be issued by a Canadian bank. No Canadian bank would be willing to go out on a limb for that sum to the virtually penniless Families Committee or even, for that matter, to the American Red Cross.

I had taught a course in secured commercial transactions, which included letters of credit, at Yale Law School, so I had some idea of what we were up against. I also knew that the expert on the subject was Henry Harfield, of Sullivan & Cromwell in New York City. His book on the subject was the commercial lawyer's bible. I called Henry, explained the problem, and asked him to draft a letter that the bank could get out of if all went wrong, but I added that it was important that such an exit not be easily perceived. The country's greatest expert went to work— *pro bono*, without fee. Bobby also got some young Washington lawyers, John Nolan, E. Barrett Prettyman, and John Douglas (all former Supreme Court clerks who later joined the department officially), to go to work with Lou Oberdorfer.

I told Bobby we would need a guaranty to the Canadian bank from a responsible U.S. party. Shortly he suggested that I try Victor Herd, chairman of the Continental Insurance Company and America Fore, in New York. I called him and made an appointment for the next morning, when John Nolan and I flew up to New York. We were accompanied by Robert Knight, a partner of Harfield's. Mr. Herd was another absolutely essential player. After Knight and I explained the situation, he said that America Fore would be willing to back up the letter of credit, but only if the Red Cross would assume the underlying liability. I think he was influenced both by Knight's knowledge of banking and by the involvement of Jim Donovan. He then asked me if all the drug shipments were insured. I was embarrassed and told him I simply had no idea, whereupon he wrote out on a sheet of yellow paper an insurance policy covering all the shipments in just a few sentences—the most remarkable and most understandable insurance policy I have ever seen. He handed it to John Nolan, who to this day has it carefully framed in his law office.

I made an appointment to see E. Roland Harriman, the chairman of the board of the American Red Cross, at his estate in Harriman, New York, some twenty-five miles north of New York City, to discuss Herd's condition. I had never met him, but he was Averell Harriman's brother, and that made me feel more comfortable. I got the FBI to provide me a car and driver (with communication via radio with Bobby if needed). There were snow flurries as we approached Harriman and began to climb the long private road up the mountain to the Harriman home. I could not help but wonder if my reception would be as cold as the weather, but I took comfort from my acquaintance with Averell and hoped that Roland would be as understanding.

Mr. Harriman was cordial in his greeting and took me into his huge living room, with its museum-quality collection of art and antiques. I told him I was about to make the most preposterous business proposal he had ever heard in his life and the only basis for my doing so was the interest of the president and the attorney general in the return of the Cuban prisoners taken in the Bay of Pigs fiasco. I then asked him whether the Red Cross would be interested in undertaking a $53 million liability on a letter of credit covering cash and drugs to ransom the prisoners. I explained that I thought it would all be secured both by the goods and by America Fore, that we were well along in securing the necessary drugs, and that I thought the letter of credit would have a possible escape clause if everything went west. I told him that we would know if we had $3 million in cash (if necessary) and the drugs by the end of the week and that the Red Cross could back out at any time in the next seven days if we did not. The seven days related to our Christmas target, just nine days away.

Mr. Harriman gulped several times and then said, "Sometimes there are decisions that simply have to be made. I think this is that kind of decision, and no amount of reflection is going to change what it is right to do. The answer is yes, we will. And though it is early, I think we both need a drink. I know I do."

And we had that drink.

He called John Wilson, who agreed with his decision and said he would contact the members of the board but was confident they would support the chairman's decision.

Thanks to some extraordinary people, the pieces were falling into place. I still needed the participation of a Canadian bank, and Robert Hurwitch of the State Department made an appointment for us in Montreal with the Royal Bank of Canada. I headed out to LaGuardia, where a JetStar was waiting with Bob Hurwitch, Henry Harfield, and John

Nolan. We arrived in the office of Mr. W. Earle McLaughlin, chairman and president of the bank, a couple of hours later, after normal banking hours. It was still snowing lightly.

Between us, we explained our mission to Mr. McLaughlin, who, while courteous, was strangely unimpressed. He expressed doubt as to the feasibility of our plan but said that perhaps the bank might be able to help in two or three months. We said our timetable was before Christmas and a good deal tighter than he apparently envisioned. He asked us if we had talked to any American banks about a guaranty, and we said we had not, but we had a commitment from Victor Herd on behalf of the America Fore insurance syndicate. Curiously, he had never heard of America Fore. He dismissed that guaranty and said he was confident that the only way his bank would be interested would be if we secured a back-to-back letter of credit from an American bank. Here was a banker wanting another bank's guaranty, and nothing else would do. Besides, he sounded awfully skeptical about the whole proposition, and I was beginning to suffer the inferiority complex I always feel when I approach a bank for money.

"Why don't you call one of the New York banks and discuss it with them?" he said. "You can use my phone."

We said that a $53 million letter of credit for such an unusual project might better be discussed in person. McLaughlin was insistent, and none of our appeals seemed to cut any ice. Indeed, he said that Canadian banks, including his own, had already done a lot of things to accommodate U.S. policy toward Cuba, and he did not know why Canada should be pulling out our dirty linen. Thus challenged, we tried to get through to a senior official of Morgan Guaranty through Henry Harfield. No luck. Gone for the day.

"Oh, well," said McLaughlin, "it's three hours earlier in California. Let me see if I can get someone senior from Bank of America on the line for you."

None of us could think of anyone we knew at Bank of America, but McLaughlin persisted and got someone, then asked me if I wanted to speak to him. Henry whispered to me, "He's an old friend of mine."

I handed Henry the phone, and a long conversation took place. At the end of it, Henry handed McLaughlin the phone. "He wants to speak to you," said Henry, giving me a wink and a smile.

The long and short of it was that Henry's friend said that while he could not commit Bank of America to a back-to-back letter of credit over the phone, it seemed to him to be a perfectly sound venture which would interest his bank. I think someone turned up the heat or else it stopped snowing, because I could see the icicles melting all around the room. McLaughlin said that in light of that conversation, if an American bank was involved in the guaranty, the Royal Bank would consider the matter, and he thought it possible even to meet our schedule.

He examined a draft of Henry's letter and, to his credit, spotted the problem that we had carefully buried. No bank would accept it, he said. We explained that it had been intentionally drafted that way and that the whole purpose was to avoid any real liability. That argument did not fly with McLaughlin, and I could see my clever scheme evaporating. No matter. We flew back to New York that evening, increasingly confident that we could bring off this project, thanks to some fine people and good luck. As we dropped off Henry Harfield at LaGuardia, he suddenly exclaimed, "My God, in all the excitement it never occurred to me that my insurance policy doesn't cover flights in military planes!" Thank goodness he had forgotten to check.

Before taking off for Washington, we met Donovan at the airport. He was impatient to get back to Cuba with everything in hand. We, of course, did not have everything in hand, but we did feel it was important for Donovan to return to make sure everything at that end was on track. His point was valid enough, but if we waited until everything was actually in hand, it would be too late to make arrangements in Cuba that could meet our Christmas deadline.

Because of the Christmas holiday, transportation was a problem. I had contacted Pan American Airways' Washington representative and asked him to provide five airplanes free of charge, three cargo planes and two passenger planes. Initially he told me it just was not possible, because of the holiday traffic. I told him I would contact some other airlines. A couple of hours later he called back and asked if older propeller planes would be satisfactory; if so, he could provide five as requested. For a 90-mile flight, anything would do. I knew Pan Am wanted to get overflight rights from Cuba for its Latin American service, but the subject never came up. Donovan had enough to negotiate without any additions.

We also had a problem getting the initial drug shipments to Florida by rail, and the drug companies wanted an antitrust exemption to coordinate shipments. We gave them one, strictly limited in time and subject matter.

Now the biggest problem was the $3 million cash. Bobby had thought the drugs would be enough, and Donovan had encouraged that belief. On Friday night, he told us for the first time that Castro insisted on the cash. I think he had always assumed it was not a real problem and that the government would come up with it through the CIA or otherwise.

But it was a real problem. Bobby was adamant. No government money. He had assured the president and others that government money would not be used, and he was not about to retreat from that position. John Nolan spoke to him at Donovan's request and told us there was no other source. It was two o'clock in the morning of December 22, and we were all still in my office. We had less than two days to raise $2,900,000 and get it to the Royal Bank of Canada (the Families Committee had raised about $100,000).

Sunday afternoon, Bobby called me and said to expect a call from Cardinal Cushing, the Catholic archbishop of Boston, who was a member of the Families Committee. He said he had explained the problem but it was up to me to see how much I could get. Bobby may have been thinking of his father's pocketbook. I'm no good at raising money, so I was pretty nervous about what one said in that regard to a Catholic cardinal.

Cardinal Cushing called and spoke in his pronounced Boston accent. It was a short conversation.

"Mr. Katzenbach?"

"Yes," I replied.

"Put me down for one million dollars." Gulp.

"Thanks," I said.

Why did I ever doubt my fund-raising abilities?

But we still had $1,900,000 to go. At Bobby's suggestion, I called General Lucius Clay, who was the chairman of the Families Committee, explained our problem, and asked him to come to the department early the next morning. Bobby arrived about 7 a.m., and the general arrived two hours later. It was the day before Christmas, and only a skeleton staff was working. I suggested Clark Clifford, a close adviser to the president, and Bobby called him and asked if he could help. He could and did. One of his clients, Richmond Oil, would donate $100,000 and offered to guaranty $900,000 more to the banks to secure the letter of credit. General Clay was working the phones furiously and by noon had $900,000. We had enough for the $3 million letter of credit, but Clay still needed to raise $900,000 to repay Richmond Oil.

"Don't worry," said the general. "Get those brave men back and I'll raise the money somehow."

So we got in touch with the New York branch of the Royal Bank, and the letter of credit was issued for the full $53 million. It was about 3 p.m. on December 24.

Lou Oberdorfer was in Florida with John Nolan, supervising the loading of drugs on the Pan Am planes. It was at a military base, and the stevedores were volunteers from the services. Jim Donovan was in Cuba, smoking cigars with Castro, letter of credit in hand. The prisoners had been moved to a military base in Cuba where the planes were to land and where the Cubans were to check our first three loads for compliance. Lou, of course, was scrupulous in making sure they complied. One last glitch came when Pan Am could not get the passenger planes to us that day. The prisoners were willing to ride out on the cargo planes, but with no seat belts, this was both against regulations and in fact potentially very dangerous, even in a minor accident like a blown tire. I called Jeeb Halaby of the FAA and persuaded him that we should take the risk of using the cargo planes to transport the prisoners. Finally—and very reluctantly—he agreed. The Christmas spirit was present and strong.

I remained in my office, watching television with most of the others who had worked so hard to get this done, as the first planeload arrived in Miami that Christmas Eve. I had not been home in four days, had bought no Christmas presents for the children or my wife, and had been sleeping on the couch in my office. But seeing those Cuban prisoners get off the plane and join their families was about as good as it gets. The last plane landed safely about 10 p.m., and the last person off was Jim Donovan. Lou Oberdorfer and John Nolan met him. He gave a press conference, explained his negotiations with Castro, and praised the Cuban Families Committee, which he represented. Then, with Oberdorfer and Nolan, he went to a phone and called my office. I got the White House operator to put him through to the attorney general while keeping me on the line. Surreptitiously I put them on the speakerphone, so all of us could enjoy the moment.

For some reason—probably Jim's ego—Bobby never really liked Donovan, but he warmly congratulated him on his success and thanked him sincerely for his efforts. Jim graciously accepted the compliments, with no mention of the help we had given him, and they wished each other a Merry Christmas. Lou Oberdorfer asked if it was okay to give Donovan a ride on the JetStar back to Washington and New York, and Bobby approved. After Jim hung up, I let Bobby know that we had been listening in all the time.

"Well," said Bobby, "I am concerned he won't be able to get his big head through the door of that small plane on his way home." Pause. "And just what have you guys been doing all this time? Sitting on your fat asses while he did all the work?" Pause. "Thanks, fellows, and Merry Christmas." Pause. "Now let's go get Hoffa!"

THERE ARE FEW EVENTS IN MY LIFE THAT HAVE GIVEN ME THE SATIS-
faction I felt in seeing those prisoners get off the planes in Miami. I know
the others who had worked so hard felt the same way. I got a warm letter from Roland Harriman saying that nothing he had ever done had
given him more satisfaction. And President Kennedy came back from the
abrazo the Miami Cubans gave him glowing with pleasure.

Jim Donovan was, of course, indispensable and had acted in a purely
private capacity throughout, albeit with a lot of cooperation from the
government. He never had authority to speak for anyone but the Families Committee. Obviously, so soon after the missile crisis, we could not
deal with Castro or he with us for political reasons. When Donovan
went back to Cuba in early February, after the last of the drug shipments
had arrived, Castro asked him about the *abrazo* and the Kennedys taking credit for the prisoner release. Donovan denied that it was in any
sense a government operation and said that he had acted throughout the
negotiations in a private capacity. Castro replied, "Good. If it had been a
Kennedy operation, I never would have released those men."

It seems to me Donovan was essentially right. Granted, it would not
have happened if the president had not wanted it to happen and if Bobby
had not provided the leadership the Families Committee lacked. But
the key people who made it happen were private: Victor Herd, Cardinal
Cushing. General Clay, Roland Harriman, and others on the Families
Committee. Henry Harfield, Bob Knight, John Douglas, John Nolan,
and Jim Donovan acted *pro bono*, and those of us in the government were
caught up in the same emotional imperative to wipe the Bay of Pigs
slate clean by getting the prisoners out. Everyone who worked on the
project shared the same emotion, even the secretaries who worked late
on Christmas Eve. Like everything Bobby worked on, it became a team
effort, with everyone pulling together. His capacity to create that atmosphere was perhaps his greatest gift.

Throughout the hectic three weeks Bobby was always there, talking
to each of us daily or more often. "How are we doing? How much have
you got in drugs? Can we get it to Cuba? What can I do? What can the
president do? How can I help?"

We did not cheat. No money from the CIA, no special treatment for
the drug companies, no favors asked or granted. Today $53 million does
not seem like much. Then it was an enormous hurdle. I have often wondered if sensible people would have tried to do what we did. We were,
of course, lucky. And once we committed ourselves, nobody was willing
to say it could not be done. What has always seemed so remarkable to

me is how people of this caliber would break their necks to accomplish a goal simply because it seemed right, and, of equal importance, how the leadership was there and made it happen.

Sometime in late January the attorney general called me and asked me to meet a monsignor representing Cardinal Cushing, and Judge Francis Morrissey, the cardinal's lawyer, at the airport. Bobby had to be at the White House. Would I take them to lunch and then bring them to his office? I took them to the Mayflower, where they had a reservation. I suggested that Judge Morrissey leave his briefcase in their room, but he preferred to keep it with him. After lunch we went to Bobby's office in the department.

I did not know the purpose of the trip, and they did not tell me. I have no idea what Bobby knew. When they entered his office, Judge Morrissey put his briefcase on Bobby's desk and unlocked it.

"We brought the money," he said. "We assumed you wanted it in small bills." And there it was, $1 million in cash!

After the monsignor and Morrissey had departed, Bobby looked at me and asked, "Do you think this is the first time an attorney general has ever been given a million dollars in cash? What do I do now?"

"Call Clark Clifford. He deals in large sums of money," I replied.

Clifford was a director of Riggs Bank, where Richmond Oil had an account. The money could be used to repay the $900,000 loan and the remainder put in the Families Committee account.

"Just send the check over," said Clark. "I'll make the necessary arrangements."

"Well," said Bobby, "as a matter of fact, it's in cash."

I would have loved to see Clark's face. But he made the necessary arrangements, and one of Bobby's assistants, Andrew Oehmann, took the briefcase to Riggs Bank and waited patiently while they counted the money.

X

FROM THE MOMENT HE WAS NAMED ATTORNEY GENERAL, BOBBY WAS determined to prosecute Jimmy Hoffa. He was convinced from his work on the McClellan Committee that Hoffa was evil, corrupt, and capable of corrupting our political institutions. The personal animosity between Hoffa and Kennedy made good press copy, and neither was interested in covering it up. More than any other aspect of his tenure, it was the "Get Hoffa" squad under Walter Sheridan that caused criticism and led to descriptions of Bobby as "ruthless"—perhaps the least apt adjective in the language to characterize him.

There was a good reason to believe that Hoffa, head of the powerful Teamsters Union, not only was corrupt, misusing millions of dollars of union dues and associating closely with leaders of organized crime, but also enjoyed thumbing his nose at law enforcement. Two criminal cases had been unsuccessfully prosecuted against him in the 1950s; in both cases the prosecution was seemingly mishandled. But failure to convict raised the question of whether it was an abuse of Bobby's prosecutorial discretion to form a group charged with investigating and seeking evidence of other crimes or whether this union leader was the innocent victim of a personal vendetta. Given what was known at the time, I think further investigation was warranted, and if Bobby had left it to Hoover's FBI, nothing would have been done. But the publicity that accompanied Bobby's every move, which was fanned by Hoffa and his union, gave the unique Sheridan group the appearance of an unjustified abuse of power.

In my role as legal counsel and then deputy, I had little to do with the Criminal Division generally, and Hoffa was a particular domain of

Bobby's. There is no question that Bobby hated Jimmy Hoffa and everything he stood for and was determined to prove that his assessment was right. He was not prepared, however, to cheat or cut corners. Hoffa was.

As was his practice, Bobby had a number of his principal assistants gather in his office to review the evidence from time to time so that any possibility of personal bias was virtually eliminated. One case, brought by the Eisenhower administration on its last day in office, was impossibly weak, and to Bobby's intense disappointment, he ordered it dismissed. The *Test Fleet* case, which involved a truck leasing company doing business with employers in apparent violation of the Taft-Hartley Act, seemed to us a legitimate one, albeit only a misdemeanor and scarcely worth the resources put into it. The nominal officers of Test Fleet included Mrs. Hoffa and the wives of Hoffa cronies. Jack Miller correctly thought the case would be strengthened if they were named defendants or at least unindicted co-conspirators. "Ruthless" Bobby would have none of it: "Mrs. Hoffa doesn't have a clue about this. She is not a criminal, and we shouldn't treat her as if she were," he said.

The case went to trial in Nashville, Tennessee, in late 1962, coinciding in part with the Cuban missile crisis The jury voted 7–5 to acquit Hoffa.

But Hoffa had had less confidence in the justice system than most innocent defendants and wanted certainty in the jury verdict. Sheridan had developed an informant, Edward Partin, who served as Hoffa's gatekeeper during the trial and who, like most double agents, had a long record of criminal offenses. He had been paroled from a Louisiana prison when he told Sheridan of a plot to murder Bobby and his family at Bobby's home in Virginia. Now he told Sheridan that Hoffa was attempting to bribe the jury and gave Sheridan detailed information that turned out to be accurate with respect to a number of jurors.

Jury fixing is a serious felony, and the evidence Partin provided to Sheridan and the FBI was strong. The result was another indictment of Hoffa, this time on felony charges. The trial in 1963 ended in his conviction and a substantial jail sentence. Appeals focused on the role of Partin and accusations of violation of attorney-client privilege, but the conviction was upheld. Later, in Chicago, a second, unrelated felony charge was tried and a second conviction obtained and upheld on appeal.

In candor, I think a number of us felt uncomfortable with Bobby's fixation on putting Hoffa in jail. But it seems to me that he was right in his determination, and to a substantial extent the record vindicates the effort. It is ironic that Hoffa's flood of accusations about his persecution should end up in a conviction for jury fixing—exactly the kind of activity that Bobby feared. Despite his strong anti-Hoffa feelings, Bobby never cheated. Partin's place on Hoffa's team and his role as a double agent might have raised problems in *Test Fleet* had there been a second trial. But it was not a problem in the jury-fixing case.

In my view, all the Hoffa cases amounted to was taking a proactive view of law enforcement. With reason to believe that Hoffa was committing criminal acts, Bobby set up for him, as he did for organized crime, a special investigative group, rather than waiting for the FBI to bring evidence of past crimes committed. The approach was obviously influenced by the investigations of the McClellan Committee, and Bobby brought many of its investigators, including Sheridan, into the department. But the important fact seems to me to be that he followed the law scrupulously, and it was Hoffa who cheated. Not only Hoffa went to jail. There were over a hundred successful criminal convictions of Teamster personnel during Bobby's time in office.

How an attorney general uses prosecutorial discretion, as well as the objectivity of his advice to the president, are perhaps the most important measures of integrity in government. The power of the attorney general is significant, and arbitrary use is a serious danger to the rule of law. The staff of the department follow the lead of the AG when they exercise on his behalf the considerable powers of investigation and interrogation. How they view him and the example he provides are crucial to the administration of justice. It is always tempting to give the president the advice he wants to hear. It is always tempting to cut corners when one is convinced of the guilt of a defendant but having trouble proving it. It is always tempting to kill a criminal or even a civil or antitrust case against a political ally, powerful party politician, or important constituent of a committee chairman. When one yields to that temptation, one damages not only the department and the administration one serves but future administrations as well. Precedent is not a useful check on power in the courts alone. It can become a political source to justify an act as well as a check. And that can begin an erosion of the checks on arbitrary power on which the rule of law and a democratic society depend. It is easier to yield to temptation when one's predecessors have already done so. Who has not heard the rationale "everybody does it," as though, even if true, that makes it right.

The rule of law is not a concept designed for courts alone, important as courts may be as an ultimate check on arbitrary government. Precedent is useful not only to know how predecessor courts determined cases but how predecessor administrations dealt with similar legal and ethical problems. Respect for law and legal precedent is effective only if it permeates all government. In our democracy, the Department of Justice is the important conscience of the executive, whose duty is to administer the law fairly and impartially. If that impartiality is pervasive because it is demanded at the top, it not only permeates all personnel but builds a pride in performance and attracts the best to a career in government— a priceless asset. Bobby was to a substantial extent a moralist, which is why he had such passion about the abuse of power by Jimmy Hoffa and organized crime. But he also had a strong sense of fairness in the use of his own power as chief legal officer. Indeed, one of his most appealing characteristics was that he almost invariably identified with the underdog, with the poor and powerless.

Identifying with the poor and powerless did not mean that one could use the enormous power of office other than in ways authorized by law. Bobby wanted law to serve those purposes, but he was always scrupulous—almost conservative—in viewing his own authority. He was adamant that one did not cheat, even for a worthy cause. The job was to make government work, not to act outside the law. Where a predecessor AG had taken a position on a matter, Bobby usually respected that position and maintained it. Where he changed it, he normally telephoned, or had me telephone, the AG involved to explain our reasoning and seek his reaction, which—in view of the unusual courtesy extended—was almost invariably supportive of the change.

It is almost impossible to overstate the importance of prosecutorial fairness and impartial law enforcement. The pressures on an AG to act politically, to look the other way when a friend is involved, to do a favor, are real. The damage done to our constitutional system when the impartiality and integrity of the department are seriously questioned, as appears to be the case today, is far greater than the general public likely appreciates. If the public tolerates political interference in impartial law enforcement, the rule of law is very sick.

While the facts are not yet public because claims of executive privilege have been frustrating congressional investigation, there is some evidence today that the department, egged on by the political operators in the White House, encouraged U.S. attorneys to investigate and attempt to indict Democratic candidates running for election in some states. Singling out persons for investigation to secure political advantage is indefensible, and no one will attempt to defend it, although it will be denied and efforts will be made to justify the acts. When such an action is in fact justifiable on its own merits, without political motivation, it is important for an administration to have acted consistently and to have an extremely strong case. The department has to earn a reputation for evenhanded administration of the laws, and it must reject out of hand any outside political pressure. The present administration does not appear to have been sensitive to the importance of both the fact and the appearance.

More subtle, but of equal importance, is the advice the attorney general gives the president. As I have already said, it is natural for an AG to think of the president as his client, amd the same is true of every general counsel advising the head of his department or agency. On the one hand, he wants to keep his client out of trouble; on the other, he wants to find ways for his boss to do what he wants to do. That works for the lawyer in private practice but not for the government lawyer. He has a broader obligation than simply representing his client, in part because the client's obligation is to faithfully carry out the law.

A government lawyer, especially the AG, who is the final voice, has an obligation to construe the law objectively, essentially as a judge would do. One can say with Attorney General (later Justice) Robert Jackson that the president should receive the benefit "of a reasonable doubt about the law," but not if what is "reasonable" gets expanded by political pressure. Of course the president wants lawyers sympathetic to his political objectives and philosophy. That does not mean trying to please the president with one's legal advice, although the temptation to do so is always there. The AG must do his or her best to be objective in seeking the intent of Congress, not an argument for the result the client wants. All attorneys general have wrestled with the problem of political pressure and efforts to promote the president's goals. I believe in the final analysis most have concluded that the president is best served by an objective legal appraisal whether he likes it or not. Essentially the president's job is to implement legislation, and he makes policy by persuading the Congress to his view.

In civil rights matters we did not see any real solution to racial discrimination without comprehensive legislation. The problem was to make southern whites accept racial equality and equal opportunity, and use of federal troops, even when lawful, did not seem the answer. Legislation was needed, and meaningful legislation was not possible. We turned to the courts, but it was obvious that courts by themselves could not produce the kind of results necessary. Civil rights groups wanted results and were prepared to extend executive power to achieve them. Bobby struggled to preserve respect for law in a federal political system.

One example of how unpleasant and trying it can be to prosecute arose when we discovered that James Landis had not filed income tax returns for several years. Landis, the former dean of the Harvard Law School, was a White House assistant charged with reorganizing administrative agencies. He was a close friend of the Kennedys—almost family—and Bobby admired him greatly, as did his father and brother. Not surprisingly, people in the administration, without the knowledge of Bobby or the president, informed Joseph Kennedy that Landis had not filed his tax returns. Apparently he told Landis and helped him to file his delinquent returns and pay the taxes, although not the penalties, which were beyond Landis's financial means. When Bobby heard of the problem from Mortimer Caplin, the head of the IRS (and, incidentally, a former professor of Bobby's at Virginia Law School), he brought it to me. It was obvious to us that both he and the president had a personal conflict and should stay out of the matter. They did.

The legal problem was that failure to file, even without any intent to avoid payment, was a misdemeanor unless the return was filed before the government was aware of the lapse. It was clear that Landis intended to pay—he had put the money aside in a special account—but it was a complicated return, and he let it slip by the first year because of the press of other matters. Subsequent years were less complicated, but the form, which he was unwilling to falsify, requires you to swear that you have filed all past returns. And here the government clearly knew of the failure before he filed.

While those of us involved did not know Landis personally, we all admired his distinguished record and his contributions to law and to this administration. We simply could not see how to avoid the misdemeanor charge. We explored all the possibilities—overwork, carelessness, psychological problems—to no avail. I even went to the lengths of asking a bright young lawyer in the tax division (later a professor at Harvard) who had been a student of Landis's and was a passionate defender to write the best defense he could. Even he acknowledged it would not hold water.

Throughout, Landis was completely cooperative and unselfish. His regret was any embarrassment his failure would cause President Kennedy, not his own, which was, of course, far worse. His law partners were supportive and loyal, particularly Justin Feldman, an able lawyer and an ardent Democrat, who argued strenuously that Landis could prevail with a psychological defense. We thought, rightly or wrongly, that such a defense would increase his embarrassment and in the end fail. We argued for a guilty plea, and we believed that any reasonable judge, on the facts and given Landis's total cooperation, would give him a short suspended sentence. Feldman brought in one of the country's leading tax experts, Dean William Warren of the Columbia Law School, who urged me to put the matter to a grand jury in Washington, convinced that the grand jury would not indict. He may have been right, but failure-to-file cases were never sent to a grand jury, and when a grand jury fails to indict, it is almost always because the prosecution wants that result and the protection grand jury secrecy affords a dumped case. I refused, pointing out that New York State had the same case and would undoubtedly bring it, causing even more embarrassment to a fine man, not to mention the administration.

I went to New York to meet Feldman and Landis in the office of Robert Morgenthau, who was then the U.S. attorney. Feldman had been Morgenthau's campaign manager in his failed campaign for governor the year before and made yet another pitch for his partner's psychological defense. Landis agreed to plead guilty, and we let him pick the date for filing our information and his simultaneous plea. While I believed that any judge would suspend sentence, I thought Landis's total cooperation earned him the opportunity to select, in effect, the judge who would sit on his case.

Unfortunately, for whatever reason, the chief judge, Sylvester Ryan, decided to sit himself. I think he enjoyed lecturing the former dean of the Harvard Law School, and instead of the expected fine and suspended sentence, he ordered a thirty-day confinement and a year on parole. The confinement, he said, was not to punish Landis but to give him "a time for reflection . . . so that you may appraise yourself in quietness." I thought then that it was an outrageous demonstration of judicial ego by an otherwise good judge, and I still do.

Landis was not well, and we arranged for him to serve his thirty days in a prison hospital. Feldman wanted him to serve it in a private hospital, the Harkness Pavillion of Columbia Presbyterian, and I refused. Feldman called Bobby, who spoke with me.

"Justin tells me I have the authority to let Jim serve his time at Columbia Presbyterian. Is that right?"

"Yes," I replied.

"Why aren't we doing that?" Bobby asked.

"I thought it would involve terrible publicity about favoritism if we let him serve his sentence in luxury."

"Is that the only reason? There is no question that I have the legal authority to order that?"

"Yes," I replied. "You can do so."

"Jim has suffered enough," said Bobby. "Make the necessary arrangements."

And I happily did. Bobby was right.

The Landis affair illustrates to me both sides of Bobby. He withdrew from the case to avoid any possibility that, if we came to the conclusion that Landis should not be prosecuted, anyone would suspect political influence. He was satisfied to let the law take its course, if unhappy with the result. But once that had occurred, his humane side prevailed—perhaps because of his friendship with Landis, but I think not. I think it was the conviction that Judge Ryan had gone too far, the sentence was unjust, and it was within his power to alleviate it. The public could judge for itself.

I hated every minute of the Landis investigation, and the only reward was getting to know a fine human being with exceptional integrity. The conviction led to Landis's disbarment, and both Bobby and I wrote letters urging that he be reinstated. Before that could occur, he drowned in his swimming pool. I have rarely felt more honored than I was when his family invited me to speak at his funeral service and I had the opportunity to say publicly how I felt about the real James Landis.

Cases involving criminal offenses by public officials are often particularly difficult because the press and the public are quick to point out political reasons for prosecuting a political opponent or not prosecuting a political friend. Appointing an independent counsel to take charge of a particular investigation and prosecution has the virtue of avoiding conflicts and is sometimes useful. But our recent experience with legislation requiring such appointments was a cure worse than the disease. There is no guarantee that an independent counsel will not use that power abusively, and removing him can create an even bigger political problem.

Ironically, the system was working as it should when President Nixon appointed Elliott Richardson, a man of known integrity, as attorney general, and he in turn appointed Archibald Cox, Bobby's solicitor general and a respected scholar and Harvard professor, as special prosecutor in the Watergate affair. When Nixon ordered Richardson to fire Cox, it was obvious to the public that the reason was not any impropriety on Cox's part, and Richardson, to his credit, refused and resigned. There was never a question about Nixon's power to fire Cox—an important safeguard—but it was clear he had no proper reason to do so. Forced to appoint another prosecutor, he was also forced to appoint a man of known reputation and chose Leon Jaworski. Jaworski, a well-known Texas lawyer, had in fact acted as a special prosecutor for the department under Bobby in the prosecution of Governor Ross Barnett for contempt because of his acts with respect to Meredith at Ole Miss.

There are times when an attorney general and perhaps his principal assistants may be conflicted in a prosecution. The proper course is to allow the attorney general to appoint a person of his choosing and to retain control over the appointment. If the department is being properly nonpolitical in its administration of the laws, that control is not a

104 | Nicholas deB. Katzenbach

problem. Perhaps that seems to some a big "if." But if the department has become politicized, as sometimes happens, the problem is too pervasive to be cured by compulsory appointment of an independent counsel. The very requirement impugns the integrity of a nonpolitical department and its head.

The publicity surrounding the appointment of a special prosecutor can easily go to his head. He can feel the same pressure to find evidence of a crime and the same fear of criticism if he fails and dismisses a case as the AG would feel. Our experience in recent years, particularly the multimillion-dollar investigation of President Clinton by Kenneth Starr and more recently the investigation of the leak of Valerie Plame's name as a CIA operative, suggests the difficulties, whether a special prosecutor is appointed as a matter of statute or at the AG's discretion. Confidence in the integrity of the department itself is the essential building block.

The department cannot and should not avoid taking on political cases and handling them as the attorney general sees fit. Jaworski was appointed as special counsel in the Barnett case because the department was representing the court itself, which had charged the governor. Most of us had taken part in the affair at Ole Miss. Bobby thought it wise in a questionable prosecution for criminal contempt of a former governor to make sure the court and the public, North and South, were satisfied with the integrity of the department's position. In candor, we did not really want Barnett convicted, because of the potential problem with George Wallace and other southern governors. Arresting and trying a sitting governor for contempt when the offense is supported by a vast majority of the citizens of his state raises obvious problems of enforcement. It was a precedent we did not welcome. Barnett, no longer governor, was narrowly acquitted.

In general, I think appointment of special prosecutors should be avoided except in very unusual circumstances. The attorney general must have the integrity and courage to deal with difficult political problems and must gain the confidence of the public that he or she can do so. To go outside the department weakens that claim. Bobby had the courage to prosecute Judge Keogh, the brother of one of the most powerful congressmen and a strong supporter of JFK, for bribery. He also successfully prosecuted the popular Democratic mayor of Cleveland. Not long after I became deputy attorney general, just before the 1962 congressional elections, I had the unpleasant duty of informing two Democratic congressmen, Thomas Johnson of Maryland and Frank Boykin of Alabama, that they were likely to be indicted by a grand jury for bribery. It was customary at the time to inform members of Congress of such a pending indictment to give them the opportunity, if they wished, to appear before the grand jury. To do so would rarely be wise, since whatever the congressman said could later be used against him in trial. An appearance tends to freeze the defense prematurely.

I made appointments to see the congressmen in their offices and was accompanied by Carl Belcher, a career lawyer who headed the General Crimes Section of the Criminal Division. In both cases the congressmen predictably denied any wrongdoing and said they wanted to testify. I strongly urged each to consult a lawyer before doing so, and I remember Mrs. Johnson telling her husband he must do so. Boykin was more difficult, in that he rattled on and on, and it was obvious that if he ever appeared before the grand jury he would hang himself. Again, I urged him strongly to consult a lawyer, but he seemed so confident of his own persuasive abilities I doubted he would do so.

Both men in fact appeared before the grand jury and were indicted nonetheless. Indeed, it was probably their testimony that strengthened the government's case, particularly in the case of Johnson. Edward Bennett Williams, the famed criminal lawyer who on prior occasions had successfully defended Jimmy Hoffa, was Boykin's lawyer. Ed decided to move to quash the grand jury testimony on the ground that the government (in this case, me) had improperly persuaded them to testify. He subpoenaed me to testify at a hearing in Baltimore.

It was my first experience as a witness, and I hated every minute of it. The Johnson case was made more unpleasant by the fact that the U.S. attorney prosecuting the case, Joe Tydings, had been a longtime beau of Mrs. Johnson's, rejected when she married the congressman. Under his direct examination, I explained that I had strongly cautioned Johnson as to the risks of testifying. I also answered repeated questions that Tydings had not urged anything to the contrary, questions obviously designed to protect Tydings from any accusations of bias and quite irrelevant.

In his cross-examination, Williams asked me if I had made any notes of the meeting with Boykin. He knew me well enough to know it was highly unlikely. I told him that I had not but Belcher had.

"Did he show you his notes in draft form?"

"Yes."

"And did you suggest any changes?"

"No."

Belcher's memos were produced, and both emphasized my advice about the risks of testifying. Williams's motion to quash the testimony was denied by the judge, and both men were convicted of bribery. Johnson's conviction was set aside on appeal, however; he had taken money to make a speech on the floor of Congress, and the Supreme Court, in a case of first impression, opined that such speeches were constitutionally protected—an opinion that surprised me. Since he took money to make the privileged speech, I did not regret the conviction, whatever the Court's rationale. It looked, and still looks, like a bribe to me.

It was not pleasant to indict two congressmen just before an election, because the indictment itself, before any evidence was presented in court or a conviction was secured, meant almost certain defeat at the polls. Because they were Democrats, delaying a vote in the grand jury until after the election would have looked political. Had they been Republicans, indicting them just before the election would have looked political. There is no good answer, except perhaps to do one's best to be sure the indictment is a proper one and conviction almost a certainty. Incidentally, a special prosecutor would have exactly the same problem.

The Department of Justice is, of course, like other departments of government, committed to carrying out policies of the administration it serves. It is "political" in terms of the constituencies from which it gains support, how it uses and allocates available resources, what legislation it seeks from the Congress, and how it deals with its congressional committees. Thus it may, for example, devote resources to white-collar crime, antitrust enforcement, or whatever fits best with the policy goals of the president. But it has the responsibility to prosecute all violations of the law, even laws it does not like and even laws it believes unconstitutional. It has some discretion, but really not much if the case, like that of Jim Landis, is clear. Further, like all departments, it must act within the law, and here it has a special responsibility, since it is the final word within the executive branch as to what the law requires. It advises the president and it advises other departments. It represents the government in court. Judges, including Supreme Court justices, have long counted on government attorneys to be honest, fair, and candid about the facts and the law. The solicitor general, whose office represents the United States in the Supreme Court, enjoys a special relationship with the justices, which reflects their respect for his office.

In giving legal advice to the president and other departments of government, the department has a special obligation to give objective analysis, not partisan argument. It is not sufficient to find a respectable argument to support what the president or his appointees want to do. It must be an argument that the attorney general is satisfied will prevail in the courts if litigated. While lawyers generally have an obligation to give clients their best advice, the consequences of mistaken prediction are different. The government exercises great power as compared with that of the average citizen or even a large business enterprise. Even more important, it has an obligation to uphold the rule of law, to "faithfully execute the laws," a concept that demands good faith. While others share that responsibility, it is the attorney general and his department that have a special governmental duty to lead the way. Any lawyer of even modest competence knows when he is skating on ice too thin to bear the weight of his argument.

XI

Relatively early in 1963 it became obvious that we would be faced with another admissions crisis at a southern university, this time at the University of Alabama at Tuscaloosa. Alabama governor George Wallace had campaigned in 1962 as an ardent segregationist and pledged that he would personally "stand in the schoolhouse door" rather than allow the admission of black students to the university. He claimed he had a legal basis for his stand, although he refrained from stating it, and eventually it turned out to be nothing more than the old Civil War argument of "interposition"—that states could interpose their sovereignty against that of the federal government, the two being equal and absolute.

Both we and Governor Wallace had learned from the fiasco at Ole Miss. Allowing violent elements of the Klan and its racist sympathizers into the picture simply led to violence and was not a solution even for those who wanted to maintain a segregated society. Governor Barnett had learned that to allow violence was politically damaging, and he was facing criminal contempt charges as well. Wallace, a talented politician, was well aware of both problems. We had learned that a large number of federal marshals was not sufficient to maintain law and persuade southern politicians that federal court orders were going to be enforced. I had learned the wisdom of being better prepared by being involved from the start.

Much of this is recorded in a remarkable documentary film by Robert Drew, *Crisis: Behind a Presidential Commitment*. Both the Kennedys and Wallace gave permission for Drew to record pretty much as he chose meetings and preparations on both sides. I had thought that the presence of a camera at the Justice Department would be inhibiting, but it proved not to be. Drew used teams of two, a cameraman who used natural lighting and a sound person with a tape recorder. Both were unobtrusive. Further, Ed Guthman assured us that Drew had agreed that final publication was in the government's control. Drew was impressive, not merely technically but with respect to his integrity. At no time did he or any of his crews discuss the issues off-camera or reveal to either side what the other was saying. The result turned out to be a unique view of government in operation.

I worked closely with Burke Marshall and Bobby on how the confrontation would be handled, and there were several meetings in the White House with the president. There were no conversations with Wallace as there had been with Barnett, trying to find a face-saving solution for the governor. It was obvious from the beginning that he would refuse to admit the students and that we would, at a minimum, have to put the National Guard in federal service. We were reasonably confident that Wallace did not want violence. The only question was whether or not he could keep order in such an explosive environment. The question remained until the end as to how he would yield. Would he get out of the "schoolhouse door"? Would he work with or against the guard in maintaining order? Would he resist in such an adamant fashion that we would be compelled to arrest him for contempt? That possibility with a sitting governor was particularly frightening in terms of the prospect of violent resistance.

We talked over these details endlessly, but we obviously could not know the answers, and we never did until they happened. We could only prepare for the worst and hope for the best.

I worked with Bob McNamara and General Creighton Abrams to be sure there was no confusion about the role of the military. Abrams, who had been a hero in World War II at Bastogne as a tank commander and who was himself built like the tank that now bears his name, was a real pleasure to make plans with. He had been brutally criticized by an angry President Kennedy during the Ole Miss affair and was determined that this time the army would be error-free. I worked with Jim McShane to be sure the marshals understood their limited role. We planned to use marshals, mostly from the Border Patrol, to drive us onto the campus in two radio-equipped cars and to protect the students if the need arose. In addition, we planned an escape route for the two students, Vivian Malone and James Hood, in the event of violence. The university campus borders on a river, and we stationed marshals and a boat on the far bank, prepared to cross the river, pick up the students, return to the far bank, and then drive them to Birmingham. We also had to make arrangements for a third student to register the following day at the university campus at Huntsville, although we believed—as it turned out, correctly—that his admission would be determined by what took place in Tuscaloosa.

There were important differences between the University of Alabama and Ole Miss. The most important difference was that the president of the university, Frank Rose, wanted to admit black students. Rose, a very capable educator and university administrator, had met Bobby when both were honored as "Young Men of the Year" by *Time* magazine before the Kennedy election, and he was anxious to cooperate in every way possible. While he could not control the governor or the politically appointed members of his board of trustees, he could and did do a great deal to prepare students and faculty for an integrated university. In addition, he provided us with valuable intelligence from time to time about the governor's intentions. Floyd Mann, who was no longer head of the Highway Patrol but who had many close friends and admirers within its ranks, also provided us with confidential information as to preparations for possible violence, through Burke Marshall and John Doar (not the FBI, which he did not trust).

We felt reasonably sure that Wallace did not want violence, but we were less sure of his ability to control a riot if it occurred. The problem, based on reports from Mann, was aggravated by the fact that there were fewer than five hundred National Guardsmen in the Tuscaloosa area, where the main campus of the university is located, and to move in additional forces would take several hours. We had no legal reason to move troops to Tuscaloosa earlier or to take law enforcement away from the governor. While we had every reason to believe he would not admit the students, based on his statements, he had not yet actually denied them admission. I was concerned that premature use of troops would in fact stir up resentment, be a cause for violence, and take away from the support and understanding that simple defiance of a court order promoted among most people.

I left for Tuscaloosa with two or three assistants and asked General Abrams to keep his staff to a minimum and to travel in civilian clothes. He did so, taking only a lieutenant colonel from the office that handled the guard and a major from the Judge Advocate General's Office—a tiny staff for a three-star general. Our base in Tuscaloosa was in the building that served as headquarters for the guard.

Here too the lessons of Ole Miss were evident. The first thing I noticed was a huge antenna in back of the building. The general who had accompanied me from Memphis to Washington after investigating communications at Ole Miss had been active. The Army Signal Corps had installed a radio communication system second to none. Indeed, if AT&T failed utterly, we had our own worldwide communication system. The office to which I was assigned had several phones with such labels as "NATO" and "Berlin," which I assumed to be direct lines. No dime in a pay phone to communicate with Bobby or the president was necessary!

We spent most of the afternoon going over plans for the *n*th time and making a few subtle changes. Being sure the governor would keep his campaign promise and stand in the door, I decided there was no point in subjecting Vivian Malone and James Hood to the insult of rejection on grounds of race. They could remain in the cars. But what should we do then? I was reluctant to leave the campus; it would look to the public like a retreat. I spoke to Frank Rose and asked him for keys to their dormitory rooms, and he obliged. I also learned that Wallace had asked the university to outline positions where he would stand and where I should stand at the "schoolhouse door." I objected to Rose vehemently, and he said he would remove the marks, but he was not able to do so.

I reported these plans to Bobby and he approved. Still angry about the marks at the door, I pointed out that we had no legal need to confront the governor, that the students could be regarded as registered without further effort on our part. Bobby said, I think rightly, that if we denied Wallace his show, the danger of violence would increase. But he was pleased with the idea of the students going to their dormitory rooms instead of leaving the campus.

President Kennedy was nervous that Wallace would deny admission and that we did not have the time or the necessary forces to insure the students' admission the same day. That was important to him; delay looked like indecision or weakness. He thought it might be preferable to put the guard in federal service immediately, which would allow us to get additional troops to Tuscaloosa. I did not really think we had sufficient basis for federalizing the guard yet, although that is one of those decisions where the president probably has considerable latitude in the exercise of his discretion. Wallace had at his disposal more law enforcement personnel in Tuscaloosa than we would have soldiers if we did not mobilize the guard that day. I was opposed nonetheless and did not feel Wallace would persist once the guard was mobilized or permit a confrontation between his Highway Patrol (reinforced by forest rangers) and the Alabama National Guard. Abrams strongly agreed with me, and the president deferred to our judgment. Although it did not occur to me at the time, I suspect that Abe had discussed that possibility with the commanding general of the guard, General Graham, who was close to Wallace and whom we had encountered in Montgomery during the violence surrounding the Freedom Riders. Graham may well have assured Abrams that no such confrontation was in the cards.

I met with representatives of the governor who instructed me on the route we should take onto the campus, which was closed to the public. While I found it annoying to be cast in a supporting role to Wallace, I was pleased that the campus had been sealed off to the public (although certainly not to the press). I met with the marshals to make sure they understood their limited role, and I met with the Alabama marshal, Norville Peyton, and the U.S. attorney, Macon Weaver. To my surprise and pleasure, both wanted to accompany me to confront the governor, an act of genuine political courage. Both were political appointees approved by the two Alabama senators, and taking the side of the law in an integration conflict showed a devotion to law that made me proud of their dedication. I learned later that Peyton was suffering from terminal cancer, and his effort was painful physically as well as dangerous to him in the future as an Alabama native.

John Doar and I went to Birmingham in the early evening to meet with Vivian and James, whom we were to escort the next morning. We met in the modest living room of one of their Legal Defense Fund lawyers, who was also present, and John told them what to expect, insofar as we knew, and answered their questions. Both were attractive as well as courageous young people and seemed to me far less nervous about the next day's events than I was. The court order to admit the students had been signed by the district court judge who had heard the case, an older judge appointed by Roosevelt who was totally unsympathetic to integration. But if he had to order desegregation, as the Fifth Circuit Court of Appeals had instructed him, then George Wallace had damn well better obey or he would jail him for contempt. We did not find that as helpful as perhaps Judge Rawes intended.

We were up a good part of the night, at first talking to Bobby and the president about our final plans. I think it was hard on Bobby and Burke to be in Washington and have to deal at a distance with all the uncertainties. Clearly a lot was at stake, and for someone as active as Bobby, it is hard not to have hands-on responsibility. The mess in Mississippi had to be on his mind all the time. His concern came through in every call. I think those of us on the scene were more relaxed simply because we were on the scene.

When I got to my motel room fairly late that night, there was another crisis. One of the horde of reporters who had come to Tuscaloosa was having a nervous breakdown and insisted on talking to me. It took us a good part of the night to get him hospitalized and calmed down.

The next morning John Doar and I were off early to Birmingham to pick up Vivian and James. On our way back to Tuscaloosa, Bobby called on the radio and said he wanted to talk to me. We stopped at a shopping center, and I went to a pay phone and called the White House collect. So much for our fancy Signal Corps system! Bobby told me that the president had a proclamation he wanted me to give the governor and that they had made arrangements to get it delivered to me. The proclamation had no legal significance that I was aware of, but there was no harm in issuing it. I think the president felt out of it and wanted to play a part. Why not? I would have felt exactly the same way. That settled, Bobby asked me, "What are you going to say to the governor?"

"I don't really know. Something about his obligation to obey the law. I haven't written anything. Any ideas? Anything you want me to say?"

"The president wants you to make him look foolish."

"Thanks a lot. Any thoughts on how?"

"Nick, you'll do just fine. Good luck!"

We picked up a copy of the proclamation and proceeded to the campus by the route instructed. The building selected by Wallace for his stand was ringed by Highway Patrolmen and forest rangers in their green jackets, all looking determined and grim. There was a forest of TV cameras and scores of reporters in an area roped off for the media. When we stopped in front of the entrance, the TV people were all over me to put on microphones. I refused. Leaving Vivian in the car, I proceeded with Peyton and Weaver to the building entrance. It was very hot, and I was perspiring heavily, half from the heat and half from nervousness. As I approached the door, Governor Wallace and a number of his aides came out.

I had never met Wallace. He was a small man but looked as fit as the former boxer he was. I was amused to note wires coming out of every coat and trouser pocket. There was no need for me to wear a mike. He had enough for both of us, and then some. As I approached the door, he held up his hand to stop me. Just for the hell of it, I kept going a few more steps. Unfortunately, it was not far enough to get out of the bright sun. That really annoyed me, because he had come out of an air-conditioned office and was standing in the shade.

We had our confrontation. I handed him the proclamation, said a few words, and listened to him denounce the central government. It is all recorded on TV, and every time I see it, I think of all the things I did not say and should have. That is, I think, a common experience for lawyers. I have never argued a case without having exactly the same feeling after-ward. I did, however, succeed in annoying Wallace by referring to the confrontation as a "show" with no purpose, since we both knew in the end Vivian and James would be registered at the university.

I returned to the car, picked up Vivian, and walked her to her dormi-tory. Frank Rose had not revealed our intention, and I believe it came as a total surprise to the security forces. To get to the dormitory we had to go through a line of green-shirted rangers. I simply pushed in between them, and in the absence of contrary instructions they let us through. At the same time, John Doar was taking James to his dormitory in a Border Patrol car without interference.

Arriving at the dormitory, we were met at the door by the house mother, whose memorable remark I shall never forget. "Oh," she said with a friendly smile, "you must be Vivian."

I told Vivian to go to her room, freshen up, and then come down-stairs to the cafeteria for lunch. I went to the Border Patrol car to speak to Bobby, who of course had been watching with the president on TV. Should they issue the order putting the guard in federal service? Yes. And then, in response to a question about what the governor was doing, I made a silly response, saying that I was sure he was thinking of some-thing. All this response did was to confuse everyone in Washington. I should have known better, but I was still angry at being put in the sun.

When I returned to the dormitory, Frank Rose was on the tele-phone. He said it was a terrible mistake to have Vivian eat in the cafeteria, and he feared some incident. I told him we had held off on using the caf-eteria at Mississippi and that had been a mistake I was not going to make a second time. Vivian was prepared to brave it. She did, all by herself, no marshals in sight. She went through the cafeteria line and then sat at a table alone. No sooner had she done so than two young women got up and joined her. No matter that they were summer students from north of the Mason-Dixon line. Tears were in my eyes.

I returned to our headquarters, where General Abrams had received President Kennedy's order to place the guard in federal service. Abe was dressed in a rumpled seersucker suit and smoking a cigar.

"Okay," he said. "Now we notify General Graham."

"I assume that will be in uniform, sir," said the lieutenant colonel.

"Don't bother," said Abe. "I think he'll know who I am."

A half-hour or so later, Abe came into my office. He said General Graham had spoken with the governor and the governor was prepared to leave quietly but wanted to say a few words first. He would leave his law enforcement units to maintain order, but there would be no further interference with the students' registration.

I was annoyed at another speech but hugely relieved to know that the governor was surrendering. I told Abe that Wallace could have two minutes, no more, and got on the phone to notify Bobby of the arrangement. My relief that a happy ending was in sight was shared by Bobby.

The governor stood again in the doorway and confronted his friend General Graham.

"It is my sad duty . . ." began the general. I could have shot him on the spot without bothering with a court-martial.

Wallace kept his word and left the campus after denouncing us once again. I had John Doar, Marshal Peyton, U.S. Attorney Weaver, and Joe Dolan escort Vivian and James through the door, with cameras grinding and flashbulbs flashing, to register without further incident. The guard was removed from federal service and the marshals were sent back to their regular duties. The next day Dave McGlathery was registered at the Huntsville campus without either incident or marshals.

Bobby and the president were obviously pleased, and that evening President Kennedy addressed the nation in one of his finest speeches. He had not intended a TV speech, but the moment seemed opportune. For the first time he called racial discrimination a "moral issue" and publicly promised meaningful and comprehensive civil rights legislation. The Rubicon had been crossed, but whether it was possible to keep that promise remained highly doubtful. It proved to be the right one.

I listened to the speech with a bunch of Alabama guardsmen who were commanded by one of my classmates at Princeton. Surprisingly, he did not complain about the speech or the students, only the timing. We were going to miss our twentieth reunion at Princeton, and he had already sent in his check. It was, he said, all my fault, and he was glad I was missing it too.

All of that seemed as trivial as it was when that same evening Medgar Evers, a prominent black civil rights leader and World War II veteran, was shot and killed by a white supremacist. We had one small victory and a very long road still to go.

Vivian stuck out her four years and received her degree from the university. While Frank Rose was as good as his promise and admitted a number of additional black students in the fall, it could not have been an easy experience for her, and it certainly was a lonely one. She had few friends, and those she had were mostly, if not entirely, foreign students. James had health problems and did not stick it out the required time for a degree. But he did return to the university some twenty years later to earn a Ph.D.

While I was confronting Governor Wallace and getting two fine young black students admitted to a state university, Lydia, unbeknown to me, was approaching the issues of school integration in a different arena. Mark Schlefer, an able lawyer and friend, had approached Lydia and a few like-minded individuals about the lack of integration of the private schools in the greater Washington area. At the time there were two black students in the more than twenty private schools in and around the District of Columbia. After recruiting a dedicated, hardworking board of directors composed of well-known blacks and whites, with Lydia as chairperson, they formed the Negro Student Fund (later, and still today, the Black Student Fund) in early 1964.

The goals of the fund were to find talented African American students lost in the miserable public school system, determine which children with supportive parents might make it in private school, raise money for scholarships, and help each student in the process of applying to and getting accepted by a designated chosen school. From the very beginning until today the project has been remarkably successful, with almost all funded students going on to college, often to elite universities.

Board meetings were usually held in our house in the evening, and often I would return home to hear vigorous discussion of many issues and difficulties: which students would receive scholarships and be encouraged to attend which school, and how to persuade that school to take a particular student. The fund began with generous donations from individuals and soon was fortunate to attract substantial funding from Ford, followed by several smaller foundations. It was wonderfully satisfying to me to have my wife working so hard and so successfully for goals similar to those that we were striving to achieve in the department.

XII

PRESIDENT KENNEDY'S ANNOUNCEMENT OF COMPREHENSIVE CIVIL rights legislation came as something of a surprise to me. We had been working on such a bill for more than a month, and Bobby had been urging the president to take this course. But the possibility of enacting a meaningful bill remained remote, and tying up the Congress in a civil rights fight posed a real problem for Democrats in the 1964 election. Apart from Bobby, there was little support among Democratic politicians for taking the risks inherent in thus dividing the country.

In April, Martin Luther King decided to make Birmingham the target of civil rights demonstrations. There were arrests of blacks for sitting in at lunch counters, and King announced a boycott of white-owned department stores until they desegregated lunch counters and began employing blacks in visible and responsible positions. Whether a boycott would have had the desired results is questionable, but Bull Connor, the Birmingham police commissioner, was outraged. He transformed an economic boycott into confrontations between Birmingham police armed with clubs and dogs and fire hoses against peaceful black demonstrators—all of which appeared in living room TVs across the country. When King himself was arrested leading a small and peaceful march and put in solitary confinement, Birmingham became the center of public attention throughout the country,

It was during that week in jail that King wrote his famous and intensely moving "Letter from Birmingham Jail," pointing out that for years Negroes had heard the word "wait" and that "wait" had come to mean "never." On his release King came up with what turned out to be a brilliant public relations coup. He enlisted black high school students throughout the city, using leaflets telling them to "fight for freedom first, then go to school." The young people had the enthusiasm and fearlessness of youth; they assembled in churches and then went forth singing and dancing down the street. Bull Connor responded as if scripted. Hundreds of young people were arrested and jailed that day. The next day, before thousands of black spectators lining the streets, more young people marched, this time into a phalanx of police who used pressure fire hoses and then dogs to break up what was becoming a riot. As the crowd dispersed before snarling dogs and club-wielding policemen, Bull Connor savored his victory. "Look at those niggers run," he shouted.

Police arrested 250 students, some no more than children not yet ten years old. It was front-page news across the country—indeed, the world—and led the TV news programs. There were speeches on Capitol Hill deploring the events, southern senators deploring the lawlessness of the blacks and liberal northerners deploring the lawlessness of the police. But there was still no great call on the Hill for legislation, and the prospects of a truly effective civil rights law were still grim. Nonetheless, Bobby told us to begin drafting an omnibus bill that could bring peace and have some chance of passage. He was sure that such a bill was necessary and, for reasons I do not know, thought it was possible. It was, after all, the department he headed that bore the brunt of the problem and the criticism.

I am not sure I appreciated it at the time, but I think that neither the civil rights activists nor the southern politicians really believed we were serious about equal rights. The civil rights leaders appreciated that we were on their side vocally and when the chips were down, but our dependence on court orders led them to think we lacked the necessary conviction. I think the southerners saw our dependence in the same way—that we were merely acting as in the past to keep the liberal Democrats in the fold and no more. Be that as it may, it was hard for any of us to see a majority in both houses of Congress for an effective civil rights law that could survive a Senate filibuster.

We began drafting a bill in mid-May. While we did not consult the civil rights leaders at this time, we knew that one provision they wanted and we did not was power for the department to interfere locally and directly with law enforcement personnel when constitutional rights were at risk. Both Bobby and Burke were adamant that we had to deal with the problem that caused the street riots, not the riots, and that the cornerstone of the legislation had to be a comprehensive public accommodations provision that required all places open to the public to be open to blacks as well as whites. Obviously such a provision would please civil rights leaders, but would they insist on the other as well? Bobby simply did not want power he could not possibly enforce.

We included a provision that would cut off federal funds to state and local governments that discriminated against blacks, and we considered a variety of other, lesser provisions. We included a provision allowing the attorney general to sue school districts directly and picked up the provisions of a languishing voting rights bill that would marginally increase the power of the federal government to sue. Everyone thought a provision on employment discrimination—a Fair Employment Practices Commission (FEPC)—was important, and no one thought it had a chance of passage. Such a bill was then pending on Capitol Hill.

We had several meetings in the White House to discuss the proposed legislation with staff and cabinet officers likely to be involved. Vice President Johnson attended some but not all of these meetings. At times the staff forgot to invite him, much to President Kennedy's annoyance. It is often hard for a strong president to find tasks for a strong vice president to do, particularly when the partnership is one of political convenience, not shared commitments. But in retrospect, not to have used LBJ much more on civil rights legislation seems incredibly stupid. Bobby must be the principal suspect, because of his aversion to the vice president—an aversion shared by the Irish mafia in the White House but not by the president. And for the vice president to be almost ignored on a subject on which he had more expertise than any of the other participants must have hurt Johnson deeply.

Bobby's dislike of LBJ had its roots in personality differences that were strongly felt. Bobby was direct, candid, and truthful. None of those adjectives could be applied to Johnson. He was the consummate politician, and he had clawed and struggled to power from a poor background and education through the use and abuse of political friendships and acquaintances. He could flatter, schmooze, abuse, reward, equivocate with the best. You could admire the skill with which he did it. Or you could see it as deceptive and dishonest, as Bobby did.

I do not think Bobby really trusted LBJ on civil rights. Part of this distrust may have been Johnson's southern background, part just Bobby's dislike of a political rather than a moral approach. He was unfairly critical of Johnson's conduct of the federal contracting program and gave him no credit for a number of pro–civil rights speeches that surely offended many supporters in Texas.

There was no conflict as to the provisions of the civil rights bill. Johnson had little to say in the meetings, and what he did say was quite

consistent with our strategy, such as it was. He talked about the importance of a fair employment provision but conceded that it could not get
through the Senate. He urged us to talk with as many senators as we
could. While he acknowledged that it would not get us any support, he
urged both Bobby and the president to talk to Senator Richard Russell,
the leader of the southern opposition and a powerful and respected man.
I think at the time Bobby may have been suspicious of the advice. I know
I was. Russell was LBJ's mentor and closest senatorial friend. But Bobby
and President Kennedy both did talk to Russell, and it served the useful
purpose of not taking him by surprise when we eventually introduced
a bill.

I spent a good deal of time getting a crash political course from Lawrence O'Brien, President Kennedy's congressional liaison, along with his
assistants, Mike Manatos in the Senate and Richard Donahue and Henry
Hall Wilson in the House. We went through the House delegation by
delegation, counting votes I was amazed at the detailed knowledge and
analytical competence of these people. We started with the presumption
that, like the predecessor civil rights acts, we would try to pass a strong
act in the House and then give away what we had to give away to get it
accepted in the Senate, since it then appeared that cloture—cutting off
debate—was impossible. Despite Senator Keating's best efforts in 1961
to lower the required votes for cloture to 60, cloture still required two
thirds of the Senate, 67 votes, and no one at the time thought it possible
to get that many votes.

Our first conclusion was simply that there were not enough non-
southern Democrats and liberal Republicans to pass a comprehensive bill. This meant that we would have to get the support of William
McCulloch, the ranking Republican on the Judiciary Committee. Bill
McCulloch was a quiet little man from a very conservative Ohio district
that had no blacks and no civil rights activists. But he was a person of
integrity, respected by his colleagues. He had supported both the 1957
and the 1960 Civil Rights Act, and so his support seemed entirely possible if our proposals were not too much at one time. If obtained, it would
likely insure the support of the Republican leadership under Representative Charles Halleck of Indiana, the minority leader. It was his policy
in almost all cases to support what the senior Republican on the relevant
committee recommended.

Vice President Johnson had expressed concern that there was not
nearly enough interest in, or pressure upon, Congress to enact the comprehensive bill we felt necessary. President Kennedy delayed submitting
his bill for a week or so while he gathered leaders from various business

and professional groups to explain the bill and the necessity of its enact-ment. The president, the vice president, and the attorney general all spoke in their quite different styles, and while they were somewhat effective, one did not get the sense that the audience was going out to join in a demonstration. The lack of real enthusiasm for genuine racial equality on the part of white America was disheartening.

The president submitted our bill on June 19. He fudged the employ-ment problem by supporting legislation already before Congress. It was clearly the most comprehensive bill any administration had ever submit-ted, but it was not going to be enough to satisfy civil rights leaders, even though they would be pleased at its scope. It is fair to say that we were guided throughout by seeking the maximum we thought possible on the theory that success was vital. Bobby, who had pushed hard for the omnibus bill, remained optimistic. He felt it was important to show the black leadership we were serious. There was a risk that failure to secure its enactment could turn the civil rights movement away from King's peaceful demonstrations into more radical hands. But despite the racist violence of Bull Connor and the "segregation forever" politics of Wallace and others, there was a real question as to whether the country was yet ready to face up to its hereditary cancer and treat all races equally. None of the legislative experts were optimistic. President Kennedy was risking disastrous failure.

Burke Marshall was dispatched to Ohio to meet with McCulloch and request that he not comment on the bill until we had had an oppor-tunity to discuss it with him, because we needed his support and the country was in real trouble. McCulloch was obliging but threw a bomb-shell into our plans. He told Burke he was willing to support a reasonable civil rights bill, but only on condition that we promise not to give away in the Senate any provisions of the bill as passed by the House. He felt personally offended—and said a number of colleagues felt the same—to have voted for politically difficult provisions, only to have them bar-gained away in the Senate to avoid cloture. Only if and when he felt convinced that no other course was possible would he consider releasing us from the commitment he sought.

That position, however principled on McCulloch's part, left us in a difficult dilemma. Even if we could get a bill passed in the House without substantial Republican support, it would be difficult, even with modifi-cations, to get Republican support in the Senate, the more conservative body. More important, everyone up to this point had assumed that the only way of getting a bill through the Senate was to buy off the southern senators with excisions, as had been done in 1957 and 1960—precisely what McCulloch wanted us to promise not to do. It seemed to Bobby that our best bet was to play along with McCulloch and hope for the best. There was not much to give away in any event, if we insisted, as we really had to, in keeping the public accommodations provisions. We were forced to wonder if we could possibly succeed, unless somehow we could get the 67 votes needed to cut off a filibuster for the first time.

In its simplest terms, we needed a strong civil rights bill that could be enacted into law. That required Republican support in both the House and the Senate. Only with strong Republican support was it possible even to contemplate passage in the Senate, which required either cloture or bargaining with southern Democrats. If this was the tactic, the issue was not how strong a civil rights bill could pass the House, but how strong a civil rights bill could get genuine (that is, leadership) Republican support in the House *and* the Senate. We needed real help from the minority leadership in *both* houses, Charles Halleck in the House and Everett Dirksen in the Senate—neither noted for leadership in civil rights.

Burke Marshall, Joe Dolan, Bill Geoghegan, and I spent a great deal of June and July on the Hill talking with members, explaining the bill and its necessity before the hearings began. I had added to my staff a bright young lawyer, David Filvaroff, to work full-time on the bill, and he not only performed with professional skill but displayed excellent judgment on political matters. There was little point in talking to hardcore segregationists or the committed liberals; the latter were in any event being lobbied by the Southern Christian Leadership Conference (SCLC), the coalition of civil rights groups. In a sense we were more interested in what the Senate would support so that we could tailor the bill in the House to something that could be supported in the Senate. Between the five of us, I think we talked to almost all the elected officials. In my inexperience, I was probably overly optimistic in interpreting courtesy as consent, but I concluded that public accommodations was not impossible and that we could, if all went well, end up with 56 or 57 votes in favor in the Senate. If that were to happen, I wondered if we could get another 10 or so to cut off endless debate and end the inevitable filibuster. The Senate had voted cloture to get a vote on the merits of the satellite communications bill. Surely we could convince even senators who opposed civil rights legislation that a vote on the merits of civil rights was as important as a vote on satellite communications.

One major problem was simply that our tactic of getting Republican support for a "reasonable" (McCulloch's word) bill in the House and then seeking to preserve it in the Senate was not accepted by the liberals in the House or by the civil rights groups. They could not accept the possibility of ending a filibuster by a vote, and thought it could be accomplished only by bargaining with the southerners. Thus they needed a very strong bill, so that there were provisions which could be bargained away—precisely what McCulloch opposed. Bobby invited the leaders of the Democratic Study Group to his office, and we had a long, somewhat inconclusive discussion. Everyone in the group, which was composed of the leading liberal Democratic members, wanted to follow the previously successful tactic of getting the strongest possible bill enacted by the House and then bargaining it down in the Senate to get it enacted there. In a real sense this was also in their own interest, because it allowed them to support every measure the civil rights leaders wanted, while our tactic would put them—and us—in frequent opposition. We needed a law with a workable public accommodations section, not a Christmas tree that would never become law.

Finally, the most experienced and thoughtful of the Democrats, Richard Bolling of Missouri, disagreed, but he saw the danger of division, which could lead to defeat of the president if no law was enacted. He reluctantly acquiesced—sort of. "If you really mean what you're saying and you are really prepared to stick with it, then I don't think it's impossible that it could succeed," he said.

When he was convinced by Bobby that we really did mean it and that we did not feel we had a workable alternative, Bolling was crucial in persuading most of his colleagues not to jump out in opposition, although, inevitably, some did. Throughout the months ahead he continued to be helpful. Perhaps the greatest irony of our tactic to secure Republican support was that it put us in frequent opposition to civil rights groups and their liberal allies on provisions we would have welcomed if only they were acceptable to our Republican colleagues. Nor could we alienate Republicans by blaming them. We were forced to work together for McCulloch's "reasonable" bill, and it was not always comfortable to do so.

Emanuel Celler, chair of the House Judiciary Committee, expressed total willingness to work with McCulloch to produce a bill both could support. But he wanted his full committee, composed of some thirty-six members, to refer it to Subcommittee Five, his pet subcommittee. The subcommittee included McCulloch, but its members, like Celler himself, were very liberal, and that caused us some concern that the bill would quickly get out of hand. Celler expressed confidence that he could control matters.

It was obviously a difficult role for Celler, who wanted to please the administration but to do so would have to vote against his natural constituency. The liberals on the subcommittee took over, convinced that the proper tactic was to vote out the strongest bill possible and then give away something in the full committee, a little more in the House, and then some more in the Senate. They saw that that tactic had worked in the past, but they didn't consider that it had delivered a mouse when what was now needed was a lion. Besides, it suited their own political ends to vote with the civil rights groups and to vote for what was morally right even if that bill could not pass in the Congress as a whole.

I left the United States to lead a delegation negotiating a law enforcement treaty in Nicaragua, and on my return three days later, our worst fears had been realized. The subcommittee (with Celler succumbing to liberal pressure) had voted out a bill that McCulloch and his fellow Republicans could not possibly support. Celler said it could all be straightened out in the full committee. He did not say how.

Burke Marshall and I went to work drafting a bill with McCulloch and Representative (later Senator) Charles Mathias of Maryland, whom McCulloch chose over John Lindsay as his principal aide on the bill. Lindsay, a liberal Republican from New York, seemed the obvious choice, because, unlike Mathias, he had been extremely active with respect to civil rights. I knew John well and liked him. He had been at Yale Law School when I was, and his older brother George had been articles editor of the *Yale Law Journal* when I was editor in chief. But I agreed with McCulloch that John was far too liberal and far too involved with the Leadership Conference to be a good choice. But he could not help but be badly hurt by being snubbed by his leader in this way.

Bobby had the unpleasant task of testifying again before the full committee, this time against provisions that the civil rights leaders wanted and many of which, but for the political need for Republican support, he favored. It put the attorney general squarely against those whom we were in fact trying to help, and it fed sentiments among blacks that ethics was all politics and we did not really understand their problems. Especially painful was opposition to a broad provision that allowed the attorney general to seek injunctions for any violation of anyone's asserted civil rights anywhere. While it was not even tied to racial discrimination—and clearly could not long survive in the House—civil rights leaders saw it as a way of protecting demonstrators. There was also a fair employment practices (FEP) provision and a significant broadening of the public accommodations provisions.

Burke and I were having difficulty getting McCulloch to commit to a bill, mainly because he did not wish to support something that the Republican leadership would not support. Halleck was opposed to the

FEP provision and somewhat on the fence on public accommodations, although we thought that at McCulloch's urging he would probably go along with a slightly narrowed provision. Public accommodations was complicated by the fact that when the president's bill was submitted to both the House and the Senate, Everett Dirksen, the Senate minority leader, had refused to be a cosponsor, because he opposed public accommodations.

While these negotiations were going on, Philip Randolph, the revered black labor leader, and others decided to have a march on Washington for jobs and freedom. While the administration was in no position to oppose the march, we were quite worried about it. There was the possibility of violence, which would be a disaster. Of greater importance was our fear that the very fact of a large demonstration would be viewed by Congress as an effort to put pressure on its members—which it clearly was—and would in the current mood of the country be counterproductive. No one from the government involved in the legislation thought it was a good idea.

It was typical of Bobby, knowing that the march would take place, to be determined to make it a success. First, he was instrumental in making it as broad in its support as possible, urging churches and labor unions to get involved so that it did not appear, as so many marches had, to be blacks versus whites. The church groups and labor leaders like Walter Reuther responded and made a world of difference. Second, he instructed John Douglas, who headed the Civil Division, to assist the organizers in every way and make sure all the logistics were properly handled.

John was an ideal choice. Center on the Princeton football team, winner of the university's highest prize, a Navy veteran, a Rhodes Scholar, a law journal editor, and a Supreme Court clerk, he nevertheless related well to ordinary people, who saw him as a decent, hardworking guy, not an Ivy League star. He was, of course, both.

John, working with John Nolan and others, did a magnificent job, coordinating with both the people running the march and the D.C. police. He worked hard with the police chief to be sure the police were helpful, friendly, and welcoming, and he got cooperation all the way around. As the buses poured in, their passengers were greeted by pleasant police officers. It was a beautiful day, and the march took on the air not of protest but of celebration. White Catholic nuns in their habits walking hand in hand with blacks, college students, union workers—there was a rainbow of faces to listen to some great speeches, topped by King's famous "I Have a Dream." It was a glorious occasion and a glimpse of what this country could and should be.

I would like to think the march was instrumental in the passage of the civil rights bill, but as far as I could see, it had no effect on members of Congress who were undecided. But it did, then and later, in the memory, have an important impact on the average American television viewer. It was, I think, the beginning of an American commitment, with respect to which Congress was, as it so often is, just a little bit behind. It is impossible to underestimate the importance of the peaceful and almost joyful atmosphere of the occasion as contrasted with the violence that had accompanied so many demonstrations in the South.

Despite the march, things remained stalled in the Judiciary Committee. We worked out a slightly modified public accommodations provision with McCulloch, but he was unwilling to commit until he had Halleck's support. In addition, labor was putting on a major push for a fair employment practices provision, and it was becoming doubtful whether we could hold enough Democrats in the committee without one. Our difficulty was compounded by the fact that the southerners, as a tactical maneuver, were supporting the liberal bill, knowing that it would not get Republican support either in the committee or in the House. Many of the Democrats simply did not believe the Republican support for a modified bill would hold up.

I met with Walter Reuther, at the request of some of the White House staff, but he was adamant that the bill must contain an FEP provision. I did not, as he put it, "understand the mood of the country." My efforts to explain that it was the votes in the House, not the mood in the country, that concerned me were to no avail. Larry O'Brien and I decided to see if Speaker John McCormack could move things along, so we met with him, Celler, Halleck, and McCulloch. To my surprise and pleasure, Halleck appeared willing to state his commitment to our public accommodations section and the rest of the draft, which would have satisfied all of us except, apparently, the Speaker. At this point McCormack stated that there had to be an FEP provision and without it he could not support the bill. Halleck said there was no way he would support FEP and walked out of the room, angry. Larry and I thought the meeting had been a disaster.

I think this was the low point. Our strategy for securing Republican support appeared lost, and we saw no way of getting a strong bill without it. Once again I feared we would end up, as on previous occasions, with little real advance. One could blame the liberals or the Republicans, but blame was not going to help solve our racial problems. Failure would be a huge blow to the Kennedy administration, and to the president and the attorney general personally as well as politically.

Bemoaning the situation with Congressman Frank Thompson, an old friend from New Jersey and a member of the House Labor and Education Committee, I asked him if he had any thoughts on FEP. He asked me if we had considered the Republican bill that his committee had voted out some years previously, when the Republicans had controlled the House. He described it as "not very good but not all bad." I discussed it with Bobby, who told me to get Larry O'Brien's thoughts. Larry thought it had real possibilities and proceeded to sic its author, Congressman Griffin of Michigan, on McCulloch. If the Republicans had voted out the bill once on its own merits, they would have trouble opposing it as part of an omnibus civil rights bill.

When I raised the Republican FEP bill with McCulloch, he was clearly interested. I think he saw the whole civil rights bill ending up with something he could not support and felt unhappy with that prospect, since from the beginning he had insisted on the strategy we adopted. If we added the Republican FEP bill to what he had already approved, he would lose no Republican votes on the committee and we might gain a couple of liberals who were on the fence. He was prepared to vote for it, but warned that he did not think Halleck would commit to it—at least, not yet.

Even with the addition of an FEP provision there was going to be a close vote in the full committee, with southerners and liberals banding together to vote for the subcommittee bill and the civil rights leaders feeling betrayed by both the president and Bobby for supporting a lesser proposal. Bobby was his most pragmatic self: "I want a bill to pass the House, not an issue." And he went on to comment that some liberal Democrats had a "death wish."

President Kennedy assembled the Democrats (excluding the southerners) on the Judiciary Committee the day before the vote. He and Bobby made an earnest and emotional plea for their vote against the subcommittee bill and for the compromise we supported. They pointed out the country's need for an effective bill and said that, like it or not, Democrats needed Republican support. There were some liberals who simply were not prepared to compromise, but there were others who would—except they did not trust Halleck to actually support the compromise, which by historical standards would be by miles the strongest civil rights bill ever if it passed. The president undertook to get Halleck's commitment personally, and this seemed to satisfy those on the fence.

JFK asked me to telephone McCulloch and go over the bill section by section to be absolutely sure of what McCulloch and Halleck were committed to. I did so, and McCulloch reiterated his support for all the provisions but said that Halleck was not committed to FEP. I reported to the president but, inexplicably and inexcusably, told him that both McCulloch and Halleck were committed to all the provisions. Apparently I thought this true, because it was only a year later, when I glanced through my notes, that I saw my own notation that Halleck was not committed.

I met with the president and Halleck briefly early the next morning, and Halleck assured JFK of his support for the bill. As he was leaving, Halleck turned to the president and said, "You do understand, don't you, that my commitment does not extend to FEP? I'm not at all sure about that."

Kennedy put his arm around him and said, "Charlie, we need a bill that will pass the House. It's almost time for the vote. Let's get the votes and get this thing out of the committee. And I'm grateful for your help."

As Halleck left, the president turned to me. "I thought you told me he was committed on FEP."

"I did and he is. Don't worry about it. He will support it. It would be a mistake to pressure him."

I honestly thought this was true, but why, I do not know. Of course, in the end he did support the bill.

Back at my office, I had a telephone call from McCulloch asking me to meet with John Lindsay and see if I could accommodate his suggestions. We met in a hotel room just before the committee meeting, and John made a modest suggestion that was both helpful and easy to accept. He had been a strong supporter of the subcommittee bill and said with the change he was prepared to switch and support his leader, McCulloch. That was a difficult decision for him, as his role as the most liberal Republican was important to him. It may well have been crucial to the committee vote.

The important job of the committee chair, Emanuel Celler, was to confine the meeting to two votes and not get involved in further discussion or amendments. Since this went against his every instinct, we carefully briefed Congressman Jack Brooks of Texas, a strong Kennedy supporter, on how to coach the chairman. He sat beside him armed with the correct text for the chair, and Celler followed his instructions. The first vote was a no on the subcommittee bill, which was the crucial one. The noes won by two votes, an indication of how much difference Lindsay made. Inexplicably, Congressman Libonati of Chicago voted yes—inexplicable because the city's Mayor Daley, at our behest, had spoken to him twice. He did not run for Congress again.

The second vote, once the danger of amendment had been avoided, was much easier, and the compromise bill passed the full committee 23–11. Bobby hailed the leadership of both McCulloch and Halleck, but the vote left civil rights leaders, even the more conservative ones like Roy Wilkins, feeling that the administration had abandoned them. It was terribly difficult for Bobby, in particular, to have to fight those we were in total sympathy with the whole way through. I suppose, in a sense, the opposition of the civil rights groups to the bipartisan bill helped throughout the legislative process to keep the support of the more conservative elements, which was essential to its passage.

It was October 29 and the bill headed to the conservative Rules Committee, where it was certain to languish for a while. The Rules Committee was chaired by Judge Howard Smith, a powerful Virginian who also led the southerners in opposition to the bill.

President Kennedy invited me to accompany him and a number of legislators and White House staff to the Army-Navy football game in Chicago. As it turned out, the president canceled at the last minute because of a crisis in Vietnam with a change of government. On the trip were Senator Dirksen, Halleck, and McCulloch. Conversation naturally turned to the bill just passed by the House Judiciary Committee. I talked about the bill all the way to Chicago with Senator Dirksen. On the way back, Charlie Halleck came into the conversation. Halleck left me in no doubt that the bill would pass the House with his support. Dirksen was noncommittal about particular provisions, especially public accommodations and FEP. But his final words to me then were "Don't worry. This bill will come to a vote in the Senate."

I reported the conversation to Bobby and the president. Both were pleased. But it was not a good time for Bobby. JFK's popularity had dropped significantly in the polls, and Bobby, probably correctly, attributed this to our problems with civil rights. He was a depressed young man when he celebrated his thirty-eighth birthday on November 20 at an office party in the department, the annual reception for the judiciary at the White House, and another party afterward at Hickory Hill.

The civil rights bill was making progress, and I was becoming optimistic about its ultimate passage. But it was not at that time popular with civil rights leaders or with the general public—it was a compromise that was perceived as too little by some and too much by others. Still, the success of getting a bipartisan bill out of the committee left the civil rights groups and labor with little choice other than to lobby vigorously for its passage.

XIII

On November 22, I went to lunch at a restaurant near the department with Joe Dolan. We had just been seated when we heard the radio behind the cashier's desk announce that the president had been shot in Dallas. We jumped up and ran back to the department, where we went to the attorney general's office. His secretary, Angie Novello, was there. Bobby was at Hickory Hill. He had had a meeting of his Organized Crime Task Force that morning and had taken Bob Morgenthau, the U.S. attorney in the Southern District of New York, home for lunch. Angie told us that it looked as though it might well be fatal and that the president had been rushed to the hospital. The FBI was keeping her and Bobby informed.

It is impossible to describe the feelings all of us in the department had. It seemed as if all the lights had gone out, all senses down. I went to my office and after a few minutes called Bobby, feeling I should but having no idea what to say. He answered the phone.

"Hoover just called me," he said. "The president is dead. I think Hoover enjoyed giving me the news."

I don't know what I said. There was nothing adequate to say. I turned on the TV and just sat. People started to come into the office: Burke Marshall, John Douglas, Harold Reis, Joe Dolan. Mostly we were just silent. The phone rang. It was Bobby.

"They want to swear him in right away, in Texas. That's not necessary, is it?"

He could not bear the swearing in. In some mystical sense I think he wanted President Kennedy to return to Washington on Air Force One as if he were still president. I think too that swearing in JFK's successor in Texas was an offensive idea to him.

"No," I said. "Not necessary."

"They want to know who can swear in the president. Does it have to be the chief justice?"

"No," I replied. "Anyone who can administer an oath—a federal judge, for example."

He rang off. I was, frankly, appalled that Johnson's people were seeking legal advice from Bobby at this time. I could understand, however, and even sympathize with the desire for a prompt swearing in as a demonstration to the world that the government was intact and functioning.

A few minutes later the phone rang again. It was Jack Valenti, calling from Air Force One.

"We want to swear Vice President Johnson in as president. The attorney general said you would have a copy of the oath."

I got up and found a copy of the Constitution and read him the oath.

He thanked me and told me that Judge Sarah Hughes was on her way to the airport to swear in President Johnson. The small group in my office departed one by one, downhearted, depressed, not knowing what changes a new president would bring and not knowing how to bring comfort to our leader in this awful moment.

At that time, the assassination of the president was not a federal crime. We had no formal role in any investigation or prosecution of the assassin. It was simply a case of murder under Texas law. Nonetheless, I kept getting reports from the FBI on the arrest of Lee Harvey Oswald as the murderer and background information about him on his visit to the Soviet Union, the Cuban embassy, and so forth. My first and most immediate concern was how well the Dallas police were handling the arrest and questioning. Perhaps my eastern, Ivy League prejudice was affecting my judgment, but I was frightened that they would mess up Oswald's arrest and questioning or deny him legal counsel, or that he would be beaten up by angry and frustrated police or put in confinement with other prisoners who would abuse him, even kill him. I could think of nothing worse than having a prosecution for murdering the president fail because of police abuse or coerced confession or denial of counsel and the like.

I made several phone calls to the United States attorney in Dallas, Harold Barefoot Sanders. I knew Barefoot slightly and knew he was an outstanding young prosecutor with good connections politically in Texas and with the Dallas police. I told him my concerns and asked him to make sure, if he could, that everything was being done properly. He reported back to me several times that things were progressing in a satisfactory fashion and that the police officials were quite cognizant of their responsibility not to abuse Oswald's constitutional rights.

I also called Bernie Segal about the problem of insuring that Oswald had competent counsel available to him. It would not be easy to get a lawyer to represent the man who shot JFK, but even the worst are entitled to a competent lawyer. I thought I had done what I could to cover those immediate problems.

On Sunday morning I was sitting at home watching television when an old friend from Princeton and Oxford rang the doorbell. Karl Harr, who had been a year behind me at both universities, was a lifelong Republican. He had been on the staff of the National Security Council under Eisenhower, and I had not seen much of him in Washington. He came around that Sunday to tell me how devastated he felt over Kennedy's death, even though he did not agree with many of his more liberal policies. We sat on the couch together watching the screen as Oswald was being escorted by the Dallas police for his arraignment on the charge of murder. When Oswald was shot and killed by Jack Ruby, we could not believe our eyes. Everything I had tried to do was wiped out in one shot.

Even without Oswald's murder, there were, understandably, many conspiracy theories in people's minds. Oswald's visits to the Soviet Union, his Russian wife, and his Communist views were the most serious, because of the obvious potential cold war consequences. It would have been almost inconceivable not to have thought of the possibility of conspiracy on the basis of the facts then known, whether that conspiracy was Soviet, Cuban, or the action of some lesser group such as organized crime or racist Rambos. A lone gunman killing the president without outside help did not seem convincing.

Nor was the conspiracy possibility held only by those who are quick to see conspiracy everywhere. President Johnson at the time thought the shooting might well have been planned by others than just Oswald, and I am not sure he was ever persuaded otherwise. My efforts to insure that Oswald was protected and not abused were in anticipation of a trial for the president's murder, which might have gotten to the bottom of things. Oswald's sudden death was sure to be gasoline on the flames of conspiracy theories.

The potential conspiracy that worried me most was the Soviet Union. I did not believe that the Soviets were foolish enough to kill our president or that they would select a frail reed like Oswald as the instrument to do so. Coming as the assassination did less than a year after the Cuban missile crisis, which had brought us to the threshold of a nuclear war, I simply could not believe the Russians would be so reckless. Nor did I think the Cubans would do so without Soviet knowledge. (I was unaware of the efforts by the CIA to assassinate Castro.) But in the atmosphere of the cold war, despite my own beliefs, I thought it essential to get all the facts out, so that if I was correct, the public would be persuaded, and if I was wrong, we would be in a position to deal with this major escalation in cold war relations. I was influenced too by the fact that a century had not eliminated any of the many theories about the Lincoln assassination, and I was seeking some way to avoid that outcome in Kennedy's murder.

The idea of a blue-ribbon commission to examine all the facts and make its conclusions public was the obvious, if not very original, solution. I could think of no other. The only person I discussed it with was Eugene Rostow, dean of the Yale Law School, who called me on the phone to make a similar proposal. I started to broach it with Bobby, but he was totally uninterested. His brother was dead. Lyndon Johnson was president. Nothing would change what had happened, and in his state of shock, he could not focus on matters beyond his broken heart.

I wrote a memo to Bill Moyers, who was the only person close to LBJ whom I knew well enough to write to. It was a badly written memo, because it suggested that the purpose of the commission would be to put to bed rumors of a conspiracy by investigating all the facts and making them public. It did not suggest what the commission would do if the facts established the existence of a conspiracy, and critics have quite justifiably pointed this out, to my chagrin. Clearly, whether or not there was a conspiracy, it behooved the administration to examine all the facts, and a presidential commission is scarcely the way to cover up a conspiracy if one exists.

Initially President Johnson did not want such a commission and thought that a Texas-based investigation under Texas attorney general Waggoner Carr was the proper course. Again, it may have been eastern prejudice, but that seemed to me a totally unsatisfactory solution. Carr, whatever his personal merits and integrity, simply did not have the resources to do the job. Further, much of the country would not trust a Texas investigation in any event. Among the many conspiracy theories floating around were those that put conservative Texas racists in the picture and even some that saw LBJ as the moving force. I do not recall the president discussing with me either the commission or Carr early in the flow of events. It could be that he thought Bobby was behind the presidential commission proposal, which might have annoyed him. And I do know he was angry at a *Washington Post* editorial that urged a commission, which I am sure he thought was my doing, which it was not.

Those days between the assassination and President Kennedy's funeral are something of a blur in my memory. I do remember a group of us going to the White House to pay our last respects to our fallen leader, a meeting arranged by Bobby to include an unusually large number of career attorneys. I remember watching the procession to the Capitol from the department as it passed directly below us; the funeral, with its foreign dignitaries and Bobby in close attendance on Jackie; and finally Bobby returning to the department the day after the funeral and trying his best to pretend things were normal. He looked like the ghost of his former self, and his efforts to tell humorous stories about events at the funeral were brave but flat.

Everything Bobby said about President Johnson was negative and often bitter. He saw a big turn to the right. He questioned LBJ's commitment to civil rights. While that commitment seemed clear from prior public statements and indeed from President Johnson's actions since Kennedy's death, Bobby simply did not trust him. He saw everything as political, not as based on conviction, and therefore as potentially changeable. I doubt there is anything Johnson could have done to change that view.

When President Johnson addressed the joint session of Congress at noon on the eve of Thanksgiving, he made one of the finest speeches of his career, committing himself to passage of the civil rights bill as a tribute to the dead president and to carrying on the rest of Kennedy's program. It was somewhat reassuring to liberals and civil rights leaders, but even this passionate commitment did not totally erase distrust for a southern president whose reputation was based on political deals. Bobby resented LBJ's wrapping himself in Bobby's brother's mantle, but he did want the civil rights bill enacted into law.

In the weeks following his brother's death, Bobby's gloom permeated the department. The joy of being something special, a cut above the other departments and agencies, that he had brought to Justice died in Dallas. We soldiered on, as did Bobby. President Johnson understood this, and while he had never liked Bobby, he made an effort, never really reciprocated by Bobby, to try to help. It was, of course, politically important to the president that Bobby stay on in office and that despite their history of estrangement, they appear to be working together. Since LBJ was a political animal, it is hard to know which motivated his gestures of reconciliation more.

For whatever reason, LBJ decided to go ahead with the presidential commission that I, and I am sure several others, recommended. He called me to tell me so and told me that he wanted Chief Justice Earl Warren to chair it. I told him I was quite confident that Warren would not accept the job and would regard it as somewhat improper for him to do so. I was told to see him and persuade him. The president also told me we would have to involve Texas attorney general Carr in some way, since his putative state investigation had now been superseded. I thought that relatively easy; he could attend all meetings as an observer.

I gathered up Archibald Cox, our solicitor general, who had the closest contacts with the Court, and made an appointment to see the chief justice that same day. Warren approved the idea of the commission but steadfastly declined to chair it. I am not sure I was very persuasive, since fundamentally both Archie Cox and I agreed with him. I called the president and gave him the news. He was not surprised. Indeed, I think he was pleased at the opportunity to turn on the famous Johnson persuasive skills. He called me later, with obvious pleasure, to tell me that he had talked to Warren and that the chief justice had accepted the assignment.

It would have been hard to pick a chairman more incompatible with Hoover's FBI than Earl Warren, whom the FBI despised for his liberal views. Hoover had, of course, been opposed to any commission, as he found it difficult to accept that the findings of the FBI were not sufficient. But he was not about to oppose the new president, through whom his close relationship with the White House had been reestablished. Also, it was obvious that the commission would be heavily reliant on the Bureau for the investigative work in this country. I selected Howard Willens, the first assistant in the Criminal Division, to be the liaison between the commission and the FBI, and thereafter I had little to do with the commission. Bobby would have nothing to do with it. Howard handled his difficult assignment competently and diplomatically. The commission was staffed with enormously able and experienced lawyers who volunteered from the private sector. There was some infighting between the CIA and the FBI, which was par for the course, and some efforts by each to cover up what in hindsight looked negligent. The Secret Service had a legitimate complaint about never having been informed about Oswald, which the Bureau sought to downplay. And Allen Dulles, the longtime head of the CIA and a member of the commission, never told his colleagues about the attempts on Castro's life, an inexcusable failure.

Bobby was in the office only intermittently in the weeks following his brother's death. He was withdrawn, pale, somehow diminished, with none of the energy he had brought to the office. He knew that the Bureau, which he had made some effort to control, was back to its old ways, in this case feeding information about him and his staff to the White House. No longer was the FBI director excluded by the fluke of a family relationship from his customary position close to the president.

Bobby was determined to carry on what he could of his brother's policies despite his diminished role. He felt that what his brother had tried to do was now up to him, especially with respect to civil rights. Since the Cuban missile crisis he had been more and more engaged in foreign policy, and now he felt frozen out of that participation by the new president. But he felt it important to carry on at least until the November 1964 elections, because only by doing so could he hope to influence Democratic Party policy in the campaign ahead. He knew Johnson needed him, whatever their personal feelings toward each other. Bobby urged all of us to work with him to achieve what we could.

In January, at the suggestion of Bobby's close friend Averell Harriman, President Johnson named him as a special representative to go to the Far East to see if he could persuade Indonesian president Sukarno to agree to a ceasefire in the troubles between Indonesia and Malaysia. Bobby was a good choice on the merits, because he was friendly with Sukarno and familiar with the background facts. He had gone on a somewhat similar trip for his brother in 1962 and written about it in his book *Just Friends and Brave Enemies*. But it was, too, an effort on the part of his friends to get him involved. Johnson was reluctant, and probably annoyed at being pressed by the Kennedy people, but he went along with the recommendation. Bobby did a remarkable job of negotiating the ceasefire. More important, from the viewpoint of those of us in the department, he returned reinvigorated, although gaunt, and plunged back into work

It became clear in many meetings with civil rights leaders that President Johnson was committed publicly and privately to getting a civil rights law passed by the Congress. It was not clear to us whether this was a matter of conviction or politics, and I am sure Bobby's skepticism about Johnson's motives permeated all our thinking. But the important point was that the president wanted the bill passed. LBJ told Bobby that it was the department's responsibility but that he was available and willing to do whatever he was asked to do. That suited Bobby, even though he thought it meant that failure was his responsibility and success, at best, was shared.

The bill was in the House Rules Committee, where it had languished since shortly before JFK's death. With all of the problems of transition, coupled with the holidays, it is hardly fair to say it was stalled there. A bill with support of both the Democratic and the Republican leadership would be voted out, and there was no indication that the Republicans would now withdraw their support, however lukewarm it was. I was confident that McCulloch was a man of his word, and I thought Halleck was also. Judge Smith would play whatever games he could to weaken the bill, and we had long anticipated that the committee would vote it out with an "open rule," meaning that unlimited amendments could be offered.

Because we thought there would be such a rule, I had put the appellate section of the Civil Rights Division (and David Filvaroff) to work on a project of publishing a rather unusual volume of questions and answers explaining every aspect of the bill and its reasoning. Harold Greene, a career lawyer who as a child had been a refugee from Hitler's Germany, was in charge, and he did a brilliant job of including every conceivable question, friendly and hostile, with clear and convincing answers. (Harold went on in his career to become a federal judge in the District of Columbia; his most famous case was the breakup of the AT&T empire.) The book was over a hundred pages long, and we provided it to all congressmen and staff who requested it, including our southern adversaries. I have no idea whether or not this unique approach (probably a remnant of my days as a teacher) swayed any votes, but I do know I had scores of messages of appreciation from congressmen and their staff members.

On a major bill such as civil rights there are many actors, and one never knows what is going on in every office every day. Civil rights and labor leaders were lobbying hard for the bill, as were various church groups. Burke Marshall, Joe Dolan, Bill Geoghegan, David Filvaroff, and I spent hours on the Hill, as did Larry O'Brien's team. I kept in close touch with Larry to see where there might be defections and worked with many Democrats to consolidate our position. Bobby was on the phone with leading Democrats, and we kept in close touch. I never knew what President Johnson was doing, but I was confident he was using his enormous powers of persuasion. What he did that was important was not give an inch on the committee's bill—nothing more, nothing less. We held to that line throughout.

The Rules Committee voted out the bill on January 30 by a vote of 11–4. The problem now was to hold the bill intact and avoid crippling amendments, and we felt we were well positioned to do so. We had organized the Judiciary Committee so that the more articulate members on both sides of the aisle were prepared to respond to various assigned provisions of the bill. Harold Greene had expanded our Q&A project into five huge loose-leaf notebooks, and the committee members and staff, led by its counsel, Ben Zelenko, were practiced in turning quickly to the pages containing the reasons for opposing particular amendments and authorities justifying the existing provisions.

The crucial debate in fact took place when the House resolved itself into a Committee of the Whole to propose amendments to the bill before voting it out to the House floor. Under House rules, the Committee of the Whole (which, as its name indicates, includes all members) can amend a bill but cannot give it final approval. This unusual procedure was crucial to our adversaries, because the votes on proposed amendments were not recorded by name in a roll call, so there was no formal record of defection. It was easy for a congressman to slip into the line supporting a crippling amendment without being held responsible. To keep the bill intact required votes, and that meant people one could count on into the small hours of the morning.

Judge Smith had his cohort of southern votes, occasionally, almost randomly, supported by conservative Republicans. We had some solid Democratic votes, usually supported by some Republicans. The trick was to be sure the votes we needed were always at hand. Frank Thompson of New Jersey took on the responsibility of providing the votes, and we helped, largely meaning that Henry Wilson and Dick Donohue from the White House made phone calls to round up delinquent members. Frank used as an enticement free alcoholic beverages, which he graciously and abundantly offered to Judge Smith's supporters as well. Gradually the Smith team diminished in numbers, which helped Frank maintain a steady majority. Frank Thompson was one of the unsung and unnoticed heroes of the House Democrats.

I sat in the gallery and watched division after division successfully defend the bill. But each time I would see some Republicans sneak over to Judge Smith's side, and I remained nervous until the end. It was particularly nerve-racking when, on one occasion, I saw Gerald Ford (later President Ford), the Republican whip, join with Judge Smith. We lost only one vote, which we were able to restore in the House during the final debate on passage of the bill. I telephoned Bobby in the small hours of the morning with the good news and left it up to him, or Larry O'Brien, to tell the president.

The bill was debated in the House for nine days—and vigorously, and successfully, defended by the designated members of the committee. I would defy any observer of American politics to find a better-informed discussion, thanks to Harold Greene's loose-leaf notebooks. Judge Smith succeeded in getting only one important amendment: the inclusion of women in the antidiscrimination provisions. We had opposed that amendment because we were concerned that it might prejudice the remainder of the bill, just as Judge Smith obviously intended. As things turned out, it did not, and the women of America owe their equal (or at least more equal) status to a southern segregationist who never in his wildest dreams would have wanted that result.

On February 10 the House passed the bill, 290–130. I think it could not have been five minutes after its passage that the president was getting Halleck, McCulloch, civil rights leaders, and lobbyists still on the Hill on the phone to congratulate them—a tribute to LBJ's political acumen and the skill of the White House telephone operators. The bill that passed was the bill the House Judiciary Committee had approved, including the Republican FEP provisions we had incorporated and equal rights for women. It was, as the *Congressional Quarterly* wrote, "the most sweeping civil rights measure to clear either house of Congress in the 20th Century."

President Johnson called me at the Capitol to congratulate me on the passage of the bill, and he also called Bobby, although Bobby, despite his pleasure at its passage, was not in a mood to discuss tactics in the Senate with LBJ. He simply emphasized the need to pass the bill in the Senate as it had passed in the House.

The next day, at a White House reception, President Johnson cornered me. He pulled up a chair for himself and one for me in the middle of the reception, and we sat there face to face. "How," he asked, "do you plan to get this bill enacted in the Senate?"

I reminded him of our commitment to McCulloch and the House Republicans that we would not bargain away what they had enacted to get it past a filibuster. "I think," I said, "we have to try for cloture. We may not get sixty-seven votes, but we have to try."

"What makes you think you have a chance for cloture?"

I had done my homework, and I thanked God for the instruction I had received from Larry O'Brien. Talking voting details with the man who knew the Senate better than anyone else was a little daunting. Nevertheless, I plunged ahead.

"I think we can get fifty-seven to sixty votes for cloture fairly easily," I said. "We have fifty-one Democrats and some liberal Republicans from New York, California, Pennsylvania, and New England who will support the bill. But not all will vote for cloture. We need at least half the thirty-three Republicans. Based on the cloture vote on the satellite communications act, there are seventy-four potential votes for cloture. We need at least seven more from fourteen senators who have voted at least once for cloture. That should be possible."

He started to cross-examine me on names. How did I get to sixty? Who were the fourteen in the pool? Why did I think any of them were possible? I told him I had talked to all the senators on the list (although admittedly before we had added FEP) and that I thought the argument that cloture was voted on the satellite communications bill was key to getting it for the civil rights bill. It was my impression that senators who had voted for cloture on that bill, whatever their motive, were embarrassed to say that a vote on the merits of that bill was more important to the country than a vote on the merits of civil rights legislation.

The president remained skeptical about cloture, but he accepted that we had no choice but to try. If we broke our commitment to McCulloch and the House Republican leadership, we would end up with nothing but angry Republicans on the right and angry labor and civil rights leaders on the left. Going for cloture was a risky gamble, but in truth it involved less risk than the alternative. I told him quite bluntly: "Mr. President, if you do anything publicly but indicate that we are going to get cloture on the bill, we can't *possibly* get cloture. If you, with your expertise, express confidence, publicly and privately, then I think we have a chance."

LBJ really had no choice but to support our strategy, however flawed he may have thought it. The Senate would be tied up for weeks or months—an unpleasant prospect. The key, we all knew, was the Senate minority leader, Everett Dirksen. But whether or not Dirksen could deliver enough Republican votes for cloture, assuming he wanted to do so, was uncertain. There was sentiment in the country for civil rights, and Republicans in the House had been responsive to that sentiment. There was far less feeling in the Senate and no great enthusiasm among many for the proposed legislation, particularly among the midwestern Republicans, who had few black constituents but who made up over half the Republican votes we would need.

At the time I was by no means convinced that President Johnson was motivated by principles of racial equality and justice, though he used them skillfully in argument. I had worked with Bobby for too long to come to any such conclusion. But I did not think it really mattered. Politics dictated the course that had to be followed, and LBJ followed it with vigor and determination.

As Congressman McCulloch had been the key in the House, so Senator Dirksen was in the Senate. Burke Marshall and I went to work with Dirksen and his legislative assistant, whose name, oddly enough, was Kennedy. The House bill was in the Judiciary Committee and would be voted out only when Dirksen, its senior Republican as well as the

Republican leader, was ready to do so. Night after night Burke and I would go over the bill line by line in the senator's back-room office in the Capitol building. Dirksen was usually joined by Senator Roman Hruska of Nebraska, a conservative who represented crucial midwestern votes, as well as Neil Kennedy. The senator would provide drinks for all, and we would proceed section by section through the bill. Burke Marshall was wonderfully persuasive, not only because he had perhaps the best analytical mind I have ever encountered, but because he explained matters in a quiet, understated way. He was highly respected even by those he could not always persuade.

The process took time, and we were lucky to get one provision agreed to every two days or so. In those meetings Burke and I discovered three important facts: first, Dirksen wanted to be sure the provision did not affect his state of Illinois in any significant way; second, he obviously wanted the bill rewritten, to appear different, even if there were no substantive changes, so that he could explain to his colleagues all the "changes" he had negotiated; and third, it behooved us to get agreement before too much bourbon had dulled the senator's recollection of what he had okayed. Burke did most of the redrafting, and while he could say the same thing a second time in different words, it got more difficult if he had to redraft a third time. Somewhat surprisingly, Neil Kennedy gradually got into the spirit of the "negotiations" and was quite helpful.

Since passage of the bill in the House, President Johnson had been preparing for the Senate debate and cloture. He, along with civil rights leaders, wanted to force the Senate into continuous twenty-four-hour sessions as a way of breaking the filibuster. Johnson's successor as majority leader, Mike Mansfield, the quiet Montana professor, would have none of that. He feared that senators would die of fatigue and said that was not going to happen on his watch. It could not have been easy for Mansfield to oppose his former leader and friend, but he stuck to his guns. Both the president and Mansfield determined to give prime responsibility for the legislation in the Senate to Hubert Humphrey, the Democratic whip and longtime civil rights advocate. It was good politics from Johnson's viewpoint. Liberals, still somewhat unsure of LBJ and uncertain of Mansfield, could never accuse Humphrey of selling civil rights short.

It was difficult for President Johnson to stay in the background, and he wanted to micromanage the bill in the Senate as he had done in the past. He kept instructing Humphrey on tactics, particularly on the importance of taking every opportunity to praise Dirksen's leadership and statesmanlike qualities, a technique Johnson often employed to his advantage. Among other things, he pointed out the need to organize his forces so that they were, like the southerners, always prepared and informed. As I discovered over time, President Johnson, in contrast with Bobby, almost always told you not only what he wanted accomplished but, in excruciating detail, how he thought you should do it. Bobby told you the result he wanted and left you to figure it out for yourself, offering help when you asked for it.

Still, President Johnson knew and understood the Senate, his advice was sound, and Humphrey followed it. Dirksen named Thomas Kuchel, the Republican whip and a liberal senator from California, to be floor manager on the Republican side, and he worked closely with Humphrey. Together they created a system whereby at least four supporters of the bill would always be on the Senate floor to challenge, debate, refute accusations, and otherwise question the bill's opponents. Together they named senators to become expert on each of the sections of the bill, and a rotation of senators on each side to be sure a quorum was present at all times. Harold Greene was kept busy filling in detailed loose-leaf notebooks.

Once a filibuster commences, perhaps the hardest part of managing the forces against it is to be sure that whenever there is a call for a quorum, fifty-one senators can be rounded up. That means they must be somewhere on the premises, whatever the day of the week and the hour of the day—not easy when a filibuster may go on for a long time, as this one was sure to do. A failure to meet a quorum call meant that the Senate was automatically adjourned for the day. A senator can only speak twice in one legislative "day," and adjournment meant a new day so the clock started all over again for the southern opposition. It is a measure of the leadership that Humphrey and Kuchel provided that in the months of debate, only once did they fail to produce a quorum.

Starting on March 9, when the motion to take up the bill was introduced, and continuing for more than three months, I met with Humphrey and Kuchel and their team captains every morning in Mansfield's office. Usually Larry O'Brien or Mike Manatos was present, and once or twice a week Clarence Mitchell, the civil rights lobbyist for the SCLC, Andrew Biemiller, the AFL-CIO lobbyist, and Joseph Rauh, a distinguished Washington lawyer who was close to LBJ, were present. Problems were aired and resolved, assignments meted out. I kept Harold Greene and his team busy doing further memos on issues the southerners were raising. The meetings resembled a locker room before a big game and were clearly important not only for what they did but for their effect on morale. More and more, the fact of efficient and successful organization gave liberals, who had been losing for years, a feeling that victory was possible. And even those lukewarm to black aspirations began to feel a stake in prevailing. As in the House, the debate was informed and very nearly interesting.

It was clear to Senator Richard Russell, the leader of the southerners (and a distinguished senator), that he simply did not have the votes to amend or significantly modify the bill. His tactic and his hope was that he could maintain a filibuster for long enough to persuade a tired majority and the president to compromise. He had eighteen senators, in addition to himself: seventeen Democrats from the Deep South and Republican John Tower of Texas. Absent cloture, nineteen could go on a very long time.

On March 26 the Senate voted to take up the bill as its pending business. With that vote, the longest debate in the history of the Senate commenced.

Initially Senator Dirksen had expected President Johnson to be willing, as in the past, to negotiate some compromise. When he found that solution unavailable, he discovered himself the focus of public attention (thanks to the praise heaped on him by Humphrey) without being at all certain he could deliver the necessary votes. He proposed two or three major amendments that were thoroughly defeated, but which I believe were simply designed to show his more conservative colleagues that that door was closed. Burke and I continued to work with him on what were essentially face saving changes. In a sense, he was trying to make up in numbers what he could not get in substance.

Senator Humphrey and his colleagues came into the negotiations, as did Bobby, and they understood that this had become a matter of saving face. They objected to some of the amendments, which was helpful to Dirksen (although Burke and I had already okayed them), before reluctantly giving way. Finally, on May 26—after three months of debate—Dirksen, Humphrey, and Bobby Kennedy had a news conference announcing the results of the negotiation. Dirksen took credit for his many amendments and was the hero of the moment nationally. Most of his Republican colleagues fell in line behind him, with some grumbling. Senator Simpson said the bill had been warmed over to make it more palatable. Some liberals were unhappy at some of the amendments that weakened the attorney general's power in small ways, but privately, Bobby welcomed the changes. The New York columnist Murray Kempton perhaps best summed it up by admiring Dirksen's skill in persuading Republicans that his amendments "were substantive changes even while he was converting them into refinements of punctuation."

One hurdle remained. Bourke Hickenlooper, a conservative Republican from Iowa, started a minor revolt against the compromise bill by insisting that there be a vote on three proposed amendments. He claimed he had seventeen Republicans with him on insisting on the vote. Humphrey was reluctant, but after consulting us and getting Bobby's okay, he agreed—but only after getting the assurances he wanted on the vote for cloture, scheduled for June 10. The three votes were taken; two were defeated and one, guaranteeing a jury trial for all criminal contempt defendants (except in voting cases), narrowly passed. Jury trials in such cases had been a constant objective of some, and it did not bother us a great deal.

The cloture vote came on the morning of June 10. I watched from the gallery as the roll call was taken. There was an eerie silence in the huge chamber as each senator called out an aye or a no. When the clerk got to Senator Clair Engle, a liberal Republican from California who was on his deathbed in the hospital following two severe brain operations, his aides carried him in on a stretcher for his final vote as a senator. He tried to speak but could not. Eventually, with great effort, he succeeded in pointing to his eye and the clerk called out "Aye." When the roll call was ending, Senator Carl Haydn, the oldest senator and a fierce opponent of cloture, came from behind the podium and voted no with enormous relief. He had promised President Johnson to vote aye if his was the deciding vote. The vote stood at 71–29. To say it was an emotional moment for many of us is a gross understatement.

The southerners were bitter and insisted on having votes on many of their proposed amendments. A few very minor changes were accepted by the joint Democratic-Republican leadership, and the bill passed 73–21 on June 19, exactly one year to the day after it had been submitted by President Kennedy. It was, in fact, a stronger bill than the one President Kennedy had submitted a year before.

After virtually no debate, on July 2 the House accepted the bill as amended by the Senate, and President Johnson signed it in a ceremony in the East Room of the White House. He was, understandably, triumphant and exuberant, as were Humphrey, Celler, Dirksen, McCulloch, and the other legislative leaders. Bobby sat in the front row, looking pale and wasted. Watching from the rear of the room, I saw him go through the motions, accept a handful of pens from LBJ, and disappear into the crowd. On what should have been a memorable day, the memories were too much—unavoidably sad, even bitter.

XIV

THE YEAR 1964 WAS ONE IN WHICH THE DEPARTMENT SEEMED IN perpetual mourning for JFK. The severity of Bobby's loss was somehow transmitted to all of us. None of us left the ship, and quite a bit was accomplished. But Justice was not the same exciting place, and one felt it never could be again.

Obviously Bobby's relationship with President Johnson tended to take any joy out of what we did accomplish. Looking back, I do not see how one could fault the president. He did not interfere with what we were doing. Indeed, he left the department alone. He let us manage the civil rights legislation as he had proposed, and while he obviously worked behind the scenes with Mansfield, Dirksen, and others, he never in any way interfered and never, to my knowledge, told Bobby what he should be doing or what he, the president, wanted done. It must have been enormously hard for this ambitious, energetic man with a wealth of legislative knowledge and experience to stay in the background, but he wisely did.

Bobby had never gotten on with LBJ, and Johnson's succession to the presidency made matters worse. It was impossible for Bobby not to see him as an illegitimate usurper of his brother's role, not to make the constant comparison between the two, to LBJ's predictable disadvantage. They could be civil to each other, but that was about the extent of it— and even that took effort. I went to a lot of cabinet meetings on short notice because Bobby just could not bring himself to be there. It was embarrassing and somewhat insulting to the president, and I am sure he blew up in the privacy of his office. Clearly it was not the way a cabinet officer should behave toward the president, but Bobby simply could not avoid it.

The 1964 Civil Rights Act was the high point of the year, but there were other accomplishments which in another time would have brought much satisfaction to Bobby. Jimmy Hoffa was convicted of jury tampering in Tennessee and received an eight-year sentence. Three months later he was convicted in Chicago of pension fund fraud and received another five-year sentence. Bobby appeared to get little or no satisfaction from these convictions. He could not bring himself even to celebrate the downfall of his archenemy.

What made it particularly difficult was that in President Kennedy's almost three years, Bobby had grown well beyond the Justice Department and to a substantial extent become the eyes and ears of his brother throughout the government. After the Bay of Pigs and his heading up the investigation of that event, he had increasingly been involved in foreign affairs, as the Cuban missile crisis demonstrated. President Kennedy actually enjoyed being in effect his own secretary of state, and he depended far more on Bobby's intuition than he did on the Foggy Bottom bureaucracy. Dean Rusk was an informed and intelligent secretary, but he was also a bureaucrat at heart. What the Kennedys admired was imaginative initiatives, which were not Rusk's strong suit. It was hard to get the State Department to respond in ways and with words that had appeal to either Kennedy.

The fundamental problem for Bobby was his brother's death. He had for three years submerged himself in his brother's presidency, not for his own ego or reputation but for his brother. All that Bobby dreamed JFK could accomplish—and he could help JFK accomplish—was gone. That dream, like the presidency, had been usurped by Johnson, a man Bobby saw as an unprincipled and crude politician who would lie and cheat to attain his personal objectives. President Johnson brought out the New England moralist in Bobby and none of the tolerance and forgiveness he often demonstrated to others. In an odd way, both men had achieved well beyond their expectations through hard work. But Bobby saw LBJ's success as the product of sleaze and manipulation, maybe even corruption. And LBJ saw Bobby's success as that of a spoiled little rich boy.

Bobby simply did not want to share the Kennedy dream with this man. Until his brother's death, he had never contemplated a life in politics, and despite his success, there was much about it that he intensely disliked. He often talked about teaching or writing, and countless times I heard him express his disgust with politics and politicians. But President Kennedy's death changed all that. He now felt the burden of succession—that he had to pick up the torch from his brother's fallen hand and carry on. But he could not bear to share that burden with anyone, least of all with what he saw as an alien Texas politician. His brother's legacy was to him a thing of beauty, to be preserved as the ideal he saw it to be. He took comfort in reading Edith Hamilton and the ancient Greek philosophers. There was a purity there he could not find in Washington.

The effect of Bobby's determination to finish for his brother what they had set out to do, however general and vague that dream might be, was to separate him even further from President Johnson. Not only did Johnson have his own dream—a remake of the New Deal, which in truth was not so far from what Bobby wanted—but it caused him to become suspicious of everything Bobby was doing or that he thought Bobby was doing. It was part of LBJ's nature to see conspiracies aimed at him, and it was not hard for him to imagine Bobby leading a move to unseat him at the Democratic convention. Bobby often spoke disparagingly of LBJ, and these remarks sometimes got back to the president, more often than not embroidered to fit his paranoia, from the Bureau and others. Since there was no plan to take over the presidency—it would have been hugely unrealistic—Bobby was not greatly bothered.

President Johnson was. There had been rumors that Bobby had wanted to dump him from the ticket when JFK ran for a second term in 1964, a highly unlikely prospect if the president wanted to be reelected, since he needed Texas and what he might still salvage in the South, but one that got some credibility from Bobby's known dislike. In 1962 a scandal involving Billy Sol Estes, a wealthy Texan and a friend of LBJ's, was investigated by the department, and while no improper connection with Johnson was found, Johnson may have seen it as an effort by Bobby to link him with scandal. Then, in early 1963, the Bobby Baker affair began to hit the press.

Baker had risen from congressional page to LBJ's right arm when Johnson was majority leader. When LBJ was elected vice president, Baker took a similar job as Mansfield's executive assistant. He was an extraordinarily talented person and knew the Senate, in my opinion, better than any senator. His vote count was precise and precisely accurate, unless for some reason he wanted to promote a mild distortion. What the press found surprising was not his ability to count votes or even to wheel and deal politically, presumably on behalf of his boss, but how he had become a millionaire doing it.

The FBI began an investigation into Baker's activities early in 1963, and Johnson may well have seen this as an effort on Bobby's part to dump him from the ticket in 1964. It got to the point where President Kennedy had to affirm that he wanted Johnson on the ticket, and Bobby denied, quite truthfully, that he had initiated the Baker investigation. Baker had obviously been close to LBJ when he was majority leader, and the press kept seeking to link them in various ways. Although the Bureau came up with a lot of information about Baker's finances, it failed to link the vice president with anything improper. Indeed, while there was much to be suspicious about with respect to Baker himself, there was no solid evidence of any criminal activity at all—just unanswered questions.

The investigation continued in 1964, and with Johnson's succession to the presidency, the press got even more aggressive, and so did Republicans, in efforts to link the new president with Baker's wheeling and dealing. How much of this LBJ attributed to Bobby Kennedy I do not know, but despite his popularity in the polls, he continued to worry about some kind of Kennedy takeover. The combination of Kennedy loyalists demeaning Johnson and Johnson's irrational fear of some kind of Kennedy coup at the convention worked to increase a tension that had always been present. While they worked together—although more apart than together—to get the civil rights bill enacted, their relations were cool. President Johnson was reluctant to give Bobby any assignments that would have put him, or his closest associates, in the public eye.

Implementing the provisions of the 1964 Civil Rights Act took time but on the whole was a lot easier than we had anticipated. Opening public accommodations to blacks was the most controversial part of the act and where we thought we would have the most difficulty. The major hotel chains had quietly supported the bill and told us they would instantly comply, which they did, setting an example. Their support was economically motivated. National convention business was impossible if they did not serve blacks. Major restaurant chains with locations in the North and West also felt pressure and complied. The FEP provisions were cumbersome and time-consuming but not of a nature to cause disorder, and this was true as well of the provisions expediting appeals in voting cases. But problems of voter registration, not covered by the act, remained.

It was Freedom Summer too, with large numbers of college students going south to attempt to register voters in the face of Klan opposition and substantial physical danger. Hoover had infiltrated the Klan and similar citizen hate groups with a raft of paid informers, using techniques similar to those he had used with the Communist Party in the 1950s—a program which we learned in the Church hearings during the 1970s was its counterintelligence program, or "COINTELPRO." At the time we knew the Bureau had informers in the Klan—indeed, Bobby had recommended such an approach to the president—and we assumed that many were paid for their information. But we had no idea of the range of illegal techniques the Bureau was using. Freedom Summer was a major concern, and the best protection we could envision was intelligence through paid informers. It had some success and then, unfortunately, got out of hand as Hoover extended it to all sorts of other groups, such as black nationalists and more radical student groups, which he treated as he did the Klan.

Apart from the Civil Rights Act and our concerns about Freedom Summer, life in the Justice Department had little excitement during the summer. Gone was the feeling that we were special, and the success of the Civil Rights Act itself led to a feeling of letdown. We had the tragedy of the Mississippi murder of three civil rights workers, Andrew Goodman, James Cheney, and Michael Schwerner, but President Johnson involved himself in pressing the FBI much more than Bobby did. I met with Mr. and Mrs. Goodman, who were understandably devastated by the disappearance of their son, and promised to keep them informed. So, I believe, did Bobby and President Johnson. I met too with Schwerner's wife, who was critical of the department for not protecting her husband and herself during their activities.

Egged on by LBJ, the Bureau sent hundreds of agents into Mississippi with huge amounts of money to buy information and in November solved the murder of the three, which, as we had suspected, involved local law enforcement officers. The possibility of getting a local jury to convict under a state prosecution at that time was slim to nonexistent. Burke decided to use the new federal law, and John Doar prepared the case, using the FBI's informer as his star witness. He eventually succeeded in getting convictions of two of the offenders for denying the three young people their civil rights—not much of a punishment for murder, but at that time a notable achievement.

As fall approached, Bobby began to formulate his own political future. At the end of the day he would occasionally get a group of us together to discuss what he should do, the choice being between trying to persuade LBJ to name him vice president and running for the Senate. The obvious objective was to become president in 1968 (or possibly 1972) and finish his brother's work. There never was any discussion of the 1964 convention in Atlantic City. That simply was not in the cards.

On its face, the vice presidency on a Johnson-Kennedy ticket seemed almost preposterous, given their relationship. Bobby felt that he had the experience and that despite personality differences, he could help LBJ. That might have been true had they been able to work together. But the real appeal to Bobby was to cut off another candidate for president.

Naming a strong candidate, as LBJ did with Humphrey, would make the presidential nomination much tougher for Bobby to attain. In any event, the problem was resolved not by discussion but by President Johnson's refusal to name Bobby or, as he put it, any member of the cabinet. The refusal to single out Bobby and linking him with the rest of the cabinet predictably brought out Bobby's sardonic humor: "Sorry to bring so many good people down," he quipped.

It is easy to understand why President Johnson was unwilling to take the risk. The rewards could have been great or, equally, could have resulted in a disastrous competition between two very strong personalities.

Most of my colleagues were planning to leave the department and return to private practice. Jack Miller, Burke Marshall, John Douglas, Lou Oberdorfer, and John Nolan all had plans for the near future. Ed Guthman and Joe Dolan would work on Bobby's staff. Bobby asked me if I wanted to be attorney general, because if I did, he said he would recommend me to President Johnson. I think he wanted me to do so, but the thought of actually attaining the job was sufficient temptation. I thought I could work with Johnson and still maintain a department dedicated to law, not politics. It would not be the department Bobby and Byron White had put together four years before. Probably no one could do that. Hoover would continue to be an obvious problem for any attorney general. Even with a brother as president, Bobby had not been able to bring him under anything approaching proper control.

I did not know President Johnson well, and of course my view of him must have been somewhat influenced by Bobby. I had talked with him on the phone several times about the progress of the Civil Rights Act and had been with him in cabinet meetings. I knew my closeness to Bobby would be a concern to him, and I was sure he would prefer to have his own person as attorney general. At the same time, I knew he was committed to civil rights and did not want to alienate its black leaders, who would prefer a known quantity running the department to someone new. I also thought he respected me as a lawyer and did not see me as a partisan political person. Indeed, he had a high regard for many of Bobby's associates, particularly Burke Marshall, John Doar, and Ramsey Clark, who was from Texas and whose father, Supreme Court justice Tom Clark, was an old friend.

I became acting attorney general just before Labor Day, when Bobby was nominated as the Democratic candidate for the Senate from New York. His opposition was the liberal Republican senator, Kenneth Keating. I did not really expect any word on my own future until after the election, and I did not then see any special problems. Most of the people were willing to stay on until the end of the year.

I was enormously fortunate to have Ed Guthman's assistant, Jack Rosenthal, stay on as public relations officer. Jack was young but extraordinarily bright and creative. The reporters who covered the department liked him for his candor, his intelligence, and his ability to suggest feature stories that were interesting and unusual—and, of course, helpful to the department and to me. While the press had understandably been focused on Hoffa, civil rights, and Bobby Kennedy, Jack got them interested in prisons and immigration problems and the lesser-known aspects of the department. He also educated me on the need to keep him informed if I wanted to avoid his accidentally putting his foot in his mouth through ignorance. He was enormously helpful in formulating ways to answer the flood of speculative questions on my future. I would have been in constant trouble without him. I was tremendously pleased, but not surprised, when in 1966 the Washington press corps voted Jack's the outstanding public affairs office in the government.

I took no formal role in the election in November, either in New York or nationally. I had no electoral experience, and neither Bobby nor the president reached out for any aid from me. I did make a number of speeches and tried to say things I believed would be helpful to the president. The most difficult part of public appearances was responding to the constant speculation about whether LBJ would appoint me attorney general, particularly when there were stories about others—Clark Clifford, Leon Jaworski, Willard Wirtz (the secretary of labor) were some of the names. The president never discussed the job with me. While I was "acting," he treated me in all respects as the attorney general and often sought my advice. He was always friendly and never critical and did nothing to interfere with my running of the department.

One of the few times my advice was sought on a matter that could be called political was on a day LBJ was campaigning in New York for Bobby. It was also the day that LBJ's longtime assistant Walter Jenkins was found in the men's room of the YMCA engaged in salacious activity. I got a telephone call from LBJ's helicopter, in which both he and Bobby were campaigning around New York State.

"Nick," said the president, "what do you think I should say about Walter?"

"Nothing critical," I responded. "I would express sadness at what happened, sorrow for the effect on his family, and support for a long-time aide."

"That's what Bobby says," he grumbled. "And Lady Bird has already gone to visit his wife."

"Good for her," I responded.

"Thanks," he said, somewhat skeptically.

But he followed the advice. Strange as it may seem, given their unhappy relationship, President Johnson appreciated Bobby's directness and political acumen on the few occasions he sought them. That they campaigned together was normal. LBJ was enormously popular in New York and wanted Bobby to defeat a popular Republican incumbent in the Senate.

One of LBJ's traits that I admired was that when he sought advice, he was usually truly seeking advice, not flattering the adviser simply by asking. In my case, at least while I was attorney general, he almost invariably followed that advice, although sometimes, because of his questions and his aggressive attitude, I could not help wondering if in fact he would. As I came to know him better, I became convinced that he wanted to do what was right, although his political style often concealed that desire.

The 1964 election was a tremendous sweep for Johnson, and I am sure Bobby was annoyed that the president led him substantially in New York. LBJ asked me to prepare the strongest voting rights bill we could draft, and Archie Cox worked with the Civil Rights Division and Norbert Schlei in OLC to do so, although the president had made clear that he was not sure if or when he would submit it to Congress. As much as I wanted progress on civil rights, I was not sure that I welcomed another several months on the Hill trying to enact a strong bill.

We were continuing to make progress implementing the 1964 act, and compliance in most of the South continued to be surprisingly good. Burke felt, and I agreed, that what was needed was less what law enforcement could do and more what the other social programs of LBJ's Great Society initiative could do to provide jobs, education, training, and opportunity for blacks everywhere. What was needed was a coordinated interagency program to promote those objectives, which we felt would be an ideal assignment for Hubert Humphrey, the new vice president–elect. He had worked all his life for racial equality, had the confidence of black leaders, and, as vice president, presumably had the time to coordinate the various departments and agencies.

We drafted an executive order for President Johnson creating such an office and function for the vice president, and I took it to the White House and explained it to him. He obviously did not like it, but at the time I was not sure why. In retrospect, I think he had decided to make racial equality a cornerstone of his Great Society and saw giving the coordinating function to Humphrey as an indication that I did not trust him, as a southerner, to do so. He wanted the credit and did not want to give it to Humphrey. In fact I did trust him on civil rights, although I could not know at that time the depth of his commitment. So I kept arguing with him about why it made sense to have a coordinator in the White House and why Humphrey was an ideal choice. He got quite angry and stuck his jaw about an inch from mine, which, I confess, made me feel quite uncomfortable. When I stood my ground, both physically and intellectually, he angrily grabbed the paper with the order, signed it, turned his back on me, and walked back to his desk. It was quite a performance, and not one within my experience, with Johnson or with anyone else. I did not know whether I had persuaded him or whether he was about to fire me.

In fairness to President Johnson, I should add that the order never worked as we had envisioned. Part of the problem was Humphrey's desire always to please black leaders without adequate consideration of other constituencies; part of the problem was the demonstrations that started almost immediately after the election and which did involve the department; and, I suspect, part of the problem was that LBJ would never really let go enough to let it work. In the final analysis, he was right and I was wrong.

Since the president treated me as if I were attorney general rather than simply "acting," I decided at the outset to act as if I were attorney general in most respects. When asked by the press about the "acting" part of my title, I responded (at Jack Rosenthal's suggestion) by saying that the title was "acting," not "interim," and as far as I was concerned I would serve until the president wanted someone else. But being "acting" is not quite the same as being appointed to the position, even though a president is free to fire a cabinet officer and replace him at any time. For one thing, I thought it presumptuous to move into Bobby's office, so I kept my own. In addition, there were initiatives I wished to take but did not feel free to pursue, the most important of which was probably to try to clarify the wiretapping and use of bugs by the FBI. The Bureau had explained that wiretaps were always approved by the AG, but it had said nothing about other listening devices. I knew that on at least one occasion in Las Vegas the Bureau had used hidden microphones, or bugs, because it had come up in an organized crime case and Bobby had asked me to be sure it no longer did so. I was not confident that this was the case, and just before Christmas my worst fears were realized.

Two reporters whom I knew well, Ben Bradlee (then Washington head of *Newsweek*, later executive editor of the *Washington Post*) and AP

reporter Joe Mohbat, came separately to my office and told me that
Cartha DeLoach, an assistant director who acted as the FBI's public relations officer (a post which the Bureau denied it had), was playing tapes
of Dr. King's sexual activities in various motels for the edification of the
press. I understood why neither reporter was willing to confront the FBI
with this charge. I called DeLoach to my office and told him what I had
heard. He flatly denied any such activity and wanted to know who had
been circulating these lies. I was totally convinced who in fact was lying,
but I was without the means to prove it. While it was possible the bugs
had been planted by local law enforcement officials out to discredit Dr.
King, I thought it more likely that the Bureau had done so, because of
Hoover's known animosity.

I consulted with Burke Marshall, who was spending his last week
in the department, and we decided the story was so politically explosive
and so clearly improper that the president should know. When I told LBJ
that I had an important matter to discuss with him, he suggested that
Burke and I fly to his ranch, where he and his family were spending the
Christmas holidays. It was my first visit to the ranch.

We arrived in midafternoon in an air force JetStar and landed on
a fairly short runway that had been constructed on the ranch for the
convenience of the president. The ranch itself was an attractive property, not pretentious, and thoroughly Texan. The president met us when
we were driven to the door by the Secret Service, and he looked very
much at home. In a way this was quite moving. He was such a big man,
with big hands and feet, and he always looked a little out of place in
Washington's more sophisticated southern and eastern society. Here his
size was dwarfed by the countryside, and his cowboy hat looked right at
home. So did he, and his obvious pride in his property was contagious.
He took us on a brief tour of the ranch—not the grand tour I was to
get on a later occasion—pointing out the things that interested him
with a joy that was genuine. It was not only my first visit to the ranch
but, in a sense, my first contact with Johnson the man rather than Johnson the political leader. He knew the trees, the plantings, every inch of
his ranch and the people on it, and was enjoying showing the sights to
these two eastern dudes.

I told him, with help from Burke, of my problem with the Bureau,
what it was doing and the risk to everything he was planning with
respect to racial equality if it continued to play the tapes. I apologized
for having to bring him the problem but did not believe I had the political muscle to stop something the FBI denied it was doing. He listened
attentively, asked an occasional question, and then moved on to different

subjects. Like Bobby, he was a good listener. He gave us no indication of what he intended to do, if anything.

He talked about his landslide victory and the opportunity it gave him to pass legislation dealing with education, job training, and poverty programs. He was warm and attentive to both of us and said many times to Burke how sorry he was that he was leaving the administration and how much he would be missed. He was happy that John Doar was staying on. He insisted that we stay for supper and wanted us to spend the night. That we were close to Bobby was never mentioned, even hinted at. One would have thought we were both his choices. Nothing was said about my continuing role as attorney general.

Finally we were permitted to leave. But first we had to say goodnight to our hostess. Lady Bird had already gone to bed, but that did not stop LBJ. He insisted we accompany him to the bedroom and say our goodbyes to her there, which would have been even more embarrassing if she had not been such a lovely and gracious lady who understood her husband so well.

One of the reasons I was anxious to get back to Washington was the Justice Department Christmas party. Bobby had started the idea of a party for underprivileged children at Christmastime in the courtyard of the Justice Department, and it had proved a great success, not just with the kids but with the lawyers as well. There were professional entertainers who volunteered their services in the Great Hall of the Justice Department (I remember that the young Bill Cosby had the children rolling on the floor with laughter) and pony rides, clowns, and treats in the courtyard. There were lawyers dressed as clowns or Santas, or in any costume they could find or make, and a couple of hundred squealing children at any given moment. To work in as many young ones as we could, we had them come in buses in shifts. It was a terrific morale-builder—a real office party. I do not think the FBI participated, and I'm not sure J. Edgar would have made a great Santa Claus in any event.

I was determined to keep the tradition going, and while I did not have the persuasive powers Bobby had had in the years his brother was president, I was pleasantly surprised by the reaction of local stars, the Washington Redskins, and other heroes. Bobby and Ethel were pleased to help, and they did. Their ponies were more used to young children than the U.S. cavalry detachment's were. It was fun.

When I look back on those Christmas parties and think of Bobby, it is with both sentiment and admiration. He loved children and was active in helping clean up and rehabilitate playgrounds in the district, a project he put Barrett Prettyman, another former Supreme Court law clerk, in charge of. He suggested to Barrett that maybe the kids would love to play in an old World War II fighter plane no longer in service. When Barrett called the commanding general, the conversation went something like this, according to Barrett:

"Do you have any old planes stripped down so they could be used in a playground here in the district?"

"Yes, but they are all spoken for, and it would be over a year before there is any possibility of one here."

"Oh, the attorney general will be very disappointed."

"You are calling for the attorney general?"

"Yes."

"How many do you need?"

"Would three be too many?" asked Barrett, adding two to the one he was hoping for.

"Okay. Is the end of the week soon enough?"

But it was not simply Bobby's love for children that led to the Christmas parties. He had a wonderful instinct for how to bring people together, to build a team, to get everyone involved. The parties were one of many ways he did so.

Christmas passed, and Lydia and I got the same present, a lithograph of the White House, that President Johnson gave to other cabinet members. He continued to call me frequently but never said a word about my continuing as attorney general. We prepared suggested comments for his upcoming state-of-the-union message, and preparations were made for the inaugural balls. I thought surely before the inauguration I would hear something. The rest of the cabinet was set, and only I was "acting." I simply could not imagine what his problem was. If he was concerned about my loyalty to him (rather than Bobby), surely four months was enough time to make up his mind.

The State of the Union was given on January 14, and I marched into the House with the cabinet. It was a great speech, one of LBJ's finest, most of it written by Dick Goodwin. Any doubts I had—and I am not sure I had any—about Johnson's commitment to civil rights vanished. The speech was mostly about his Great Society program. It was well delivered and well received.

Shortly thereafter he called me over to the White House. He told me that John McCone was resigning as CIA director, a fact which was hardly a secret. Would I be interested in taking his place? I could not have been more surprised or had less of an idea what to say. It was not a job I wanted or one I thought I was qualified to perform.

"Mr. President," I said, "I really do not feel qualified for that post. I have no experience in intelligence work, and I think you would be making a mistake to put me in that job. I want to serve you and my country and be a part of what you are trying to do. So I will do whatever you ask me to do."

I could not tell his reaction. He said nothing further, but I assumed the offer was designed to clear the way for another attorney general, and I was disappointed.

The inauguration came and went. It was my first (and last) inaugural experience. Lydia and I attended three or four fancy balls. She looked beautiful, and I had purchased a new dinner jacket, which, given the salaries of the time, I could ill afford. We were treated like royalty, as if I were a cabinet member, not just some interim appointee.

The same was true the next day. We were invited along with members of the cabinet to a fancy luncheon given in the Capitol by the Speaker before the parade, and I was seated as if I really were AG. We attended the swearing in, sitting in seats in the front of the grandstand, and then we rode in the parade in a new red Buick convertible past cheering crowds along Pennsylvania Avenue to the White House. In front of the White House, we sat in the grandstand where the president reviewed the seemingly endless parade of high school bands. It was an exciting and heady experience for both of us. It would have been a little more so if I had not been conscious of the "acting" I felt was engraved on my forehead and, despite everyone's courtesy, the feeling that I was somewhat of an imposter. Nobody treated me as such, certainly not the president or his staff. But nonetheless I felt uncomfortable.

But more serious than my personal feelings was the problem of holding together a workable Justice Department. I could not recommend appointments to vacancies to the president until he appointed an attorney general. Not unreasonably, people wanted to know who they would be working with, and obviously a new AG would have his or her own ideas about who should head the various divisions. I still had a number of good people in the first assistants who stayed on when the assistant attorneys general went back to private practice, but some of these wanted to know their future as well. Only John Doar felt secure as Burke's successor.

Abe Fortas, the president's close personal adviser and one of Washington's most prominent lawyers, counseled me to be patient. I had had Abe as a professor at Yale, and I felt that he had turned down the job himself and probably supported me despite his strong dislike for Bobby. I had worked with him as legal counsel on Puerto Rican matters, and I believed he had a high regard for me as a lawyer. He was one of the most skilled advocates I knew, and he spoke in a soft Virginia accent. His wife, Carolyn Agger, was a well-known tax lawyer. The two of them, without children, enjoyed living on two high incomes in their Georgetown estate, where Abe, an accomplished violinist, often performed on his Stradivarius violin with visiting virtuosos such as Jascha Heifetz. I did not think either of them was interested in Abe's giving up his partnership in Arnold, Fortas & Porter for the $25,000 annual salary of the AG.

It was easy enough to carry on the routine work of the department. But Bobby had shown that much more could be done, and I at least wanted to take a crack at some innovation too. By the beginning of February, I felt that five months of "acting" was long enough. I wrote a letter to the president by hand, telling him that he needed to appoint an attorney general for the sake of the department and the success of his own administration and that I could no longer continue to serve in an "acting" capacity. The next day Fortas telephoned me to tell me I was crazy to put a gun to the president's head and that LBJ was furious. I told him the letter expressed my feelings and that the president was entitled to know them.

Two or three days later I got a message from the White House saying that the president would like Mrs. Katzenbach and me to come for tea at six o'clock. I told Lydia and sent a car to pick her up and bring her to my office. I was fairly certain that LBJ had made a decision, and I thought it a good sign that he had invited Lydia.

When we arrived at the White House, we were escorted upstairs to the family living quarters, where we were met by the president and Mrs. Johnson. President Johnson was at his most charming; this tall, gaunt, sometimes crude man could turn on the charm when it suited him.

"Nick," he began, "I wanted Lydia to be here when I told you that I was naming you attorney general. For the past five months you have done everything I asked, you have given me good advice, you have sought to do justice in a fair and evenhanded way. You are the person I want as attorney general."

I thanked the president and said I hoped I could live up to his expectations.

Lady Bird chimed in, gracious as always. "Lyndon has spoken so often about you, and it is such a pleasure to welcome both of you into the family," she said.

Tea turned out to be supper with the president and Mrs. Johnson. The president went on about the election and the opportunity it presented to pass a program that would make a reality out of his Great Society—education, poverty programs, model cities. He talked knowledgeably about each and about what could be done. He brought in civil rights, the demonstrations for voter registration, the problems of black arrests, including that of Dr. King, in Selma, Alabama, and the need for a stronger voting rights bill. But despite these strongly felt concerns, he kept his emphasis on the other programs he was sponsoring in an effort to lift the poor, so many of whom were black and Latino. I was tremendously impressed by both his grasp of details and his passion. It was his passion that moved me most, because for a brief time the politician, the wheeler-dealer, the often crude manipulator disappeared, and I had a glimpse of what I assumed his devoted followers must have seen in him and many of us had missed.

Of particular interest to me was his discussion of crime and the need to do something about it. The increase in crime statistics—state and local crime, not federal crimes—had been prominent in the election, with Barry Goldwater, the Republican candidate, blaming the increase on civil rights demonstrations and the new legislation. The president was correct that crime was a major public concern, and whenever you have a national concern, attention seems to focus on the federal government, whether it is a federal responsibility or not. I was opposed to rushing into federal legislation, and actually, I think the president was too. But he felt that something had to be done, and I suggested a national crime commission to make a study and recommendations. I thought we might be able to persuade Thomas Dewey, the renowned Republican prosecutor and former presidential candidate, to head it up, and LBJ liked the idea.

He promptly sent my nomination to the Senate, and I went around to see the leaders as a courtesy. I was not particularly concerned about confirmation. I think the only surprise I had came from Senator Robert Byrd of West Virginia, who wanted a clearly unqualified lawyer supporter appointed to the federal district court. He said that if I refused to recommend this man to the president, he would not vote for me, and he was as good as his word. My testimony before the Judiciary Committee was short and uncontroversial, and the nomination was taken to the floor, where it passed relatively easily over predictable southern opposition, which was more for the benefit of constituents than serious opposition to me. Apart from civil rights issues, I got along quite well with the southerners.

When I got back to my office, I had a call from Senator Eastland.

"Nick," he said. "I had to vote against you. I'm sorry, because you know I'm for you. But that SOB Javits insisted on a roll-call vote, and I simply had to vote against you."

"That's perfectly okay, Senator," I said. "In fact, it's probably good for both of us."

"Oh, I'm so glad you feel that way," Senator Eastland replied.

I was sworn in at the White House shortly thereafter by Byron White. President Johnson said some flattering things, and Bobby and Ethel were prominently present. So was my family, my sons having come down from school in New Hampshire. They were a good deal less impressed than my eighty-year-old mother.

I now felt legitimate.

THE NEWEST Supreme Court justice, Byron White, swearing me in as his replacement as deputy attorney general in the attorney general's office. Bobby is holding the Bible.

A MEETING in the Cabinet Room with President Kennedy over the rise in steel prices. The smiles reflect the fact that U.S. Steel had just rescinded its price increase, probably as a reaction to the antitrust suit brought by Bobby. Lee Loevinger, head of the Antitrust Division, is standing on Bobby's right.

SENATOR KEATING (right) taking public credit for the nomination of Thurgood Marshall (left) to the Second Circuit Court of Appeals. My necktie in the middle is my failed effort to represent JFK at the Senate confirmation hearing.

JIM MCSHANE (left) and John Doar escorting James Meredith to register at Ole Miss. I have never known three braver men.

FACING OFF with Governor
Wallace at the University
of Alabama. The governor
probably enjoyed his show
more than I did because he
stood in the shade and I was
under the hot sun on a very
hot day. Still, I did get in both
the first and the last words.

VIVIAN MALONE, escorted by Joe Dolan, going through the "schoolhouse door" to register as
a student at the University of Alabama.

JACK ROSENTHAL (standing) advising me on an air force plane. Even in the air Jack kept my feet on the ground.

WITH Harold Reis and John Doar in my limousine. Harold thought we looked like members of the Mafia.

BOBBY consulting with Burke Marshall, Norbert Schlei, and me. Norb succeeded me as legal counsel, and, just as notably, blindly followed me onto a plane bound for Mississippi on September 30, 1962, the day of the Ole Miss riot. I think this is a rare picture of three former editors in chief of the *Yale Law Journal* all giving advice at the same time. Obviously the advice was not good enough.

IN THE Rose Garden with LBJ and Bobby. I am telling them to get to their corners and come out fighting.

BYRON WHITE swearing me in as attorney general in the White House. Lydia is standing behind White, and behind her are our sons, John and Chris, dragged down from Exeter, New Hampshire, for the occasion. The elderly lady with the black hat is my mother.

RIDING in the 1965 inaugural parade. Despite the cold weather, Lydia loved the convertible. So did I.

AFTER I became attorney general, LBJ wrote Lydia suggesting she post "No Smoking" signs throughout the house.

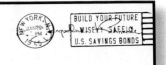

NEW YORK, N.Y.
JAN 29
PM
1965

BUILD YOUR FUTURE
WISELY SAFELY
U.S. SAVINGS BONDS

The Attorney General ✓
Department of Justice
Washington
DC

January 28 1965

Dear Dick

I just heard this afternoon that
you had been Named Attorney General.

Nothing that could happen now
could make me as happy as hearing that.

What a wonderful day it must be
for you — I cannot believe it is true —
I was hoping against hope for so long
that it would happen

Now all the things you did and
cared about will not be undone —

I RECEIVED many letters of
congratulations when I was
named attorney general, but
none meant more to me
than this one, from Jackie
Kennedy.

Please accept my deepest congratulations

Love

Jackie

Martin Luther King, Jr., Vice President Hubert Humphrey, and me at a meeting in Humphrey's office to discuss voting rights legislation. The meeting was a result of an executive order. I had recommended putting Humphrey in charge of civil rights, but the vice president turned out to be sometimes more accommodating to demands than was realistic. Since I was responsible for getting the legislation enacted, I suppose this was poetic justice.

President Johnson signing the letter transmitting the voting rights bill to Congress. I am the delivery boy.

THURGOOD MARSHALL and me in our morning suits on the opening of the 1965–1966 Supreme Court term. Thurgood was before the Supreme Court so often that he owned his; I rented mine.

MAKING our entrance at the dinner dance we threw for the U.S. attorneys. The event was a huge success, and this is one of my favorite pictures of Lydia. The younger generation referred to us as "bird's nest and baldy."

IN Mobile, Alabama, after my Emancipation Day speech on January 2, 1966. The speech, written by Jack Rosenthal, was so successful that I wished I had written it myself.

MEMBERS of the Crime Commission enjoying a working lunch in my office. From the way Jim Vorenberg handled the agenda at these meetings, it was easy to see why the Harvard Law faculty elected him dean.

WITH Myrl Alexander, who headed the federal prison system, visiting one of many prisons. With Myrl's enthusiastic support, I made a major effort to improve the care, education, and job training of prisoners to prepare them for their return to society.

SENATOR DIRKSEN and me outside his office. He was an effective leader and speaker, but his mellifluous voice led some to refer to him as the "Wizard of Ooze."

IN THE Vietnam years, Security Council meetings were largely replaced by Tuesday lunches in the White House living quarters, to which I was only rarely invited. I attended this one because Dean Rusk was out of town. Here, Dick Helms has his back to the camera. On the president's left are Bob McNamara, George Christian (the White House press secretary), Jim Jones, and Walt Rostow.

CLARK CLIFFORD, Dean Rusk, Marvin Watson (LBJ's chief of staff), and the president in the Situation Room discussing the capture of the U.S. communication ship *Pueblo* and its crew by the North Koreans in January of 1968. The White House Situation Room always added a touch of drama and urgency to a discussion.

THE SITUATION ROOM during the Six-Day War. Around the table from my left are Clark Clifford, Walt Rostow, Hubert Humphrey, LBJ, Robert McNamara, McGeorge Bundy, and Dean Rusk. It was at this meeting that LBJ called for a cease-fire.

SAIGON, 1966. From left to right are Ambassador Lodge, Prime Minister Ky, Bob McNamara, myself, and General Wheeler. I don't remember what was funny.

MEETING with Prime Minister Indira Gandhi in New Delhi in 1968. Despite the summer heat, I did put on a suit and tie.

MEETING with Marshal Tito in Belgrade after the Russian invasion of Czechoslovakia in 1968. Tito was tough and unconcerned.

LYDIA learning a dance step from an African expert. Her husband, as usual, is not joining in.

NOT my favorite cat, but beautiful nonetheless. President Mobutu of the Democratic Republic of the Congo strokes his pet while Wayne Fredericks and I watch.

XV

I MOVED INTO BOBBY'S OLD OFFICE ON THE FIFTH FLOOR. THE JUSTICE Department was constructed during the 1930s by the WPA, and it is a beautiful building with wonderful painted murals of famous legal events in history, including Moses receiving the Ten Commandments. The AG's office is huge, with a high, ornately designed ceiling, a large mural over the entrance door, and a wood-burning fireplace—a room so spacious that Bobby and Byron used to throw a football back and forth to each other for amusement. I think the deputy's office, which is directly under-neath, on the fourth floor, is about the same size, but it never seemed as big to me. Past the fireplace is a smaller conference room, then a dining room, a kitchen, a bathroom, and, up a short flight of stairs, a small bed-room. A private elevator opens into a small hall by the conference room. Over the door from that hall to the main corridor is a beautifully carved message that reads, in essence: "The Department wins its case whenever Justice is done."

I had recommended Ramsey Clark to be my deputy, in part because I knew the president wanted him and in part because so many of the other assistants had told me they would be leaving. I liked Ramsey. He was good on civil rights and well liked by its leaders, and he was a person of high principles and ethical standards, although sometimes a little rigid in his views. There were better lawyers available, but none more idealistic in his view of what law should accomplish. I thought we might work well together.

The passage of the 1964 Civil Rights Act and the general feeling of liberation that had led many young people into the South for Freedom

Summer now were leading to more and more demonstrations and picketing for voting rights. Dr. King was having increasing difficulty keeping his younger followers in line with his peaceful tactics. Success in the passage of legislation led to demands for more. Scattered but often serious violence occurred throughout the South, and it was increasingly clear to all that the voting provisions of the 1964 legislation, which mainly expedited appeals in cases where registration was denied, were woefully inadequate. Decisions were in the hands of state court judges, who routinely denied blacks the right to register, usually on literacy grounds. Dr. King wisely decided to focus the attention of his young supporters on voter registration. The place was Selma, Alabama.

The department was familiar with Selma. We sued in 1961 for failure to register black voters, won on appeal, got an injunction against further discrimination—and nothing changed. Despite the injunction, in a population of almost 30,000, more than half of whom were black, fewer than 500 blacks were registered. As though to underline the point, shortly after passage of the Civil Rights Act, Sheriff James Clark and his deputies, wielding cattle prods, arrested some 50 blacks on the courthouse steps as they sought to register.

From King's viewpoint, Selma was ideal and Sheriff Clark a perfect foil. By late 1964 he had focused his attention on Selma, and soon thereafter the nation's attention was similarly focused on this obscure town in Dallas County. On the day before President Johnson's inauguration, Sheriff Clark arrested more than 60 blacks seeking to register. Those arrests sparked further efforts by blacks to register. Another 150 were arrested. On February 1, King led some 250 blacks to the courthouse steps, where all, including King and Ralph Abernathy, were arrested for an unlawful parade. When black children poured out of school in protest, Clark's deputies, with cattle prods and billy clubs, forced the frightened youngsters to march some six miles out of town, where they let them "escape." Arrests continued, and soon more than 2,500 blacks were in jail. As King noted in a letter to the *New York Times*, "There are more Negroes in jail with me than there are on the voting rolls."

King was released from jail and returned to Atlanta, but the protests continued in Selma and in nearby Marion. It was too awfully predictable that violence would occur sooner or later, and it did, when several hundred protesters in Marion were assaulted by police and state troopers. Jamie Lee Jackson was shot by a trooper while trying to rescue his mother from being beaten by another. He died a week later. King seized the occasion to announce a fifty-mile march in protest from Selma to

Montgomery, the state capital, to stage a huge rally protesting voter discrimination on the steps of the capitol.

On Sunday some 600 demonstrators, predominantly black but with a few white supporters (mostly students and clergy) from the North, began the march from Selma to Montgomery despite King's absence (we had warned him of a plot against his life) and Governor Wallace's order prohibiting the march. After crossing the Edmund Pettus Bridge, they were met by state troopers and by Sheriff Clark and his deputies. When the marchers refused to disperse, they were attacked by the troopers and deputies with clubs, cattle prods, tear gas, and mounted police. A number of marchers required hospitalization, and some 40 or 50 more were treated for more minor injuries.

The event received national attention both in the press and on television, where the world could see the brutality of the attack on peaceful marchers. The press labeled it "Bloody Sunday," and the public reaction throughout the country was one of revulsion.

Seeking to take advantage of public support to get the voting rights act that the president had promised him in due course, King announced another march to Montgomery. Before it could take place, Judge Frank Johnson, one of the very few nonracist federal judges on the federal district courts of the South, issued a temporary restraining order on all marches. The president deplored the violence and announced his intention to submit a voting rights bill the following week.

I had sent Ramsey Clark to join John Doar and a number of lawyers from the Civil Rights Division to Selma to be on hand for whatever might occur. The president was on the phone with me several times about the wisdom of sending troops to maintain order. I was reluctant to do so and so advised him, although he was not happy with the advice. We did agree to send a number of marshals to an army base in Alabama and to put the army on alert. LBJ was far less hesitant than President Kennedy or Bobby to call in the army, which I attributed, rightly or wrongly, to the fact that he was from south Texas and did not carry the political freight of a northern liberal among southerners.

I did agree to hold a press conference, in which I made it clear that the president was acting on my advice that the situation did not yet call for federal troops. This took some of the immediate pressure off LBJ, and he was lavish in his praise. We talked to King about the need to obey Judge Johnson's order, although he had a lot of younger supporters who did not have his patience. President Johnson had formed a community relations group in the Department of Commerce under former Florida governor Leroy Collins to help mediate racial disputes, as Burke Marshall had done in Birmingham on an earlier occasion. The existence of the group did not make John Doar very happy, because there was always a coordination problem, aggravated by the question of who was in charge. Governor Collins, a person of considerable ability and stature, was not about to take direction from the department. He said he had worked out an agreement with King that King would lead the march but would turn back when confronted by Sheriff Clark and other law enforcement personnel.

Whether King would be able to keep this private agreement—and frankly, we were not that sure that he had really agreed to turn back—in the face of pressure from his followers was a question in all of our minds. On March 9, King led 2,000 followers, including a large number of religious leaders from all over the United States, onto the Pettus Bridge. Ramsey was observing from a Border Patrol car with radio telephone connections to my office, giving me a play-by-play account. At Jack Rosenthal's suggestion, I had invited Mary McGrory, one of the great Washington reporters, to listen with me in my office. She had been helpful on a number of occasions, and I was not concerned about what she would say if things went wrong. I did not think they would, but I was terribly nervous that my first month as AG would end in disaster.

When confronted by Sheriff Clark and his deputies, the group stopped and knelt in prayer. The law enforcement people opened up, as if to permit the group through, but King did not fall for the ruse. After the prayer the group turned and walked back, then dispersed. King had not violated Judge Johnson's order. We all breathed a sigh of relief.

But the problems of violence were not over. In contrast to the peaceful marchers, a group of Klan types beat up the Reverend James Reeb, a white minister from Boston who had joined the march. He died in a Birmingham hospital hours later, and people across the United States reacted to this crime of wanton violence. There were demonstrations all around the country, including pickets in front of the White House and the Department of Justice, demanding that troops be sent to Alabama and a voting rights bill be enacted. Many carried signs denouncing LBJ.

President Johnson was deeply upset at the lack of trust in his leadership and, no matter what he said or did, the burden of being from the South. Dr. King and the other civil rights leaders had confidence in him, but the rank and file remained deeply suspicious. At the same time, southern whites were looking for the opportunity to denounce unnecessary federal intervention. Like President Kennedy, LBJ was forced to walk a narrow line, and it was not easy for him—or indeed for any of us.

But the problem remained what it always was—the federal government was never in a position to take over law enforcement or the protection of blacks unless the situation was clear, continuing, and without a less disastrous solution. One could hardly expect blacks who were seeking to assert constitutionally guaranteed rights to accept this, and of course they did not. But unless troops could be seen to have a specific, defined, and terminable function, such as admitting students to a university, sending the army presented huge problems of function, withdrawal, and the danger of confrontation with local law enforcement charged with a similar function. Once troops take on the normal functions of civil law enforcement, here or abroad, it is difficult to formulate plans of disengagement and withdrawal.

Demonstrations calling for more federal involvement following the Reeb murder continued, and young demonstrators invaded the Department of Justice building, sat down in the halls, and insisted on meeting with me. I had no problem meeting with a small number of leaders but insisted that they must leave the building after the meeting. Eventually they promised they would, but after our meeting they changed their minds. I had the guards remove them physically (and humanely) and secured the building. I treasure one picture of a young white girl being carried out by two large black guards, smiling and laughing, as she was obviously enjoying the experience of demonstrating for black voting rights and being removed by two blacks.

Governor Wallace maintained that he wanted peace and was opposed to violence, which made the legal basis for using troops more difficult. There was no reason to doubt him, but the problem—always the same problem—was that he saw black demonstrations for constitutional rights as the cause of violence when whites reacted violently. But his position made it difficult for LBJ to act as he wanted to. He invited Wallace to a meeting in the White House on Saturday, March 13. He asked me to attend and to persuade Burke Marshall to be present. I arrived early, at his request.

What the purpose of the meeting was or what the president intended to accomplish, I had no idea.

"Write me some demands I can make on Wallace," he ordered.

"What kind of demands?" I asked.

"I don't give a damn. Make them as outrageous as you want."

So I did, having no idea what their purpose was. They were certainly outrageous: why don't you register all the blacks to vote, integrate all the schools—questions like that. The president glanced at them, smiled, and put them in his pocket. Burke arrived, as did Richard Goodwin, LBJ's special assistant. Then the president's secretary buzzed him to say that Wallace had arrived, and he left the Oval Office to greet him.

Thus began a political performance that was pure LBJ at the very top of his form.

We could hear the president's booming voice through the open door. "Come over here, Lem," he said to the head of his Secret Service guard, a native of Alabama. "I want you to meet your governor."

They came into the Oval Office, the president beaming as though his dearest friend were visiting him. "This is Nick Katzenbach, my attorney general," he said, adding mischievously, "but of course you've already met. And Burke Marshall, and Dick Goodwin."

Wallace introduced his treasurer, Seymour Trammel, who had accompanied him. We all sat down, the president in his rocker and the governor on the couch next to him.

The president was dominating in every respect. Physically, Wallace was a man of small stature, a former middleweight boxer. LBJ towered over him even when both were sitting. After some small talk, the president began an absolutely virtuoso performance, flattering Wallace, then confronting him, pretending to seek his advice, then giving him hell. It went on for almost an hour along these lines:

"George, I know you're a man of peace and that you don't approve of all this violence that's been going on in Alabama."

"Oh, yes, Mr. President. It's just all these agitators coming in and disturbing our way of doing things."

"Like all those people you see picketing and demonstrating outside the White House?"

"Yes, Mr. President. Exactly."

"Wouldn't it be great if we could put a stop to all this demonstrating?"

"It sure would, Mr. President."

"Well, George, I'll bet we could. You saw all those reporters and television cameras out there when you came in?"

"Yes, sir. I sure did."

"Well, why don't you and I go out there and tell all those folks that you have decided to integrate all the schools in Alabama?"

Hesitation, then a slight stammer. "I can't do that, Mr. President. That's up to the local school boards, and I don't have any power over them."

"Don't you shit me about your power in Alabama, George. I know who runs that state."

Then LBJ would change the subject and seek Wallace's views on Vietnam. After some friendly exchanges, the president would go back to my outrageous notes and seek to have all blacks registered, demonstrations protected, and so forth. He talked of Wallace's place in history, of the opportunity that civil rights presented, of the need to unify the country, not divide it. At times he was harsh and demanding, at others flattering and cajoling. I have never seen a political performance to compare with it. It was like a violin concert by a virtuoso, with every note perfection. At the end, Wallace declined to meet with the press and left quietly and inconspicuously through a side door.

After Wallace departed, I accompanied the president to the Rose Garden, where the press and TV cameras were patiently waiting. The president was almost manic in demeanor, obviously pleased with his performance, as indeed he should have been. He forcefully denounced the violence in Selma and announced to the press that he was sending a voting rights bill to the Congress that week and that I was there to brief them on its contents.

I whispered to him, "Mr. President, isn't this meant to be on background?"

"By God, you're right," he said in a loud voice. "This briefing is on background. Turn off those cameras." One would have thought it was Cecil B. DeMille, not the president of the United States, talking. "CBS," he shouted, "your camera is still on. I can see the red light. Turn it off."

And thus began the most public "background" briefing of my career.

On Monday the President determined to address a joint session that evening on voting rights. Doing so put his prestige squarely behind the bill, which was something of a political risk. The congressional leadership was divided. Mansfield and Dirksen had urged him not to do so, but LBJ was now firmly committed and felt the need to reassure black leaders by once again demonstrating that commitment publicly. That evening at nine I joined my fellow cabinet members marching into the House and heard the greatest speech of Johnson's presidency. It was written by Dick Goodwin and edited and revised extensively by the president. It came out pure Johnson in its passion and simple eloquence. In common, I suspect, with many others, I almost fell out of my chair when the president spoke.

"But even if we pass this bill, the battle will not be over. What happened in Selma is part of a far larger movement which reaches into every section and state of America. It is the effort of American Negroes to secure for themselves the full blessings of American life. Their cause must be our cause, too. Because it is not just Negroes, but really it is all of us who must overcome the crippling legacy of bigotry and injustice."

A dramatic pause and then the words of the anthem of black protest: "And we shall overcome."

The chamber went wild.

I called the president the next morning (along with many others) to tell him what a great address it was. He was obviously pleased at the reception his speech had received, and told me and others with a happy chuckle how, when Dirksen did not immediately stand to applaud the reference to the black anthem, he had paused until the cameras were focused on his friendly old adversary and waited until the senator, conscious of the TV camera, finally rose to his feet.

The voting rights bill was submitted to Congress. At the suggestion of the president, I had asked Chairman Celler to hold hearings immediately and continue with night sessions. The president was anxious to build on his address to the Congress and create a sense of urgency about voting, in the hope that this would serve to calm the demonstrators and avoid further violence. Further, he was concerned that the demonstrations might now spread to the Hill and be a problem in getting votes from those who felt they were being coerced.

Judge Johnson heard the case in Selma with respect to the demonstrations and authorized King to lead a march from Selma to Montgomery, as King had originally planned. He issued his order on the same day Celler began the hearings. My testimony was, I think, the best opening statement I ever made—and I did not write a word of it! Harold Greene and Jack Rosenthal stayed up all night preparing it. It gave a detailed history of the efforts of blacks over the years to register to vote in Selma, examples of the bias of registrars applying literacy tests, and then the frustration of lawsuits lasting months or years, with racist judges delaying decisions and then denying registration. Its power—and it was powerful—lay in the excruciating detail that Harold Greene had provided. Indeed, I learned a lot myself as I read my testimony, though I did not volunteer that fact to the committee. Southern members of the committee were obviously embarrassed by the facts I detailed. Congressman McCulloch graciously said it was the best opening statement he had ever heard.

The testimony was important, because no one, not even those with strong racial bias, was willing to defend a denial to blacks or any other citizen of the right to vote. But people were willing to defend literacy tests—a defense that even in their view required even-handed administration. Our bill, ingeniously drafted by the solicitor general, Archibald Cox, was designed to get rid of the tests completely in those places where their administration was biased. To avoid naming names, he devised a legislative presumption of bias and a suspension of literacy tests where less than a specified percentage of the voters were registered. That presumption could be appealed to the court of appeals in the District of Columbia, thus reversing the burden of proving bias. The attorney general was given broad discretion to send federal registrars into those states or districts covered to insure fair registration if local registrars were not applying the law properly. The presumption covered the Deep South effectively and also picked up parts of Alaska and Arizona. That annoyed the senators from those states, but I could not help wondering if there had not in fact been discrimination against Indians in those places.

After my rather long opening statement, I returned that evening to continue my testimony before the House committee. Even in the evening the large hearing room was packed. Burke Marshall accompanied me. Not far into the questioning, the female committee clerk leaned over Celler's shoulder and whispered, "The president is on the phone for Mr. Katzenbach."

Unfortunately the chairman's microphone was turned on, and her voice could be heard all over the crowded room, to the huge amusement of the audience.

"Why don't we take a brief recess," said the chairman.

I went to the phone.

"Nick," said the president, "I've been watching the TV news. It says Wallace has sent me a message saying he cannot afford to protect King and his followers on the march. Doesn't that give me the authority to mobilize the guard to do so?"

I knew the president had been anxious for many days about protecting King and wanted to put the Alabama National Guard in federal service to do so. It was, of course, the governor's responsibility to do that, but if he was unable or unwilling, the president had authority.

"I should think so," I said. "But we should wait to see exactly what Wallace said to you."

"Okay." The agreement came a little reluctantly.

I went back to testifying. Some ten to fifteen minutes later, the clerk went to the chairman. He turned the microphone off, then turned it on again.

"Let's take another short break," he said, to the amusement of the crowd. Again to the telephone.

"I have Wallace's message," said the president. He read it to me.

"That's enough," I said. "You can tell him you are ordering the guard into federal service."

"I'll put a girl on. You dictate a reply."

I did, and returned to the witness chair. This time less than five minutes passed before the same act was repeated and I was on the phone again.

"Yes, Mr. President."

"Nick, that girl didn't take shorthand. Dictate it again."

So I did. He also asked me to come to the White House and explain to others in the cabinet and staff why he was federalizing the guard at this point. I did that too. So much for night hearings.

In any event, it was the Senate's turn to act first on the bill. Senator Mansfield asked that the bill be referred to the Judiciary Committee with instructions to report it out in two weeks, a provision southern senators objected to vehemently but in vain. The Senate committee had a majority of liberals, so there was no real question that it would be voted out, but there was a question of how much delay Chairman Eastland and his southern colleagues could manufacture; hence the two-week deadline.

The Selma-Montgomery march began on March 21 and continued peacefully with protection from the Alabama guard in federal service over a five-day period. Given the violence that had accompanied its beginning and the contrast of the guard now marching beside the tired but peaceful marchers, protecting rather than molesting them, it gave a huge public opinion boost to the Voting Rights Act. There was an especially dramatic moment when the marchers camped overnight in a field in Lowndes County, perhaps the worst county in Alabama with respect to race, and literally hundreds of sharecroppers, carrying small children and leading others, streamed in from all directions to join them in order to hear a sermon from Dr. King.

When the cadre of some 500 marchers neared Montgomery their numbers began to swell, and by the morning of the final day there were as many as 25,000, waving American flags, marching up Dexter Avenue to the state capitol. Flanking them were thousands of jeering and cursing whites shouting threats, with the guard on each side of the avenue between the groups *but facing toward the black marchers as though protecting the white hecklers.* Shades of Ole Miss! Conscious of the PR disaster, Jack Rosenthal told the guard commander, Major General Carl M. Turner, Jr., that he should turn around the troops, whose job was to protect the marchers. A white Alabaman through and through, he refused. Jack called me, I called Cyrus Vance, now deputy secretary of defense, and five minutes later the troops were turned around. Vance had not forgotten Ole Miss, and even racist generals obeyed orders.

Activity on voting rights continued in the Senate committee. Testifying before the Senate Judiciary Committee essentially meant arguing with Senator Sam Ervin of South Carolina. Senator Ervin, a former member of his state supreme court, was a fine lawyer and a more than competent scholar on constitutional issues—with the sole exception of race. He would ask me a question about the Constitution, and I would reply by citing the relevant decision and its reasoning. The senator would respond: "I don't think that case was rightly decided." And he would go on to cite an older case taking a more conservative view, often one which the Court itself had overruled.

I never could figure out just where to go, other than to repeat the later case. Since Senator Ervin tended to monopolize the hearings in this fashion, few other committee members bothered to attend, and I had never seen the chairman, James Eastland, at a hearing involving civil rights.

One afternoon Senator Ervin (to my relief) had to leave, and who showed up to take the chair but Senator Eastland. He began asking me questions about voter registration in Mississippi. Fortunately for me, Harold Greene and his staff had prepared spreadsheets covering several years of registration attempts and failures by both one or two whites and many blacks, county by county, in Mississippi. It was almost embarrassing, because on each question I would hit the ball out of the park with an answer that showed conclusively the extent of bias and prejudice against black voters. Yet Eastland kept coming back for more until the hour of adjournment. I wondered what I had done to our relationship, which, aside from civil rights, was of importance to the department.

I had not been back in my office five minutes when my secretary buzzed me. "Senator Eastland is on the line."

I picked up nervously. "Yes, Senator?" I asked, as though I did not know why he was calling.

"Nick," he said. Then a slight chuckle. "You know too goddamned much about the state of Mississippi." And he hung up.

Somehow the liberals on the Judiciary Committee were not tending to business, and they allowed several weakening amendments to get into the bill. On the final day the bill was to be reported, the committee was meeting in the Capitol in Senator Dirksen's conference room. I was in the small sitting room so familiar from the 1964 act, so I could be a resource for the bill's supporters. Before the start of the meeting, Senator Eastland said that he would give me a choice: the bill would be reported out either in its present form or exactly as the president had submitted it. To me that was a no-brainer, but not to the liberal members of the committee. Led by Senator Jacob Javits, Republican of New York, and Democratic Senators Philip Hart, Edward Kennedy, and others, they explained to me that they had the votes to defeat the prior changes and add some provisions they thought would strengthen the bill. So back to the conference room they went. I could hear Senator Ervin's melodious voice patiently explaining the Constitution (as he saw it) to the Young Turks. I waited and waited in the sitting room.

About three hours later, Senator Javits and his cohorts traipsed in, looking a little haggard.

"Progress?" I asked.

"Not exactly," said Javits. "Ervin has been talking the whole time. It's a mini-filibuster."

Senator Hart took the bull by the horns. "Nick, would you speak to the chairman and see if that deal is still on the table?"

They left and Senator Eastland came in, smiling. I had no idea what to expect, but I asked the question.

"Certainly," he said, to my surprise.

And so the committee voted out the president's bill just as he had submitted it.

XVI

THERE WAS NEVER A SERIOUS QUESTION THAT THE VOTING RIGHTS BILL would pass. But it took a little longer than expected because of disputes about relatively small issues. Liberals wanted to strengthen the bill and seized on a provision banning the poll tax to do so. I did not want the provision, because the constitutionality of the poll tax was already in the courts, and I was quite confident that the Supreme Court would find it an unconstitutional burden on the right to vote. If the law contained a prohibition, I thought the Court might postpone its decision until the legislative ban was before it, which could delay a decision a couple of years. Teddy Kennedy was leading the forces for legislative prohibition in the Senate, and Bobby asked me how strongly I felt and whether Teddy's amendment was a problem for me. I told him I was pretty confident we had the votes to defeat Teddy, so if it was doing Teddy any good politically, there was no reason for him to lay off. I was right about the Senate, but the close vote and fight in the Senate led liberals in the House to take up the same cause, unfortunately with King's support. Senator Dirksen, again with the help of Neil Kennedy, prepared a lengthy set of questions and proposed amendments. Once again I spent hours revising language in more or less meaningless ways to satisfy him. I had been sympathetic with the need in 1964, but he really did not have a leadership problem in 1965.

The southerners delayed matters with endless amendments, and eventually Mansfield called for a cloture vote, which was successful. The House passed several minor amendments and restored the poll-tax prohibition. Judge Smith held up the bill for a month in his Rules Committee, and eventually it went to the floor, where it passed by a substantial bipartisan vote. At the conference committee, the House accepted the Senate version of the poll-tax prohibition, which simply urged the attorney general to seek such a prohibition, and in mid-July both houses accepted the committee compromise.

President Johnson was elated. He went to the Capitol for an elaborate signing ceremony and made a quite eloquent speech. In the department we had spent considerable time planning how we would implement the act, particularly the power to send in federal registrars. That had been offensive to the South and somewhat controversial in Congress. It passed because the only alternative—more lawsuits—just did not have any appeal after Selma. Nonetheless, we determined to use the power carefully and only when necessary. Our whole philosophy had always been to try to make southern officials obey the law, not do the job for them. In a sense federal registrars were like federal troops; using them meant we had failed to get southern registrars, like southern sheriffs, to obey the law. We wrote criteria for registrars that would be the basis for how well they were doing their job and whether federal registrars were needed—for example, remaining open sufficient hours to permit voter registration without unnecessary delays or long lines. We solicited complaints and investigated them.

We went to work immediately after the act's passage. Predictably, compliance was uneven. There were districts that simply were not willing to register large numbers of blacks; there were others that did not want federal registrars. We did our best to make federal registrars a last-resort solution. Once again our guiding principle was to attempt to persuade local officials to comply with the law, not to substitute federal registrars for local ones if the job could be accomplished in another way.

Shortly after the act took effect, I had a call from a disgruntled Senator Eastland. "These civil rights agitators want to come on my plantation and register all the Negroes there, and I'm damned if I'm going to let them. I want you to call them off, or I'll have them all arrested for trespassing," he grumbled.

"Senator," I said, "you know perfectly well they wouldn't pay any attention to what I said, and I can't be involved in hindering registration. Why don't you simply make sure all of them are registered? They will all vote for you anyhow, and you can tell the people trying to come on your property that to do so would be pointless and they can check with the local registrar's records if they don't believe you."

"You think that would work?"

"Seems to me worth trying."

"I'll do it," he said. "But Nick, don't you dare send any of those federal registrars into Sunflower County. I simply won't have it."

"I won't," I said, "as long as your registrar follows all our guidelines."

"Now, listen here. If she doesn't, you let me know before you send anyone into Sunflower."

Actually, she did a good job, and we never sent federal registrars to Sunflower County, much to the disappointment of many civil rights workers, who, understandably, wanted to embarrass the senator.

I kept the president informed of our plans, and I believe he was in agreement, although neither of us liked the criticism we knew we would get from civil rights groups, which wanted more registrars all the time. The Civil Rights Commission joined in, publicly criticizing me and the division for going too slowly. We stuck to our policies and believed they were right.

I went to Martha's Vineyard for a short vacation with my family immediately after the act was signed into law. Bob and Margie McNamara were visiting us over the weekend. That Saturday morning the phone rang. It was the president—and it was the morning after the Watts race riots in Los Angeles. We knew nothing about them.

LBJ explained what had happened. Violent rioting and looting had broken out in Watts, born out of frustration and with no particular objective other than venting fury at racial discrimination. The rioting was serious, and the president thought he ought to send in troops. I told him my advice was to stay out of it. The governor of California, Pat Brown, was a well-known liberal, as far from George Wallace as a governor could be. The riots were his problem, not the president's. Brown had a huge National Guard contingent, and he could put them into service as needed. But it would obviously be to his political advantage to involve the federal government as a partner, and I had no doubt he would be willing to ask for troops as a means of sharing both political and fiscal responsibility with LBJ. I thought LBJ should stay out of it—express confidence in Governor Brown's ability to handle it fairly without outside help.

The situation in Watts was not, of course, a response to the leadership of the civil rights groups or a peaceful demand for recognition of constitutional rights. It was a spontaneous reaction to years of being second-class citizens, to not having jobs, to living in de facto segregated ghettos. Whether the rhetoric of the civil rights movement or its leaders, or that of the president and the rest of us, helped spark it, I did not know.

The president did not like my advice. Given his commitment to civil rights, I think he felt a responsibility to be involved. He told me I should come back to Washington. I said of course I would, but that I could not see the point of it. He hung up, I think a little angrily. A minute or two later the phone rang. This time the White House operator asked for McNamara. Obviously the president did not know we were together. I could hear only Bob's end of the conversation.

"Mr. President, I heard Nick's advice and I am in complete agreement with him . . . Yes, Mr. President, I'm in Martha's Vineyard . . . Yes sir, I have a plane over at Otis Air Force Base, and I can get back immediately . . . Yes sir, he can come with me."

So we got ready to give up our weekend in the sun and surf. Five minutes later the phone rang again. I picked it up, and it was a White House secretary.

"Mr. Attorney General, the president says there is no need for you and Secretary McNamara to come back to Washington. He asked me to call you."

All of which was very typical of LBJ. He did not like my advice, but—at least when Bob agreed—he accepted it. It would be petty to insist that we go to Washington, but he was not going to let us have the satisfaction of his saying so directly to us.

I think my advice was correct—the problem was, absent any denial of constitutional rights, a matter for the state. I also think the president was concentrating so much on insuring those rights for black citizens, and doing so as he had in Alabama, by placing the guard in federal service, that he lost sight of the difference between peaceful demonstrations and unlawful rioting. To feel responsibility for their welfare was an honorable position, and I respected him for it. Probably neither of us sufficiently appreciated that Watts might be a precursor of further black discontent leading to violent response elsewhere outside the South, as did in fact occur in 1967.

In a less serious vein, the Watts riots knocked my picture off the cover of *Time* magazine. *Time* ran a feature story on the voting rights legislation, but not a painting of me on the cover. *Sic transit gloria.*

Despite the criticism of civil rights leaders, the registration of voters in the South went quite well. It had been carefully planned by John Doar well in advance of the law's enactment. He had civil rights lawyers assigned to voting districts throughout the South to make sure of compliance, to listen to complaints, and to make recommendations. While blacks were never more than about a fifth of the population eligible to vote on a statewide basis, in some rural districts they were a majority, and when the next elections took place we had a few black local officials, including sheriffs, take office. The act itself changed the political face of the South in many respects, not the least of which was moving the Democratic "solid South" into the Republican column. We had anticipated white efforts to dilute the significance of the black vote through various redistricting plans, and the division was quite effective in using the act to blunt these efforts through litigation.

I HAD WANTED TO KEEP ARCHIE COX AS MY SOLICITOR GENERAL. He was a distinguished advocate, a proper Bostonian, and someone who worked enormously long hours perfecting the government's briefs. He was also a proud man and perhaps a little stubborn. When I asked him to stay, he said that he would if the president asked him to do so. Given Archie's closeness to the Kennedys, LBJ was not about to ask him either to leave or to stay. Despite my efforts with the president, he would not ask him to stay on, so Archie resigned.

The president asked me if Thurgood Marshall, the great black advocate then on the Second Circuit Court of Appeals, would be a good appointment. Obviously my answer was yes. I assumed at the time that LBJ had in mind eventual appointment to the Supreme Court if a vacancy occurred, but knowing LBJ, I doubted that he had made any promises. Politically it was a great appointment, welcomed by the court and by civil rights leaders as well, who I feel sure made the same assumption that I did. Nonetheless, I was sorry to lose Archie, whose enormous integrity (later demonstrated as special counsel in the Watergate affair) would be missed.

It would be hard to imagine two more different solicitors general than Archie Cox and Thurgood Marshall. Both were fine advocates, but there the similarity stopped. Archie was always the serious scholar and teacher, with a passion for getting the smallest detail right, editing and reediting briefs to change a word here and there or clarify a difficult concept for the nth time, often working into the late night to do so. Indeed, I remember having to tell him that our budget could not stand his editing the page proofs of briefs, which was expensive in the technology of the sixties. Thurgood was one of the world's great storytellers, and he loved an appreciative audience. He was interested in the big picture and had a fine mind that could effectively separate the wheat from the chaff. He had no interest in details, or indeed in some of the issues in his office, and left the editing of briefs to his subordinates once he was satisfied with the general argument. He often went home in midafternoon to be with his lovely wife and two young sons. He was as far from the Boston Brahmin and Harvard professor as it was possible to get.

Not long after the Voting Rights Act became law in August, South Carolina filed a bill of complaint in the United States Supreme Court alleging its unconstitutionality. Such an action invoking the Supreme Court's original jurisdiction was almost without precedent, at least in modern times, and was totally unexpected. Nonetheless it was welcome, because it provided a quick way of answering any constitutional questions and putting them to rest. The Court accepted jurisdiction and expedited the hearing. The case was captioned *South Carolina v. Katzenbach*, but I did not feel as threatened as Fort Sumter or as if the first shot of Civil War II was being fired. That had happened at Ole Miss.

I spoke to Thurgood and told him I wanted to argue the case myself, which I think did not surprise him but may have disappointed him a little. Still, I pointed out, he had argued some of the great constitutional cases in the Court and I wanted a turn. He graciously accepted my wishes and spent many hours preparing me for the argument, along with some of his colleagues in the solicitor general's office: Louis Claiborne, a southerner from New Orleans, who was one of Thurgood's favorites, and Bob Rifkind, a fine young New York lawyer whose father was one of the great advocates of the time.

I wanted to argue the case not simply because of its importance, but because I knew the act backward and forward from our efforts in Congress and, of equal importance, from our many discussions in late 1964, when we were preparing its text and arguing the constitutional and legal issues it posed. In many ways I was already prepared, and I knew that whatever came up, I would not be caught short of knowledge. I had argued only one case in the Supreme Court previously, but I loved appellate argument and was quite good at it. The sessions with Thurgood were obviously useful, despite my familiarity with the act's background and history, but beyond that they were fun. Not only did Thurgood have the opportunity to tell some wonderful stories, but he had a marvelous way of injecting humor as well as substance into the practice questions he would pose.

"I'm Mr. Justice So-and-so [using his real name]," he would say, before posing a complex and multifaceted question.

After a minute I would respond: "Thurgood, the act doesn't say any such thing."

He would look up with a broad smile. "I told you I was Mr. Justice So-and-so."

The only difference of opinion we had was related to my desire for the opinion to say that "Attorney General Katzenbach argued the case *pro se*," that is, for himself. Thurgood insisted (quite rightly) that the language I wanted was inappropriate, because although I was named as the defendant, the government was the real defendant and I was not personally defending myself. I thought it a unique twist that might amuse lawyers. He said he could never persuade the Supreme Court clerk who scheduled argument and reported decisions to do so and refused even to try. When, the following March, the Court handed down its opinion, there was my language, right in the first footnote. How Thurgood managed it I have no idea, but despite his protests, he enjoyed doing it.

I also consulted Archie Cox, not only to take advantage of his huge experience with the Court but simply because he was the principal draftsman of the act and deserved a voice. He told me that he would argue for a group of states that had entered the case on the government's side as *amici curiae*, "friends of the court"—traditionally, other parties who have an interest in the outcome and can, with the court's permission, assist it with argument. So I knew I had someone behind me to pick up the pieces if I flubbed the argument. He also told me how he would argue the case if he were in my place.

The case was scheduled for argument on January 17, my birthday, which seemed to me a good omen. The Court had scheduled two hours a side instead of the usual fifteen or thirty minutes. I allocated thirty minutes to the *amici* and wondered how on earth I would fill up an hour and a half. To say I was nervous would be a profound understatement. I had rented the customary morning suit, and Thurgood joined me at the defendant's table in the front of the courtroom. While a morning suit—striped gray trousers and a black cutaway coat with long tails— is not required for lawyers arguing before the Court, it has long been customary for lawyers representing the United States. Needless to say, the room was as crowded as the law permitted. Lydia was there with Cissy Marshall, Thurgood's wife, and Marion White, Byron's wife, in the special section reserved for guests of the justices. I began to have second thoughts as to whether my arguing the case was a good idea. I hoped I would survive.

I listened carefully to the argument of South Carolina and the questions of the justices. Nothing new there, and I felt better. When the chief justice turned to me, I went to the podium without collapsing and began what turned out to be a lively argument, with many questions from the justices. As always happens to me on such occasions, once the first words were successfully out of my mouth, I relaxed and began to enjoy the experience.

In the Supreme Court, as in many other courts, there are lights that tell you when your time is expiring. I had set the yellow light for two minutes from the end of my time. When the red light comes on, your argument time is over, and the Court is very strict in enforcing it. You may finish your sentence, no more. Shortly after I had begun my argument—or so it seemed—the yellow light came on. To that point everything had gone well, as far as I could tell. Justice Black was in the middle of a question. "You must know, Mr. Katzenbach," he finished, "that Section 5 is unconstitutional." I opened my mouth to respond as best I could. The red light came on.

The Court decided the case in March and was unanimous on all points in our favor except Section 5, to which only Justice Black dissented. The result was not surprising but was certainly pleasing. I may have been fortunate that the red light came on when it did. It would not have been easy to refute Black's argument, although the issue was not central to the act's purposes. Section 5 dealt with the ability of the attorney general to take state voting legislation to the District of Columbia court of appeals before it became effective if he believed it violated the act. Courts are constitutionally limited to hearing actual disputes—"cases or controversies"—and cannot give what are called "advisory opinions" before an actual dispute has arisen. Justice Black believed that Section 5 called for such an opinion, since the case would be brought by the AG before people voted or sought to vote in an actual election. As a practical matter, it was important not to have an election first that we would then have to contest.

In its political impact, the Voting Rights Act was by far the most important legislation of the time and changed the political face of the nation. The Democratic Party lost the solid South, as both Presidents Kennedy and Johnson had feared and believed would be the case. More importantly, the black vote was sufficiently important, even though not decisive on a statewide level, to change southern politics and get blacks elected to office in state and local elections. It is that simple fact which broke down the caste system that had prevailed. But the minority vote by itself has not been enough to insure genuine social and economic opportunity, though it has helped.

The sad footnote to this history is that despite renewals of the act, there are still efforts to dilute the power of black votes by gerrymandering voting districts so that black voters are dominant in a few districts and powerless in others. Worse is using the provision against voter fraud as a device to prevent the poor from voting, by requiring, for example, drivers' licenses or other costly and unnecessary forms of identification, a subtle way of discriminating against the elderly and the poor.

XVII

VERY SOON AFTER MY CONFIRMATION AS ATTORNEY GENERAL, I DETER-mined to straighten out as best I could the problem of FBI wiretaps and listening devices, or bugs. I had no illusions that I was going to bring the FBI under my control; I had seen Bobby, with his brother as president, have only partial success and matters revert to their normal status when LBJ became president and Hoover's access to the White House was restored. But I did think it was possible to institute a more orderly procedure on wiretaps and bugs, particularly since President Johnson said he was opposed to all such devices. It was an attitude on the president's part that I found puzzling, since it never seemed to me to be consistent with his love of gossip, which the Bureau fed.

Hoover came to my office to congratulate me on my appointment and to express his strong desire to work closely with me and my assistants. He could not have been more cordial. When I told him I thought we should set tighter rules on wiretaps, he professed complete agreement with me, noting that other agencies, primarily Treasury and Defense, seemed to have no rules at all and were engaged in such activities. That was news to me, and I said I would take up the matter with the president.

I had discovered that when the attorney general approved a wiretap, his office kept no record of the approval. Further, once a tap had been approved, the FBI regarded it as approved forever. Thus, if an AG many years ago approved a tap, the Bureau felt free at any time to reinstate it without further approval, so a successor to the office had no knowledge of the tap. I said I thought permission for a tap should expire in a reasonable time and suggested six months (which was too long, but I thought a good starting point). Hoover, to my surprise, said he had always felt the same way and agreed with me. I then took up bugs and said that I thought these too should have the attorney general's specific approval each time, particularly since they often involved trespass. It was not clear to me just how the attorney general could approve a trespass, but then again, according to Hoover, he had been given a general permission by my predecessors to do so at his discretion and without informing the attorney general. I was, frankly, astounded to hear this, but welcomed Hoover's view that bugs should be treated in the same way as wiretaps.

Had I not been familiar with some of Bobby's problems with the Bureau, and had I not been misled by the FBI on at least two prior occasions, I think I would have felt that dealing with the FBI was easy. Hoover continued to be cordial, telling me various stories about the FBI in the past or his experiences at various social occasions. He was garrulous, and most of what he said was not clearly relevant to any current business of the department's. In point of fact, he appeared somewhat senile. Obviously I would have to send a memo setting out our understanding in detail, which I did. I also learned an important lesson: meet in Hoover's office, not in mine. It was far easier for me to get out of his office than to get him out of mine.

Throughout my time in the department, the Bureau remained something of a puzzle to me. Clearly Hoover was showing his age of almost seventy, and it was not clear to me to what extent he was in fact guiding his subordinates. He was always friendly and, at least on the surface, cooperative. But it was virtually impossible to know what was really going on. Joseph Kraft, the very knowledgeable columnist for the *Washington Post* (and an old personal friend), wrote an article calling Hoover the perfect bureaucrat, and there was a good deal of truth to what he wrote. If the attorney general made a written request, it would be either complied with or responded to. But one could never be sure of verbal directions to the FBI.

More exasperating was never knowing what the Bureau was doing. For example, I discovered through accident that my department budget was in fact reviewed by Bureau agents. The chairman of the House Appropriations Subcommittee, John Rooney of New York, borrowed FBI agents to audit and assist him on his committee's review. They could and did make recommendations about department requests. No wonder the FBI always got what it asked for! Perhaps some attorney general in the past had given Hoover permission to lend his agents; perhaps he simply did it on his own.

In theory the AG could fire Hoover. In fact, even a president would have paid a heavy political penalty for trying. Appointed to head a small and insignificant investigative bureau in 1924, Hoover had built that bureau into the competent and powerful Federal Bureau of Investigation. In the 1930s it had gone after America's best-known criminals—John Dillinger, Baby Face Nelson, and many others—and made the G-Men the heroes of the decade. Hoover had a brilliant public relations person in Lou Nichols, and as I can recall, every kid wanted to grow from being a junior G-Man into the real thing. Because of the Great Depression, Hoover was able to hire extremely competent personnel, most of them with legal or accounting degrees or with laboratory experience, and build them into an exceptional organization. He ran it with military precision and discipline, and every success, every arrest, was carefully managed by Nichols to milk every ounce of favorable publicity. There was no man better known or more admired by the general public than J. Edgar Hoover.

At some point in his remarkable career, this conservative southern bureaucrat acquired a taste for the power of his office and not only capitalized on his reputation but began to abuse the office by compiling information on political figures, which increased his power. He became feared by politicians for the information he either possessed or they feared he might possess, as well as admired for accomplishments the Bureau in fact brought off. He loved to share with presidents bits of gossip and bits of real information (not always distinguishing which was which) about their political opponents, and he became suspicious of every liberal idea as having a Communist origin and subversive purpose. He ruled his FBI with a combination of discipline and fear and was capable of acting in an excessively arbitrary way. No one dared object.

Hoover and his longtime friend and deputy director, Clyde Tolson, spent a good deal of time at the races in Pimlico. They took expensive vacations at well-known exclusive resorts, all paid for by "friends." I do not suggest actual corruption, but any other person in the department who did this would have been fired for accepting favors of this kind. Hoover was in essence untouchable and thus out of effective control. The Bureau never made a mistake, because it took pains to cover up any errors and did so effectively. The agent who stepped out of line found himself reassigned to a hopeless job in a far-off place. The FBI ran its own shop. It got information from others but did not reciprocate. It was a principality with absolutely secure borders. In Hoover's view, it was the job of the attorney general to defend the FBI, not to guide it.

I think most of my predecessors (other than Bobby) simply accepted the Bureau as a fact of life. One could get on with Hoover, and the

Bureau was usually amenable to a request. It investigated cases and presented them to young prosecutors. On most federal crimes it did not need outside direction. Only when it came to matters the FBI disliked did attorneys have to spell out what was needed. In the Civil Rights Division, for example, John Doar and his assistants had to make it clear in excruciating detail what they wished the FBI to investigate, whom it should interview, what questions it should ask, and so forth. Agents hated the work, primarily because Hoover hated the civil rights movement and its leaders. He was, of course, from the South and shared dominant southern views of racial inequality.

The FBI had a White House liaison (itself a bad idea, as it allows White House staff to use the FBI without informing the AG). That liaison was Cartha "Deke" DeLoach, my principal liaison with the FBI as well and an agent whom I never trusted. At no time did he ever tell me what information he was sharing with the White House or what, if any, requests people there had made of the Bureau. When I asked, he would blandly tell me that all such information was confidential. It gave me a very uncomfortable feeling, but to tell the truth, I doubt it was very important. The Bureau did get itself involved in the 1964 Democratic convention in ways that were totally improper, but I believe it did so at the request of the president himself, who was paranoid about Bobby Kennedy's taking over the convention and more concerned than he should have been about the Mississippi Freedom delegation trying to unseat party regulars. The FBI prided itself on staying out of partisan politics and generally did, but in my opinion DeLoach had poor judgment, and Hoover was tempted by his dislike of both Bobby and blacks.

On one occasion I did get a memo from the president attaching one he had gotten from the Bureau with a question for me about it. Since I had never seen the FBI memo, I told the president I knew nothing about it, which evidently surprised him. More important, I took the occasion to call the memo to Hoover's attention in writing. I told him I had no problem with his communicating directly with the White House but that it could be confusing to the president. Therefore, in the future all such memos should indicate on their face that the attorney general either had or had not seen them. The president supported me, and that cut down considerably on the communications, but it was still possible for the FBI to transmit information without a covering memo.

I saw Hoover only rarely and Tolson almost never. Indeed, except for accompanying Hoover to the races, I could never figure out what, if anything, Tolson did. Perhaps I should have spent more time with Hoover. But except on rare occasions, like the aftermath of the assassination of

President Kennedy, when I was trying to review with all the relevant agencies how best to coordinate intelligence and activities, there was little gain in doing so.

I did pick up the newspaper one day to read a huge headline saying that "Hoover Calls King the World's Greatest Liar," so I knew I would have to traipse down the hall to his office and discuss it with him. He could not have been more pleasant or more contrite. "I know, I know why you are here. I'm very sorry. I told DeLoach it was a mistake to see all those women reporters. I never speak to the press. But he insisted and I gave in. Terrible mistake. One of them asked me about Dr. King, and of course I simply felt obligated to tell her the truth."

With an apology like that, what more could I say? After all, King had committed the world's greatest sin, in Hoover's view. That was not King's occasional sexual adventures. It was the fact that he had criticized the Bureau.

I think with respect to wiretapping and bugs the Bureau accepted and generally abided by the process I established. I say "generally" because in the 1970s, Senator Church's committee investigating the Watergate scandal and other administration excesses came up with two memos informing me of two bugs planted in Dr. King's hotel rooms that I had not approved. The Bureau did not claim that I had approved them, and under the rules, my approval, if I was available, was required in all situations. I had been available on the dates involved and testified that I did not recall seeing these after-the-fact memos, even though they contained my initials, and that I strongly believed I would recall them if I had. It is hard for me to believe that the FBI would have blandly sent me a memo informing me that it had failed to comply with the rules on bugs with no mention of why it had failed to do so. However, I think this was an anomaly and that compliance was in general good.

I am less sure of taps by other agencies. The president issued an order that all taps and bugs must be approved in writing by the attorney general. Since I had virtually no requests from Treasury, the CIA, or Defense, they must have stopped using the devices, used the FBI, or never bothered to get my permission. In my experience, intelligence agencies hate to have to explain or justify what they are doing to third parties. To do so necessarily requires them to reveal information they regard as highly confidential. Beyond that, most taps and bugs are in fact fishing expeditions that involve the invasion of privacy of persons not involved in a legitimate investigation, and they only occasionally lead to important facts. It is always difficult to articulate a persuasive ground. Hoover, who never voluntarily cooperated with other agencies, was delighted at the effort to handcuff their wiretaps by forcing them to seek my permission, and saw this as a way of getting information from them that they might not otherwise have shared with the Bureau.

The FBI's prior practice of planting bugs without the specific approval of the attorney general involved me in one of the few (I think only two) disagreements I had with Bobby. When the case of Fred Black, a close associate of Bobby Baker's (LBJ's former assistant in the Senate), was on appeal to the Supreme Court, Thurgood Marshall discovered that a bug had been placed in Black's hotel room and had inadvertently picked up a conversation with his lawyer. This had not been revealed in the courts below, because there was nothing of significance in the conversation and the department attorneys involved had had no knowledge of it. Now we knew of it, Thurgood rightly felt it must be revealed, whether or not important, to the Court. The problem lay in the fact that Hoover insisted the bug was authorized by the attorney general under existing policy well known to the attorney general. Bobby was equally adamant that he had no knowledge of any such policy and had not authorized the bug.

The Bureau depended on a letter from Attorney General Brownell which it said authorized the Bureau to install a bug in exceptional circumstances. It was a possible, though I thought somewhat strained, reading. In his organized crime investigations, Bobby had listened to many conversations that were obviously the product of bugs, and the Bureau depended on this fact to show his knowledge of the practice. Bobby said he thought such tapes had been obtained from local law enforcement officials and he did not know they were the FBI's work. The issue was further complicated by the fact that some of the attorneys working on organized crime believed the tapes had been made by the Bureau at the direction of the attorney general but never said so.

Knowing Bobby as I did, I believed him. He was as truthful as anyone I have ever known. But I doubted the Court would simply take his word, and I thought most people would regard it as improbable that he had never asked questions about the tapes he had listened to. Thurgood was obviously skeptical, but he did not know Bobby as I did. Together we worked out a mealy-mouthed explanation in a footnote that satisfied the Court but did not satisfy either of the protagonists, by simply affirming that the FBI had installed the bug under what it believed was a long-standing authority known to the attorney general. Both Bobby and Hoover, and to a lesser extent Thurgood, were furious at me, but (as Bobby later admitted to me) it avoided an unpleasant showdown in which I doubt Bobby could have prevailed.

There had been growing concern about what was perceived as an increasing crime rate throughout the country. While these were ordinary street crimes—muggings, theft, arson, armed robbery—not federal violations, there was much interest in Congress and with the president in taking some kind of federal role. The president had been enthusiastic when I had suggested a commission to study the problem and report to him on measures the government might take. I had suggested Thomas Dewey as a possible chair, because he was a famous prosecutor and Republican presidential candidate who I thought would be respected by all, despite his age. When I called Dewey on the phone, however, he declined and expressed the strong view that the attorney general should chair the commission. He thought it important that the department be committed to the commission's recommendations and responsible for their implementation.

I reported the conversation to President Johnson and suggested that he might be better able to persuade Dewey than I. I do not know whether or not he tried, but a couple of days later he called me and said he thought I should chair the group. I had talked to Hoover about the commission, and it was difficult to read his views. He was somewhat skeptical, and I think he felt that if there was anything to be done, the Bureau could do it. But he said of course the FBI would cooperate in every way, and he had no problem with my choice for the commission's executive director, Professor James Vorenberg of the Harvard Law School. I had known Jim since he came to work with me straight out of law school in the Air Force Counsel's Office in 1951. Jim was very bright—he had been president of the *Law Review*—and, of equal importance, very affable and good-natured. In 1951, Secretary Thomas Finletter had gotten permission to give direct commissions to one or two of the best law graduates in the country, so technically Jim was a second lieutenant, although he never owned a uniform, to my knowledge. Nor did he ever learn how to salute. But he earned the respect of a number of senior officers, who never suspected he was a mere shavetail and admired the quality of his work and the gentle good humor he always displayed. He left the air force to teach criminal law at Harvard, where many years later he became dean.

I had no doubts about Jim's intellectual capacity, and I thought him an ideal personality to run the commission, despite his relative youth. Youth, of course, was not regarded as a handicap by either President Kennedy or President Johnson. My selections of commission members were passed by the White House and, as I recall, approved. I do not believe the president had any suggestions or personal desires, and I had tried to achieve a commission with expertise and diversity in every sense of the word. It was composed of state and federal judges, prosecutors, leaders of the bar, police chiefs, a university president, a newspaper publisher, a prominent civil rights leader, the head of the League of Women Voters, and a metropolitan mayor. They came from all over the country. One member, Lewis Powell, later went on the United States Supreme Court. It turned out to be an active, congenial, and participatory group, and its members had very close to a perfect attendance record.

The underlying philosophy of the study was to try to understand common crime and how to bring it under better control. Jim was insistent that we see law enforcement not in terms of its separate institutions—police, prosecutors, courts, prisons, parole, release—but in terms of how these institutions interact with one another in a process that is important to understand. That understanding affects how we see the total process and where we see the greatest opportunities to address the problem. We were particularly interested in just what role the federal government could and should play in our federal system without destroying the states' basic responsibility.

To assist in the process, Jim put together a large and extremely competent staff, assisted by scores of consultants and experts in every field. A lot of time and effort was spent to determine where the emerging technologies would take us, in terms of both their use by law enforcement and their use by criminals. A lot of time and effort was also spent trying to sort out statistics and the different criteria used in their classification and compilation. We attempted to state appropriate roles for the federal government, the states, and municipalities. We developed over a hundred specific recommendations for improving the criminal justice system.

When our report, formally *A Report by the President's Commission on Law Enforcement and the Administration of Justice*, eventually came out, in late 1966, it was well received by those involved in law enforcement and generally by the Congress. It encouraged police and others to come up with innovative ideas that the federal government could finance through the Justice Department on an experimental basis. What worked could then be replicated with some confidence and what did not work abandoned. That did unavoidably put the department in a position of selecting the most promising programs, which did not always sit well with representatives of losing localities. Congress pushed—as predictably it would—for block grants rather than our highly selective process, and eventually succeeded in persuading my successor as attorney general, Ramsey Clark, to yield. I doubt he had a choice.

The report itself was some 300 pages, and in addition we published a number of detailed studies on particular aspects such as courts, juvenile delinquency, prisons, narcotics, and so forth, providing supporting detail for the experts involved. The recommendations were often on ways to prevent crime through better-organized community efforts with youth, alternatives to the criminal system, and means for keeping families together and involved through changes in both welfare and schools—diverse suggestions going well beyond what we normally think of as law enforcement. In addition, many of the recommendations called for additional training of professionals, especially in the use of technology and ways of exchanging information and sharing expertise. There were suggestions for cooperative training of judges, prosecutors, and police officials. One of my favorites, and a very successful program, was one we arranged for police chiefs at the Harvard Business School, in administration and financial planning and controls. The chiefs were more than willing to give up their vacations for a Harvard "degree" that gave them a far better understanding of the skills needed to run a large organization.

It is always hard to measure the impact of such a report, and in many respects it has been ignored by politicians in recent years, when the prevailing mood has insisted on more punishment as an answer—longer sentences (often mandatory); more power to prosecutors and less to judges; fewer efforts at education, job training, and rehabilitation; and huge increases in the number of prisons and the costs of internment. Not only does this approach demonstrably cost more, but it breeds more violence and more often than not leads to a brutality I cannot associate with a decent society.

Unfortunately, crime is a more difficult problem than simplistic approaches can resolve, even at great expense. Punishment is but one element in deterrence, and while most of us find satisfaction in catching and punishing the bad guys, it is only a piece of the process. Overcrowding, inadequate medical care, mixing the mentally ill with the sane, brutal treatment, and failure to prepare prisoners for their release back into society in the long run increase violent crime rather than deter it. Of equal or greater importance is the damage these actions do to our human values and sense of decency. We have to look at and understand the whole process if we are to be successful both in dealing with criminal behavior and in preserving our own ethical standards. Most professionals understand this, so I find it satisfying to know that even today among trained professionals our report is still not only remembered but used and respected. I think of it as a real and important achievement. Today, as in the sixties, it is important to think of the problem as the title of the report indicates: *The Challenge of Crime in a Free Society.* Every law has to satisfy both sides of the equation.

During my time as attorney general, I tried to improve some of the prison practices and got laws on work release, halfway houses, and the like enacted, with the support of many conservative Republicans, such as Senator Roman Hruska of Nevada. I think I was motivated in part by the Crime Commission and in part by my own experience in Italian and German prison camps during World War II. Fortunately, I had outstanding federal corrections commissioners in James Bennett and Myrl Alexander, who were helpful to the Crime Commission and anxious to put into effect many of its recommendations.

When I took over from Bobby, morale in the department had suffered greatly from the death of President Kennedy and from Bobby's loss of special status as the president's brother. But the professional quality of the personnel remained high, and staff members were devoted to their responsibilities. Within the department itself, probably the single most important factor is the leadership of the AG and his assistants in their dedication to fair and nonpolitical enforcement of the law. Once the career staff is convinced that integrity is in fact the foundation of all policy, their loyalty, capacity for hard work, and dedication are a joy to observe.

A potential problem that concerned Bobby and that we had frequently talked about was control of U.S. attorneys. The problem stemmed from the fact that U.S. attorneys are political appointees of the president who, like judges, are recommended by state political leaders, usually the senator if he is a member of the president's party. They were usually young, not always very experienced, and ambitious about attaining higher elective office or a judgeship. Thus there was a danger that their loyalty might run to the senator involved and that political ambition could lead them to use the power of their office for improper political purposes. The problem, as we saw it, was making sure that their loyalty ran to the AG and that they did not engage in improper activities.

Control for the most part rests with career attorneys in the department who oversee the work of U.S. attorneys functionally and who have to approve the bringing of cases or the commencement of investigations. Usually the experience of the career attorneys is helpful and appreciated in the field, but this is not inevitably the case. Obviously the department has an interest in taking a consistent view of the law throughout all its offices, so a large part of the supervision is making sure that all the lawyers are on the same page of the same book. Consistency is of little interest in the field, where the desire is to bring a case or use a legal interpretation of a statute that is helpful to the case at hand. So close supervision is important, and so is the willingness of the U.S. attorney to accept that guidance from Washington, even if in his opinion it adversely affects a case of local importance.

Bobby's relationship with his brother was helpful both in avoiding bad appointments and in exercising appropriate control. So too was the way he involved many of the U.S. attorneys in the investigation of organized crime and his skill in making them part of his team. I was fortunate in inheriting U.S. attorneys loyal to the department and in having John Reilly in the deputy's office to help retain them and examine the qualifications of new appointments.

When I succeeded Bobby and was confirmed as AG, I wanted to find a way of gaining loyalty similar to that Bobby had attained. I think it was Reilly who came up with the idea of bringing all the U.S. attorneys to Washington for a conference and suggesting that they bring their wives. Since we paid for the attorneys' travel and hotel rooms, the trip was affordable for them, and we arranged a marvelous black-tie dinner and dance at historic Anderson House. Ramsey Clark and Thurgood Marshall and their wives joined Lydia and me in the receiving line, and President and Mrs. Johnson joined us all for a brief visit and a chance to meet the guests. The service orchestras entertained and played for dancing until the small hours of the morning. As Lydia will affirm, I am not much of a party person, but this one was really special. It would be difficult to overstate the enthusiasm and pleasure of the U.S. attorneys and their spouses.

I think the party was enormously helpful in winning the loyalty of the U.S. attorneys, and generally I had no problems stemming from differences. Judge Cox in Mississippi tried to hold me in contempt for a refusal to prosecute a black whom a white grand jury wished to indict for perjury (no perjury had been committed, but Cox refused to accept my view and that of the department lawyers), and the U.S. attorney for southern Mississippi, Robert Hauberg, followed my instructions not to indict the black witness as the judge and grand jury wished, even when the judge held him in contempt too. Cox's efforts, which were totally improper and unjudicial, were rapidly set aside by the circuit court.

I did have a slight disagreement with Edward Hanrahan in Chicago, Mayor Daley's choice for U.S. attorney. He wanted to call a leading organized crime figure, Sam Giancano, before a grand jury and ask him questions about a relatively unimportant matter but one to which he knew Giancano would plead the Fifth Amendment. Organized crime leaders really had to do this in order to preserve their code of silence. We would then grant him immunity, and when he refused to answer, we would jail him for civil contempt for the life of the grand jury. I was reluctant to do so, in part because of the obviousness of the tactic and in part because I thought it likely that Hanrahan would ask too broad a question and thus give the witness too broad an immunity. Eventually I gave in, after having Hanrahan thoroughly coached and writing out the only questions he was permitted to ask. It all worked as scripted, and Giancano went to jail until he answered the questions before the grand jury, which of course he never did.

The witness's jail term expired automatically with the end of the grand jury's term some twenty months later. Hanrahan was back in town, wishing to repeat the identical exercise before another jury and jail Giancano again. It was obvious that Giancano would never answer the questions and that this was just a device to put him in jail. Not wishing to anger a court and lose power entirely in cases where the threat of jail might in fact get valuable testimony, I refused. Hanrahan returned to Chicago, held a press conference, and said he was prepared to put the organized crime leader back in jail but the attorney general simply did not want that to occur and had refused to explain why.

Hanrahan was better at PR than he was at law.

But Hanrahan was an exception, and most U.S. attorneys were interested in fair prosecutions for the crime committed. Our U.S. attorney in a midwestern state, I think Kansas, called me about a bank robbery that bothered him. The defendant, a criminal with past convictions, was identified by the bank president as the robber, and several employees confirmed the identification. His alibi was that he had been in the home of a Jewish couple in Florida at the time of the robbery. Despite a life of crime, he had never robbed a bank before, and it seemed to the prosecutor quite unlikely that he had robbed this one. On the other hand, the prosecutor was sure he could secure a conviction from a local jury based on the bank president's testimony as against the alibi witnesses' regarding whom some prejudice was likely. Edward Bennett Williams was the defendant's lawyer, so a conviction would be quite a feather in the cap of the U.S. attorney. But the thought of convicting a man he believed was probably innocent of the alleged crime bothered him.

I asked Ed Williams, whom I knew and liked, to come to my office, and he said his client would never rob a bank but agreed that he would probably be convicted on the bank president's testimony, supported by that of his subordinates. Some years before I had served on the board of the New Jersey Diagnostic Center, a somewhat unusual, if not unique, institution that diagnosed prisoners' mental state, especially any tendency toward violence, as a way of assigning them to prisons or assisting the parole board considering their release. Dr. Ralph Brancale was a national expert on the administration of drugs designed to get at the truth of past events. Williams and I agreed to send his client to Brancale, with the understanding that the results of the examination would not be used at trial by either side.

Two or three weeks later, Ralph Brancale called me on the phone. "Nick, you have no idea what crimes this man has committed. But I am absolutely confident he did not rob that bank."

The U.S. attorney dropped the case and incurred the wrath of the bank president and other local citizens. But in our justice system, a man can be convicted only on evidence of a crime he committed, and both the U.S. attorney and I felt better, even if less popular.

XVIII

THE MAJOR DIFFERENCE BETWEEN BEING ATTORNEY GENERAL AND being deputy attorney general is not simply the increased responsibility in decision-making but the demands of the Congress, the press, and the public on one's time. Fortunately, as I have said, I inherited an outstanding public relations officer in Jack Rosenthal, as Bobby had in Ed Guthman. Jack had been Ed's assistant and was extraordinarily skillful in dealing with the press, and therefore in essence with the public. He also was responsible for getting my congressional testimony and my outside speeches into shape and for suggesting which reporters I should talk to, about what, and what invitations I should or should not accept. Each of these tasks is crucial to the AG's doing his job in a reasonable way. In a democratic society, much of government is public relations, informing the public in a serious way about what one is doing and why. There is an important difference between information and advertising, and while in a sense one is trying to sell policy, reason rather than slogan and fact rather than fiction should be the instruments. In truth, one is trying to develop a view as well as convince others of its merits.

One of the things Jack impressed upon me from the outset was that he had to know what was going on in the department and in my own thinking. If he did not, he would inadvertently say the wrong thing and make us look deceptive. I told him that he was welcome at all staff meetings and that the door to my office was always open to him. When he told me about a speaking invitation I should accept and why, he would suggest a few topics as possibilities, and I would select one. Then we would discuss in general terms what I wanted to say on the subject.

Jack would get some young lawyer in the appropriate division to write a first draft incorporating and elaborating on my ideas, which he would then edit and rework himself before giving it to me for my comments. I would make changes or suggest some additions and give it back for a final editing. If the lawyer writing the draft disagreed with my thoughts, he was welcome to come to my office and discuss them with me. I learned a lot by preparing speeches. It was typical of Jack's good judgment that the cadre of speechwriters were young but extraordinarily able. They included Adam Walinsky, who later worked on Bobby's campaign and ran for attorney general of New York; Peter Edelman, who also worked for Bobby and was nominated by President Carter for the court of appeals; and Stephen Breyer, who is now an associate justice on the Supreme Court.

I describe this process in detail because it made me feel as though the speeches I gave were in fact mine. The main ideas were mine, and what I did not like, I edited. The language was sometimes mine, more often Jack's, but it felt like mine (which may have been wishful thinking on my part). When we discussed the final draft, Jack would tell me what the press would seize on, and he would adjust the language so we could control the one or two possible leads. The accuracy of his predictions as to the lead was only further evidence of what a good reporter he was. It would be hard to overstate the extent to which I depended on his many talents.

I made a lot of speeches, although I suspect nowhere near the number Bobby did. Only a few are memorable to me, but they stand out for one reason or another. One of Jack's ideas was that I should go south after the Voting Rights Act was passed and make a speech on voting to a predominantly black audience in Mobile, Alabama. He promoted an invitation from a group of black organizations engaged in voter registration for me to make an address at their celebration of Emancipation Day on January 2, 1966.

President Johnson thought it a great idea. Senator John Sparkman of Alabama was less enthusiastic but did not strongly object. Mobile was an ideal city, because it was in the vanguard of southern cities trying to cope with the changes wrought by the civil rights acts. Mayor Joseph Langen volunteered to introduce me, and Alabama attorney general Richmond Flowers also joined me on the podium. Both were extremely popular with black citizens.

The talk took place in the city auditorium with an audience of some 4,500, almost all of whom were black. I talked about the Voting Rights Act and emphasized that while we wanted voluntary compliance, we were prepared to send in registrars where necessary and that we would not tolerate efforts at voter intimidation. I singled out fear and voter intimidation and stated in very strong terms that we would deal forcefully with any efforts by the Klan and others to interfere with the right to vote. I praised my audience's efforts to get voters registered and to the polls and spent some time singling out some of the black heroes of the movement—Thurgood Marshall, the solicitor general, professionally; Vivian Malone, whom I had escorted into the University of Alabama, a daughter of Mobile; Albert Turner, who left his bricklaying job to spend all his time registering black voters in rural Alabama; and others. I quoted frequently from some of President Johnson's eloquent speeches and ended up with words of hope: "A century ago it was Lincoln who emancipated the Negro. A generation hence, we may very well recognize that it was the Negro who helped emancipate the nation." It was an exhilarating experience.

The Mobile Bar Association had invited me to lunch the next day, and I had arranged to meet with the U.S. attorneys from the southern states that morning. It was not easy or, for that matter, very safe to serve Kennedy or Johnson as a government lawyer in the Deep South, and I admired the courage of these young men. All were southerners, but they believed in law and faithfully did their duty, even though it usually ostracized them socially and professionally to do so.

I was pleased to have been invited to lunch by local lawyers and was therefore somewhat surprised when the president of the association, Jack Gallalee, decided to take advantage of his introduction to denounce all of my activities with respect to civil rights. He spoke of "an unhealthy policy of giving in to pressure and creating mob rule," adding that he hoped my presence and remarks "would not cause violence or create a disturbance" and ending by expressing his "prayer that the administration's views don't spell the end of constitutional government in America."

Coming on the heels of my Emancipation Day speech and a meeting with my U.S. attorneys, this unusual breach of southern courtesy was annoying. The six U.S. attorneys who were at the luncheon were, like me, visibly angry. I made a brief response, trying my best to contrast measured words with his rhetoric. I said that I was confident that "so long as we test our policies in the courts, and they are affirmed by the United States Supreme Court, I don't believe we need fear the end of constitutional government." Then I added—perhaps a little overkill, but irresistible— "This might even be the beginning."

Predictably, the attack was picked up by the northern press and reported to my advantage. What surprised and pleased me was that both it and my Emancipation Day speech were fairly reported in the *Mobile Register.* The paper did note, a little sarcastically, that I had arrived in Mobile with seven assistants, "all white." This particularly irritated Wiley Branton, my light-colored black special assistant, a well-known Texas lawyer who was one of the seven. Even the *Birmingham News* favorably reviewed my visit to Mobile and praised both blacks and whites for their peaceful efforts to integrate in Mobile. I returned to Washington encouraged. In Mobile, at least, most white political and business leaders were facing the realities of integration and beginning to work with local black leaders to that end. I was unhappy that lawyers were not in the vanguard.

In many respects my Emancipation Day speech was a high point of my many talks. It was the only time I (or any other government official) spoke to a large, predominantly black audience in the Deep South. Even Senator Sparkman had the grace to call me and praise my speech.

One of my most carefully planned and interesting talks was also my most embarrassing speaking experience. In the fall of 1965, Leon Jaworski invited me speak to the Rotary Club of Houston. Leon, one of the outstanding lawyers in Texas and a member of the Crime Commission, had been after me several times to come to Houston, and I finally accepted. Going to the president's home state, I particularly wanted to do well. The speech obviously should deal with civil rights, and when Jack and I talked it over, we thought of the modernity of Houston, its rapid growth, and its leadership in space, technology, and medicine. But its public schools were still segregated, and it seemed a marvelous opportunity to gently chastise the most modern city in Texas, with its prosperity based on knowledge, for its much too "deliberate speed" in desegregating its schools. My two Texas associates, Ramsey Clark and Barefoot Sanders (who now headed the Civil Division), were enthusiastic. So too was Jack Valenti, a Houston native, close to LBJ in the White House.

The problem, which I did not discover until I was seated at the luncheon and the speech had already been distributed to the press, was simply that it had not occurred to any of us to examine the Rotary Club itself. Had we done so, we would have learned that its president was the superintendent of Houston schools! It would now appear as though I were abusing their hospitality to criticize their president. With the speech already given to the press, there was nothing I could do but simply confess my ignorance at the outset and deliver the speech. It was a good speech but delivered with reluctance.

Again, to my pleasure and surprise, the speech was favorably reported by the press in Houston, who thought it made more sense than the superintendent did. Valenti said it was good for people there to get this message, and that made me feel better too.

Most of my speeches were to various bar associations around the country, and the subject was usually something on criminal law, often the work of the Crime Commission. I annoyed Walter Annenberg's *Philadelphia Inquirer* by being opposed to the death penalty, although my opposition was not for the usual reasons. My objections rested—and still rest—not so much on moral grounds as on two related reasons: capital punishment defendants often are not assigned competent counsel and consequently are denied a fair trial, and the emotion raised by the possibility of death (often combined with the perception of poor representation) has led judges to find error where none would likely exist. The precedents thus established carry over to other felony cases and tend to distort and needlessly handicap the criminal process by increasing the chances of technical errors. I also think that the most heinous crimes are often committed by the mentally ill, which poses the Hobson's choice of executing the mentally ill or executing only those whose crimes are far less brutal.

I think it was my views on the death penalty that annoyed Mr. Annenberg. I was never sure. His paper opposed everything I did or said, and the reporter who covered the Justice Department told Jack that his editor had told him not to file a story favorable to me. I minded the criticism less than the frustration of never understanding why.

I also made a number of speeches to civil rights groups and their allies, and the content was predictable rather than memorable. I think what makes a speech memorable to the speaker is usually not its content but surrounding circumstances. I do not recall my talks to bar associations, but I do remember visiting Midland, Texas, to speak to the state judicial conference, simply because I was invited by Judge Perry Pickett. Perry had been the bombardier on our plane in North Africa early in World War II when we were shot down in the Mediterranean after sinking five ships with six bombs—quite a bombing feat! He was a prisoner with the rest of the crew in Italy but successfully escaped and eventually made his way home. It was a real joy to see him again, and it was that reunion, not the speech, which made the occasion memorable.

I also have a vivid memory of a speech to the Anti-Defamation League in New York, because it was the only time I ever received a standing ovation for my opening words. The speech came immediately after news that Coca-Cola was closing its bottling plant in Israel under threat from several Arab countries that they would cease doing business with Coke. My opening line was "Welcome to the Pepsi Generation." It took about five or ten seconds to sink in, and then my audience was on its feet. Would that such opportunities occurred more often!

I suspect my most unusual speeches were the Christmas Eve visits I made to federal prisons, especially one with a number of youthful offenders. My own experience of Christmas as a prisoner of war made me think of these youths, most of them about the age I was when I was in prison camp. It is an incredibly lonely and depressing time, and while I could not help that much, I could give them something different and unexpected to take their minds off the loneliness that accompanies incarceration. I think it may have made some of them feel better. I hope so. It made me feel a little more human.

While their experience was very different from mine, I told them that at least I could understand the loneliness of the holiday season away from family and friends, far from home like many of them. I also told them how wonderful the day would be when they would regain their freedom, and how important it was to make the best use of that freedom they could. That was the resolve I had made as a POW, and I hoped they would do the same. They should start preparing for it now, by studying and reading, as I had done in prison camp, so that when the day finally came, they would be ready to take advantage of it.

I worked hard on all my talks, as did Jack and the others who helped prepare them. I often modified my views as a result of discussions with those helping with the substantive presentation. If one thinks of such speeches as a means of communicating with the public about what one is thinking and doing, they can be an important part of the process of governing in a democracy. Not only do they inform the public, but they help to bring the department head closer to the people who are doing the real work. They can relate what they and their colleagues are doing to what the attorney general is talking about. And it gives the reporters who are covering the department a context for their stories, a much more in-depth look at the department than they get in day-to-day press releases. It is important to be honest and candid, not only because the problems of government are never easy and there is always room for honest difference of opinion, but also because you get useful criticism if you are willing to risk seeking it. If your speeches are simply bland recitations of well-known administration policy, neither the audience nor the speaker profits.

XIX

Since President Kennedy's death, and especially since Bobby's departure from Justice for the Senate, I had gradually gotten to feel more comfortable with President Johnson. In many respects I was as different from LBJ in background as Bobby had been—thoroughly eastern, educated at elite institutions, with a mixture of idealism and pragmatism. LBJ was poorly educated in the formal sense; very Texan in his demeanor, his accent, his storytelling; and extremely intelligent. His almost rough exterior, tall with enormous hands and big facial features, made it difficult for people easily to see the first-rate mind he possessed. He understood government better than anyone else I have ever met. Part of this was his experience as a legislator and part of it was an extraordinary innate ability with people. He could persuade, flatter, cajole, intimidate—depending on the problem and the person—and he had a sixth sense of when to apply the pressure and when to turn it off. He loved the power of the presidency and the arsenal of political weapons that go with the office. And he knew how to use them. He could be kind. He could be mean. He knew what he wanted and was determined to get it.

Succeeding John Kennedy in the presidency probably made governing more difficult for Johnson. He had relatively little expertise in foreign affairs compared to Kennedy and lacked the good looks, the easy grace of the Harvard-educated son of a wealthy father, the quick wit, the carefully cultivated charm of the eastern elite. His skill was in the legislative process, the winning of support, the knowledge of a person's strengths and weaknesses, the wheeling and dealing that put together legislative majorities. That contrast was rarely to his advantage. It made him easy to caricature, and it made it easy to see his faults and be blind to his considerable strengths. In retrospect, I think Bobby's dislike was rooted in that contrast. It was difficult to see this man as the idealist I believe he was, in part because he never would have acknowledged those dreams to anyone, perhaps not even to himself. He loved politics because he was good at it. But he never lost sight of the fact that government had goals, and politics was a means, not an end.

During the several months I was acting attorney general and LBJ was trying to make up his mind as to whether he could trust someone close to Bobby as AG, he always treated me with respect. I had been concerned that he would turn to close colleagues to give him legal advice—to Abe Fortas, or Jim Rowe, or Clark Clifford, for example—but while he may have tested what I said with them, he always took my advice. Neither then nor after he named me attorney general can I recall any occasion when he wanted me to act in any way I thought improper or to do any favors for political reasons. I was repeatedly flattered that he sought my advice and, after some discussion, followed it. At all times I felt completely comfortable from an ethical viewpoint.

Despite the bias I began with, inherent in our different backgrounds and undoubtedly inflamed by Bobby's dislike of him, I began to feel comfortable with this president. He called me with some frequency on the phone, usually about civil rights but occasionally about other stories in the news. I kept him informed of matters that I thought might get the attention of the press or someone in Congress, usually through his assistant for domestic affairs, Joe Califano. Joe was a great help in keeping me informed of what the president was thinking and accurately reporting my views to him. Joe was an excellent lawyer and an honest broker. If the president did not like my advice he would call me, but more often than not Joe explained it to him persuasively. I disliked calling the president directly unless it was really necessary, because I never knew what he was doing or who was with him, and I hesitated to disturb him if he was in the midst of something important.

Far more often he called me to inquire about some story he had read in the newspaper or heard on TV. Like all presidents, he was always concerned about leaks to the press, but there were few from the Justice Department, because lawyers are used to constraints of confidentiality about cases and the good ones hate press conferences. Nonetheless, leaks can happen, and I remember one vividly, though I have forgotten the subject matter. A reporter called me with a story that was both wrong and damaging about some proposed changes, I think, in legislation. When he insisted that my "no comment" would lead him to publish, I told him where the story was mistaken. The next morning I got a call from the president.

"Nick, did you see that front-page story in the *Post*? It had to come from Justice."

"Yes, Mr. President."

"I want you to find who leaked that story and fire him."

"I'm afraid I can't do that, Mr. President."

"What the hell do you mean you can't do that?" He was angry.

"Mr. President, you're the only person who can do that. I leaked the story."

Silence, then a chuckle. "By God, that's the first leak in government I've ever uncovered!"

And that was that. But I heard him complain often about other leaks, sometimes bitterly. And he occasionally acted in an almost childish manner when news he had been planning to announce leaked out. I remember he intended to appoint Lloyd Cutler as undersecretary of commerce, but when that possibility appeared in the paper, he changed his mind. And I recall once he was chuckling when I entered his office shortly after another cabinet officer had departed.

"What's the joke?" I asked.

"Tomorrow Drew Pearson will report that I'm going to name so-and-so to . . ." He named the person and the post.

"How do you know?" I asked.

"Because that's what I just told your cabinet colleague, and I'll bet he can't wait to tell Drew."

"So what's so funny?"

"It isn't true," said the president, laughing even harder.

In actuality I think many of the leaks that bother presidents come from the Oval Office itself.

I had to put together my staff in Justice to replace the assistant attorneys general who had resigned after the election, and the president did not try to put in his own people or foist off some political obligations on me. He made one or two suggestions but left the decisions up to me. The recommendations he did make were fine. Indeed, on occasion they were almost amusing. I had found a very able tax lawyer who, after twenty-odd years in practice with a major firm, was teaching at a noted law school. When I sent his name and résumé to the president, LBJ called me.

"I don't want another academic in the Justice Department heading the Tax Division. I want a skilled practitioner."

I pointed out that my candidate fitted that requirement after years of practice.

"Yes," said the president, changing ground. "But I don't know him. I want someone I know. It's a very sensitive position."

"Mr. President, how many tax lawyers do you know?" I asked. "I doubt you know any except Carolyn Agger."

Carolyn, Abe Fortas's wife and law partner, prepared LBJ's tax returns.

He laughed. "You're wrong. I know Mitch Rogovin and Mort Caplin." Mort was head of the Internal Revenue Service and Mitchell Rogovin was his general counsel.

"Well," I said, "Carolyn won't take the job, and neither will Mort. Can I have Mitch if I can persuade him to come?"

"Okay," he said. And I did.

I had suggested Ramsey Clark as my deputy because I knew the president wanted him, and I was confident I could continue to work with him. I recommended another Texan, Barefoot Sanders, to head the Civil Division. I had worked with him at the time of President Kennedy's assassination and come to have a very high opinion of him, as had Bobby. The Criminal Division was tough. Jim Vorenberg was running the Crime Commission, and my other choice had just been made dean of a prominent midwestern law school. The president suggested Fred Vinson (I suspect the name came from Fortas), son of the former chief justice. I checked Fred out, and he got, and deserved, high marks, so I accepted him. The closest LBJ came to seeking a political favor was his suggestion of Ed Weisl. Ed was young but had a good academic record, and his father, a close friend of the president's, was a distinguished lawyer. I discussed the appointment with Ramsey, since I had in mind his old post as head of the Lands Division, and Ramsey thought he would be fine. As it turned out, he was. To head Antitrust I recommended Professor Donald Turner of Harvard, probably the country's most highly regarded antitrust authority, and the president agreed. It was a good team in which I could have confidence as to both ability and integrity. Perhaps of equal importance, I did not feel I had to watch my back. They were people I felt I could count on.

President Johnson and I were too different in background and life-style to become close in any but a professional sense. The same could be said of Bobby and me, although Bobby was a far more open person. But I did feel with both that my relationship was friendly and relaxed, without any hidden agenda. I respected the president as a person as well as president, and as he grew to trust me, he was more relaxed and friendly with me. To some of his staff I remained an outsider, a Kennedy crony, but by others, such as Moyers and Valenti, I felt accepted.

I went quite faithfully to cabinet meetings, not because they were particularly interesting or important, but simply because (remembering Bobby) I did not want the president to feel I was not on his team. He quite regularly singled me out to say something on civil rights, because it was important to him. This was especially true when we had the Voting Rights Act before Congress. LBJ knew his legislative program and often knew it better than some of his cabinet officers knew their piece of it. Particularly after the 1964 election, he was constantly prodding all of us to get legislation passed while we had a large Democratic majority, because he did not think we would have it after the midterm elections.

In the public mind, cabinet meetings are important. In some respects they may be, but they are not meetings where policy is determined or decisions are made. It is useful for the president to gather his team together from time to time, particularly at the beginning of an administration, when cabinet members do not know each other well, or when, for the same get-acquainted reason, there are new cabinet appointments. Meetings can also be useful for the president to explain a policy that is getting public attention, particularly critical attention, so the members know the party line. In addition, President Johnson used them to push and explain his legislative program so all would understand what was going on and help each other where they could. Often meetings were held with no particular purpose that I could discern.

It was, of course, very exciting to spend so much time in the White House, talking with the president, something I had never imagined I would ever be doing. Add to that the magnificent White House state dinners at which Lydia and I were regular guests. LBJ liked Lydia because she was unlike many cabinet wives, having her own views, which were intelligent, often from a different perspective from most of Washington society's, and anything but carefully politically honed. She also was particularly good at getting people to talk, usually about their favorite subject, which generally turned out to be themselves. It is a quality that makes her a superb psychoanalyst. President Johnson was an interested observer who instinctively saw exactly what she was doing even when he succumbed to it himself. She also has a maverick quality that he (like her husband) found appealing.

State dinners are full of pomp and ceremony and the kind of events you remember for a long time—if you do not go to too many. The food and wine are excellent, and the various service orchestras provide some beautiful background music. The company can be fascinating or boring—that's luck of the draw. There is an inevitable sameness about them, but in fairness, it is a quite lovely sameness. Washington society thrives on them, as do business moguls and Hollywood stars.

Of more interest and intimacy were the invitations for a weekend at Camp David. Lydia and I would go to the White House on Saturday and fly to Camp David from the White House lawn with other guests on one of the presidential helicopters. It was a relatively short flight, thirty or forty minutes to the mountain retreat created by the WPA and run by the navy for FDR, who named it Shangri-La, after the place in James Hilton's *Lost Horizon*. It was renamed by President Eisenhower for his grandson, David. Isolated from the public and hidden in a part of the beautiful Catoctin Mountain Park near Hagerstown, Maryland, it consists of several log cabins for meetings, entertainment, sleeping accommodations, and recreation facilities. There are bowling alleys, tennis courts, a putting green, and a large swimming pool. Dress is informal, and there are several beautiful nature walks to be enjoyed.

Weekend guests can be as varied as the president wishes, and the weekend can be devoted to recreation or to business, or some of both. I am not sure LBJ ever really relaxed, except perhaps back home on his ranch in Texas. Our visits to Camp David usually included some members of his White House staff, another cabinet member, and an outside guest or two, all with spouses. There would be a business meeting in the afternoon, and then free time the rest of the weekend. Dinner was lavish but informal—sometimes a Texas barbecue, quite a contrast from the White House. After dinner there would be the latest first-run movie. I found it interesting that the president could never sit through more than a few minutes of a moving picture. He was far too keyed up and active to be a passive viewer.

I recall on one occasion the outside guest was Billy Graham, which meant a sermon on Sunday morning. Lydia was less than excited at the prospect. With an uncle as a former canon of the Washington Cathedral and a cousin as Episcopal bishop of Massachusetts, she had had all the formal religion she felt she needed at a young age and doubted Billy Graham's ability to rekindle piety. Nonetheless, we dutifully attended the sermon. Such is the power of the president!

That afternoon we were sitting by the swimming pool, and the president, in a deck chair a few yards from us, spent the whole time on the telephone instead of relaxing like the rest of us. I could not help wondering if some international crisis was brewing in some far corner of the world, or if Vietnam was exploding. Finally I asked Bill Moyers.

"No crisis," he responded. "He's talking to friends in Texas about what's going on in local politics."

On reflection, I think that is how LBJ relaxed.

While he used Camp David, as all presidents have, as a means of getting out of Washington and the White House to a more comfortable and private setting, it was his ranch in Texas that really invigorated LBJ. It is located in the hill country of south Texas, country he loved and felt thoroughly at home in. He took enormous pride in his land and its cultivation, his friends and neighbors, "real" people who shared his love of the land. By my eastern standards it was a huge piece of property—some 500 acres—but not by the standards of his native state. He knew every inch of the ground and loved it.

I did not visit the ranch often, perhaps only three or four times. It was usually on business, and a part of the time would be spent discussing whatever problem he had on his mind. After that he would get on an old fire engine that some admirers had presented to him and drive me around—me sitting beside him in my Brooks Brothers suit and tie, LBJ driving in his ten-gallon hat, flannel shirt, and blue jeans. He would point out sights of interest, and when he saw one of his black workers in a field he would stand up (the fire engine still moving), wave his hand, sound the siren, and shout, "Come over here, boy, and meet your attorney general."

I would cringe beside him. It was almost as if he did not associate any of his workers with the civil rights leaders he regularly met with in Washington, although I am sure in fact he did. It was just a southern way of life that he was used to and felt comfortable with, just as he often did with the stories and jokes he told about blacks. They made me feel uncomfortable, but this president who did so much to secure equal rights saw no impropriety and no inconsistency between his stories, where blacks were the butt of a joke, and his convictions about racial equality.

There were deer on the ranch, and he enjoyed taking his visitors hunting. Frankly, it was not my idea of deer hunting, since it all took place seated in an old Cadillac convertible parked on a dirt road. One could shoot the deer from the seat without getting out. It did not seem to me very sporting.

On one occasion I recall, two or three Texas congressmen were in the party, one of whom was Congressman George Mahon, chair of the House Appropriations Committee. We shared the view that this was not the way of true sportsmen. At the same time the president was insistent that we hunt, and I did not wish to appear an eastern wimp in front of all these Texas he-men. At that moment, inspiration struck in the form of a brilliant legal analysis.

"Mr. President," I said, "as much as I'd like to shoot a deer, I don't think I should. I don't have a Texas hunting license and I'm not even a citizen of Texas. There are reporters around, and I'm concerned, frankly, that one of them will report that your attorney general broke the law."

LBJ looked at me. "By God, I never thought of that. You're absolutely right. I'm sorry, but it's better if you don't shoot."

Congressman Mahon winked at me.

I think it was on a visit to the ranch in December 1965, when we were discussing LBJ's coming state-of-the-union speech, that he asked me to prepare a memorandum for him proposing a constitutional amendment creating a four-year term for congressmen. The more I thought about it, the worse the idea seemed to me. It meant that the House would always or never run with the president, and that either destroyed its independence or exaggerated it. But LBJ was insistent, so I devised a complicated scheme that combined staggered four- and two-year terms, which tried to preserve the merits of having half the House running in presidential elections and half in midterm elections and staggering the two halves. I was not enamored of it, but it was the best I could do, and I still thought the existing system better.

The president liked my proposal and a similar one, unknown to me, that he had persuaded Professor Richard Neustadt of Harvard to draft. He used the four-year term in the state-of-the-union and, predictably, got a standing ovation from members of the House. The idea of not having to run for reelection every two years had instant appeal. Then came their second thoughts, critical press commentary, and the realization that such a change had far-reaching and unpredictable consequences.

LBJ retreated in a very LBJ-like way. "I knew that four-year proposal was a mistake," he would say, "but I let these two professors talk me into it. These academic types just don't understand the real world."

I ran into Dick Neustadt shortly after the president's speech, and he told me that he had been as opposed as I had to the change.

The story illustrates a side of President Johnson that I never understood. After a while I became convinced that he had persuaded himself of the truth of his comment and thought that we, not he, really had originated the proposal. But how could this possibly be the case? Yet many times I saw similar instances of statements that were not true, statements one would normally call lies. When things did not work out as he had thought they would, he was able to conjure up an explanation that had little or nothing to do with fact and then become convinced that that was how it had happened. It was, I believe why Bobby thought of him as a consummate liar and one of the reasons he lost credibility with the press and the general public on Vietnam. Over time I became convinced that, for whatever reason, this was how he remembered it and he was not consciously lying. We all tend to see ourselves in a favorable light and to engage in wishful thinking. Lyndon Johnson, being bigger than life, tended to do so on a larger scale than most of us.

One day when I was in the White House well into the early evening and the dinner hour, he surprised me with a statement and then a question. "You know, this place is a lonely place when Lady Bird is off somewhere and I'm alone. You never get to meet real folks. It's all ceremony. Why don't you invite me to dinner some night with some of your friends so I can get to know you better?"

Nothing could have surprised me more. The idea of having the president of the United States to dinner had never occurred to me. It also made me nervous.

"Okay," I stammered. "You name the date."

He did.

I went home that night for a late supper and told Lydia that the president had invited himself to dinner. As with all things, she took it in stride.

"Who shall we invite?"

That was not easy. Many of our friends were newspaper people—Tony Lewis, Joe Kraft, Sandy Vanocur, and their wives—but that seemed out. Others were closely associated with Bobby and Ethel Kennedy, and that seemed out. Finally we settled on the Jim Vorenbergs, the Frank Thompsons (my favorite congressman), and the Jean Gordons. Dr. Gordon was a psychoanalyst I had known since high school, and his wife had been a classmate of mine at Yale Law School. All were old friends of ours, although none of them knew each other. We decided not to mention the president when inviting them.

Lydia made the arrangements—not so easy when your guest is the president. But we circumvented most of the Secret Service's problems by using the Justice Department chef and hiring two waiters cleared for White House dinners. The menu was Lydia's, and as always it was both good and imaginative. We invited our guests for thirty minutes ahead of the president.

After our guests had been seated and served drinks in the living room, there was a knock on the front door, and Lydia went out to greet LBJ. You could hear his booming voice in the living room, which was in the back of the house.

"Jesus!" said Jim. "Is that who I think it is?"

It was an interesting evening, and I think the president enjoyed himself. He did most of the talking. Some of it was stories, often with a racial joke; he was oblivious of the black waiters. When we went to the living room after dinner, Lydia said, "Mr. President, we don't know much about your childhood. Why don't you tell us something about it?"

LBJ then began some fascinating reminiscences of his parents and childhood in south Texas. I think Dr. Gordon and my wife particularly enjoyed his stories, and I could almost hear the psychoanalytic gears grinding when he described his mother dressing his brother in girls' clothes.

There was not, to my recollection, any discussion of current politics, civil rights, or Vietnam. I doubt there was another dinner party in Washington that night about which the same could be said.

XX

DESPITE THE EXCITEMENT OF BEING ATTORNEY GENERAL AND ALL THE lavish social life that involved, in 1966 the atmosphere in Washington became almost depressing for me. The excitement of new civil rights initiatives and dealing with violent crises was diminishing as black voters got registered throughout the South—which was exciting for them but not a crisis for us. The previous year had been dominated by my appointment as attorney general, the Voting Rights Act, the creation of the Crime Commission, and the passage of the Immigration Act, which eliminated national quotas and was signed by the president with great fanfare on Ellis Island. As 1966 progressed, Vietnam more and more dominated the news. Dr. King took his crusade north to Mayor Daley's Chicago and began to demonstrate for peace in Vietnam. The youth of America were turning from demonstrating for civil rights to protesting the war, and prosecuting draft evaders and draft card burners seemed to be the growing mission of the Justice Department.

I felt almost burned out. Much of the excitement was gone. I had no desire to prosecute Muhammad Ali, the great boxing champion, for draft evasion by questioning his claim to be a conscientious objector or young people who burned draft cards—if indeed they were not just faking it, as was often the case. The FBI was busy looking for Communist influence in every demonstration and in every youth organization opposed to Vietnam, and Hoover was still grumbling over the dispute with Bobby about who had authorized the bug in the *Black* case.

It was on such a day in early fall that I received a call from the president. "Nick, George Ball wants to resign as undersecretary of state, and

I have some names of possible successors. I'd like to have your thoughts on them."

He named two or three people, none of whom I thought particularly strong. Ball had been strong in his pessimism about Vietnam and his opposition to escalating the war. The fact that his opposition had not prevailed did not mean that his voice was unimportant. The president's suggestions for his successor were far more hawkish.

It was not the first time the president had sought my views on personnel outside Justice, and while I was sure he was asking many others as well, I was flattered and pleased, as always, that he asked me. I expressed some of my reservations about the names he had given, and then, to my utter amazement and I expect his as well, said, "Mr. President, may I make a suggestion for the job?"

"Sure. Who do you have in mind?"

"Me."

"Are you serious? You'd take the job?"

"Absolutely. I've always been interested in the State Department."

He paused a minute. "Well, I can't let you go. I need you right where you are."

After he had rung off, I thought about my spontaneous and totally unpremeditated act of volunteering. I did not regret it, but I certainly had not thought it through. Johnson's presidency was getting to be dominated by Vietnam as it had been earlier by civil rights, and I was no longer in the eye of the storm and thus was unable to influence direction. I knew little about Vietnam, but it seemed to me from afar and ignorance that there ought to be a way to put the killing to an end. If so, I would like to try. For whatever reason, I was increasingly dissatisfied with what I was doing at Justice, where we seemed to be just marking time.

I doubted anything would come of my offer. I did not mention it to anyone but Lydia. And for some time nothing did.

Then, late one afternoon at a meeting of the Crime Commission—I think it was the final formal meeting—I got a call from the president. "You still want to be undersecretary of state?"

"Yes, sir."

"I talked to Secretary Rusk, and he says he would be delighted to have you. Would you recommend Ramsey to succeed you?"

"Yes, Mr. President. I think he would be a good appointment. The civil rights leaders all like him."

"That's what I thought you'd say. Of course, his father would have to resign from the Supreme Court if I appointed Ramsey, to avoid any conflict."

"I really don't think that's necessary, Mr. President. As long as he doesn't sign the briefs or appear before the Court, there's plenty of precedent that no conflict exists."

"Oh, no," said the president. "I've talked to Tom Clark, and he agrees with me and says he will resign. So I'm going to go ahead with your appointment, and I would like to announce it tomorrow."

"Okay," I said with a gasp. It was not so much that Dean Rusk approved of me, which I did not doubt, but the fact that LBJ would gain another appointment to the Court that had led to his change of heart.

That gave me a lot to do. I had to tell my staff in Justice, and I knew that would be difficult; some would be unhappy and all somewhat mystified as to why I would voluntarily give up a cabinet post for a formally lesser position. I did so late that afternoon, and it was a pretty grim session. I felt as though I were jumping ship and leaving some good friends behind. Maybe I was making a mistake. Yet this was no longer the department populated by old friends from years back—from law school and even before. Gone were Burke, Byron, John Douglas, John Doar, Lou Oberdorfer. While their replacements were able and loyal, I did not feel the same ties of affection and common purpose that old friends have.

Jack Rosenthal stayed on after the meeting and told me that he would like to go to State with me, not as a public information officer but in a substantive position as my special assistant. I had no doubt that I could pick my own staff, and Jack's willingness to help cheered me up no end after the rather somber meeting. That he would do well in a substantive position was beyond question. Like all really good newspaper people, he was bright, curious, and knew how to ask the right questions. It would be a comfort to have a familiar face and a person I totally trusted go with me. I was a lot less confident that I was making the right move than I had been when I spoke to the president. While I knew international law and had even coauthored a book on the interplay of international law and international politics, I had almost no experience in international affairs or diplomacy. The confidence I had in my ability as a lawyer did not automatically translate into confidence in my new post.

Jack helped me put together a really exceptional staff. As my second assistant, Jack found Lawrence Eagleburger, and we hit it off from the start. Larry was a Republican who had been in the Foreign Service and was persuaded to return. He knew the people, was tough and exacting in his demands for excellence when he received memos or asked for information, and was an enormous help. I was not alone in my admiration. Later in his career he was deputy secretary, and he then succeeded James Baker as secretary of state. He was direct and candid, never hesitating to tell me if he thought I was wrong. He did not have the reserve of a typical Foreign Service officer and could be counted on for honest opinion. The final member of my little team was John Franklin Campbell, a young Foreign Service officer who had worked for George Ball and would be useful in the transition.

I wanted people around me who were bright, knowledgeable, and not afraid to speak their minds. The only way I can deal with policy problems is to hear different viewpoints and have frank discussion of issues. If I am wrong, I want to be told so, and why. I want to explore alternatives and be satisfied that other possibilities have been examined. But I do not want those discussions to leave the room, because the questions I ask or the hypotheses I suggest may not reflect my views. Those who know me are used to this approach. That was the way I had tried to run Justice, and it was the way I wanted to learn my new responsibilities. It is the way I believe government officials, including the president, should be informed about decisions they must make. With this team, along with Benjamin Read, who ran the secretariat and kept both the secretary and me informed as to what was going on, I felt as comfortable as possible for one in such unfamiliar surroundings. The secretariat is in a sense the nerve center of the department, to which the most important cables or memoranda come. It is located between the offices of the secretary and the undersecretary, and both count on its head to know where the latest crisis is.

Before I began my new job, President Johnson gave me some thoughts. He wanted me to make a priority of exploring a negotiated peace in Vietnam along every avenue possible. Vietnam was getting in the way of the Great Society, and he desperately wanted to get the United States out on honorable terms if that was possible. Both escalating costs and criticism were adversely affecting legislation and, more important, budget requirements. Second, he wanted me to look at personnel in the State Department, because despite his admiration for Rusk, he felt that the department was simply not responsive to the president (shades of President Kennedy's similar frustration, shared by Bobby, though I did not mention that similarity of view). It took too long to get an answer to his questions. Third, I should take a trip through Africa and talk about what we had accomplished with respect to civil rights here in the United States. He had suggested this latter project while I was AG, so it did not come as a surprise.

XXI

AFTER ALMOST SIX YEARS OF COMMUTING FROM OUR HOME IN Cleveland Park to the Justice Department, it was strange to go to Foggy Bottom. Despite some familiar faces and new but friendly ones, I felt a stranger in my new, modern offices. It was difficult not to wonder if I had been temporarily insane in volunteering to take this job.

Dean Rusk could not have been more welcoming and went out of his way to make me feel comfortable in my new surroundings. Throughout my time in the department he was always available, helpful, friendly, and kind. He knew we had some disagreements on Vietnam, on personnel policy, and on administration, but he also knew I took those disagreements to him, not to the public or the president. We got along well, even though I could never understand just who Dean Rusk was or what he wanted his world to look like. He was a very private, very self-controlled person.

I joined the department shortly before the annual dinner for all the Washington ambassadors. Virginia Rusk had planned an imaginative menu, which had famous specialties from various states around the country, which she shared with Lydia. Lydia brought me the menu and the invitations, saying that the menu was fine but the invitations would never do. It took only a minute to see why. Each invitation contained a reproduction of a beautiful old engraving of a New Orleans kitchen, replete with black slaves. Lydia said she had mentioned it to Virginia, who did not seem concerned. I knew Dean was from Georgia, but I also knew he was a strong and courageous supporter of civil rights. In some embarrassment, I showed him the invitation, muttering something about

African ambassadors and my own role in civil rights. Dean saw the problem instantly and told me not to worry, that he would take care of it.

In a sense he did. When the invitations went out, the picture had been touched up. The slaves were now all white. What the ambassadors from African countries thought, I never found out. But in a way it was Dean's method of fixing a problem.

I had a lot to learn about the department, and I set about trying to do so. Much of my time was spent reading the intelligence briefings and then the more important cables from our embassies around the world, along with our replies. With little background, there was not much I could contribute substantively, but just reading them and asking questions was a good way to get familiar with my job. Ben Read was great at giving me background and recent history, telling me Rusk's views to the extent he knew them. Larry Eagleburger had already read most of them by the time I got to the office and was prepared to help me understand the substance. They were good teachers, and I began to feel comfortable with the routine fairly quickly.

In addition, I tried to meet and learn from the various senior officials, some of whom I knew and many of whom I did not. This included such outstanding statesmen as Averell Harriman and Ambassadors Llewellyn Thompson and Foy Kohler (both experienced Soviet experts). In addition there was Arthur Goldberg, now our UN ambassador; Eugene Rostow, the undersecretary for political affairs (who had been dean at Yale Law School when I taught there); Robert Bowie (a Harvard Law professor with the title of counselor), and the various assistant secretaries, with either regional responsibilities such as Europe, Latin America, Africa, East Asia, or functional ones such as the UN, NATO, intelligence, legal adviser, and congressional relations. I discovered that one of the perks—and State had many compared to Justice—was that you could have anything from a sandwich to a fancy lunch served in your office, with wine and cocktails to boot! This made it possible to learn what was going on in a pleasant way. I tried hard to encourage some of the informality that Bobby had been so good at promoting in Justice. I wanted to know what people were thinking, not just the official policy of the department, and to some extent I succeeded. But at State it often went against the grain, particularly with the younger officers, and with everyone except Averell Harriman there was a caution in straying from department policy. It was difficult to have a discussion about the pros and cons of what we were doing in various parts of the world, what alternatives were worth considering, what the risks of failure were. It was hard for me to accept that everything was going well or even as anticipated when I looked at the problems of dictatorships of the right or left in Latin America and elsewhere. Perhaps it was respect for the secretary. Perhaps it was fear of politicizing the department, which was far from my intent. There were still memories of Joe McCarthy and his Communist witch hunt.

Our post–World War II foreign policy was largely a function of containing the Soviet Union and its Communist allies. Constructed by such foreign policy greats as George Marshall, Dean Acheson, and George Kennan, it employed a series of military alliances such as NATO, SEATO, and CENTO, coupled with regional organizations such as the Organization of American States, the European Community, and the United Nations and its agencies. For most of the postwar era, the United States effectively used its economic power to control this array of economic, political, and military institutions. It was difficult for countries to maintain a neutral posture between the two superpowers, and neither encouraged it.

The policy of containment—the so-called cold war—was not an issue politically at home. Both parties embraced it, and it had strong appeal to those who had fought in World War II. Veterans tended to see that bloody war in terms of British prime minister Neville Chamberlain's capitulation in negotiations at Munich and the failure to deal with Hitler's aggressive expansionism and the somewhat similar stance of Japan in Asia. There was a determination not to allow military conquest and a willingness to join collectively to prevent it. In addition, it was an obvious tactic of the Soviet bloc to foment revolution, assist Communists in overthrowing non-Communist governments, and then to consolidate the new Communist state in the Soviet or Chinese sphere of influence. Our retaliatory efforts took the form of military and economic assistance programs to bolster non-Communist governments.

My purpose here is not to review our foreign policy, nor did I go to the State Department with any intention to argue for major changes. What I had not fully appreciated was the effect of this seemingly simple policy on the department. The cold war had led to the huge growth of our foreign policy apparatus in a relatively short time—not simply the State Department, but also the Department of Defense (including its massive technical intelligence effort) and other departments in foreign economic assistance, food programs, arms control, and so forth, not to mention the UN, the World Bank, and the multilateral defense, economic, and political organizations already mentioned. In all of these the State Department played a role, often a leading one, and the sheer weight of numbers created a bureaucracy of horrendous proportions. More important, these other players meant that the State Department was rapidly losing its leading role in foreign affairs, because in terms of money and numbers of Americans engaged in foreign affairs, it was a poor relation. Fewer than 5 percent of the government officials stationed overseas were State Department employees.

Going from Justice (where we rarely had to coordinate with anyone) to State soon made me conscious of the difference. To some extent, the building itself reflected the change. My office on the seventh floor was adjacent to that of the secretary and close to those of three or four other high officials. There was an enormous reception area for visitors, and getting an appointment even for relatively senior officials could often be a chore. At a minimum, one had to go through an aide first. Gone was the informality of Justice, where anyone could simply walk in to see if I was busy, or I could walk down the hall to hold a conversation with the person working on a problem. When I asked a question in Justice, I was accustomed to getting an answer quickly. In State, you had to understand the system. Otherwise it was like dropping a stone in the ocean and waiting for it to float back to the surface. It usually did, in written form, with at least twenty initials indicating those who had read it and approved. Little wonder, with so many clearances to be obtained, that the system so often was tardy in responding and then produced a bland response.

President Johnson had complained about the vanishing primacy of the department and its unresponsiveness and charged me with improving matters. I sought to get Thomas Schelling, a distinguished Harvard economist who was expert in administration theory and practice, to help reform the department. He was reluctant to take on the chore for personal reasons, particularly after he began to appreciate the enormity of it. In a sense, so was I. It was obvious that Rusk simply was not that interested, and I began to appreciate that reformation of a serious kind really should not be undertaken six years into the secretary's tenure unless it is a high priority for him. The problems really were—and I suspect still are—extremely difficult.

As I worked with Schelling, I discovered that the problem was not simply the increased multilateral aspects of foreign policy but also resulted from two other factors. First, at least thirty-four government departments and agencies now had foreign liaison duties as a result of treaties or agreements or just simply because common problems were more easily resolved by negotiation than by unilateral action. Of the almost 50,000 U.S. nondefense personnel abroad, fewer than 10 percent worked for State. Other departments and agencies also had bigger budgets, with Defense accounting for some 97 percent of the dollars

America spent abroad. Second, the personnel system at State was a mess. The rapid expansion of the Foreign Service during and after World War II had created a personnel picture that resembled an hourglass: there were a number of new recruits in grades 5 through 7, a smaller number in grades 3 and 4, and far too many in the top grades, 1 and 2. One consequence was simply that officers were getting assignments that were no better than those they had had ten years before; second, competition for promotion and good assignments was such that a single bad appraisal, or even a lukewarm one, could effectively damage a career, and as a result officers became increasingly cautious and less aggressive; and finally, the situation had led to the creation of many unnecessary jobs in attempts to occupy senior officers until something better showed up.

Foreign Service officers were recruited from the best of our college graduates, took stiff exams for entry, and began as a highly motivated, intelligent, and well-trained group. By 1967 there were serious morale problems, which in my judgment required some tough personnel decisions. I made Dean Rusk aware of the problem, but he was averse to taking the unpleasant measures necessary to turn the hourglass into a pyramid.

I recall one occasion when I said, "Dean, do you have any idea how many special assistants you have?"

"Of course," he replied. "I can count them on my fingers. It's either seven or eight." And he began to name them.

"Wrong," I said. "In fact you have fifty-nine."

I handed him a list, which he looked at and then commented, "Well, it's a policy department. Good to have a lot of senior people looking at what's going on."

While the dominant policy of containing the Soviet Union and its Communist allies was a factor in almost every decision, that did not mean there were not many potential ways of forwarding that goal. In my opinion, there were lost opportunities in Africa and Latin America— lost in part because of the difficulty of getting a large bureaucracy to come up with and test imaginative proposals. There is no question that there are many variables in foreign affairs and that it is essential to be well-informed before one acts. Often doing nothing may be the least risky course of action. But there are also times when opportunity is lost through hesitation, through unwillingness to take some risk, and it is important when one does nothing that that decision is conscious and not simply the result of lost opportunity through bureaucratic delay. It was the apparent inability of State to come up with ideas and the pros and cons of each that frustrated the Kennedys. Their style was to seek and weigh alternatives, and it was a style to which neither the department nor Dean Rusk apparently could adjust.

Given guidance, the department was very good at implementation. Foreign Service professionals were skilled at the art of explication and persuasion once policy was set. But the skill and imagination that the department had shown in coming up with a policy of Soviet containment, of rebuilding Europe through the Marshall Plan, of creating organizations such as NATO and the World Bank, seemed to me to have been lost. Yet the intelligence and skill remained, stifled, I felt, by the sheer weight of numbers and a dominant philosophy of caution.

Another piece of the problem lay in the secretary's multiple obligations. With over a hundred embassies in Washington, not to mention the various delegations to the UN, congressional committees, and meetings of multilateral organizations abroad, the secretary's calendar left little time for thought or reflection beyond reacting to the day's cables. Another secretary might have used some of his staff to explore and develop initiatives, but Dean Rusk valued his relationship with the president and, quite unlike Bobby, did not encourage his assistants to take leadership on issues or explore new ideas. I do not mean that he in any sense tried to muzzle their opinions. He was far too decent and far too professional for that. But if he did not promote or endorse their views, they went nowhere. Thus, George Ball, my predecessor as undersecretary, was free to object to the war in Vietnam and explain his views to President Johnson, but he could expect no support from Rusk, who consistently supported our forces there, although initially he too had been cautious about a troop buildup, as indeed LBJ had been.

Actually Dean was more passive than this description sounds. He once said to me that he thought it very serious if the president and the secretary were in disagreement. I thought that was both true and obvious. But he went on to say that for this reason he always wanted to know how the president felt before he offered an opinion. To me, that seemed a serious abdication of responsibility. It also helped to explain why leadership in foreign policy so often—at least in my opinion—fell to more aggressive people outside the department.

Frustrations presidents feel about the nonresponsiveness of the department may in fact often simply be the frustrations of foreign policy, of being unable to get your own way. Not only must the activities of our own bureaucracies be coordinated, but we must also get the cooperation and support of other countries. Their leaders have political problems at home just as we do, and their problems may frustrate our desires. Most of the time the events the president does not like are those that, despite everyone's best efforts, we are unable to influence as we would like, not the result of incompetence or unresponsiveness. The president's involvement in foreign affairs often comes precisely because there is no good solution from an American viewpoint and his choices are all unsatisfactory. There is often a temptation to blame the messenger for the message.

Given the enormous demands on the secretary's time, coupled with the international responsibilities of other departments and agencies, it was perhaps inevitable that much of the responsibility for foreign policy had migrated to the Security Council and its staff in the White House. Here was a mini–State Department staffed by bright people, many of them Foreign Service officers, who could get information from those they knew in the department quickly (quickly because it did not represent a department view or position) and put it together with intelligence and information from other relevant departments, and whose head had direct access to the president, with no other duties in any way comparable to those of the secretary and no need to deal with over a hundred ambassadors, the UN, regional organizations, or congressional committees.

I think President Kennedy was right to disband the mini–State Department which had built up in the White House as staff for the national security adviser and to try to make the department play its traditional role. But the temptation to move decision-making to the White House is always there, and the role of national security adviser has grown since the death of President Kennedy. Even with as scrupulous a national security adviser as McGeorge Bundy, who did his best never to go behind the back of the secretary, it was an unfair fight. The president—any president—is likely to turn to the person in the White House who is informed, near, and available for advice. The secretary of state is far too isolated and occupied with the minutiae of foreign policy around the world, except perhaps in times of crisis.

I think this institutional inability to come up with creative ideas was most importantly a result not only of the factors I have discussed but of the secretary's own personality. Dean Rusk was a foreign policy professional, not a political personage, and totally uninterested in using emerging information technology to make the department more efficient. He was almost always satisfied with the status quo if he felt it did not endanger the United States. He had little interest in remaking the world and little confidence that a great deal could be done in that regard. He had enormous respect for the president's views and saw it as his job to do his best to carry them out rather than influence them. This basic attitude was displeasing to the Kennedys, both of whom were essentially activist. President Kennedy was interested in foreign affairs and wanted to leave a mark, but he got precious little help in defining goals from Dean Rusk. On the other hand, LBJ, while an activist in domestic matters, was both inexperienced and essentially uninterested in foreign affairs. He wanted his Great Society program, and unhappily for him and his administration, Vietnam got in the way. He tended to see foreign affairs through the same domestic political glasses through which he saw all government, that is, the views of Congress and public opinion. He was less interested in the merits of the domino theory, which was the basis of our intervention in Vietnam, than he was in the domestic political consequences of a change of course.

I failed in my efforts to make over administration in the State Department, and that failure was pretty obvious to people in the department, pleasing to some and disappointing to others. The only exception was minor by comparison with what I had wanted to do. Early in 1966, LBJ created a Senior Interdepartmental Group (SIG), chaired by the undersecretary, whose members were the deputy secretary of defense, the national security adviser, the director of the CIA, the directors of the Agency for International Development (AID) and the U.S. Information Agency (USIA), and the chairman of the joint chiefs. LBJ had quite specifically intended it as an instrument to restore leadership in foreign affairs to the department. It had never interested either Rusk or George Ball and had been essentially moribund since its creation. It had a powerful membership, and I thought it might perform a role not unlike that of the Security Council and become in essence a responsive arm of the president.

My staff came up with the suggestion that if I could persuade Arthur Hartman to join my staff and run the SIG for me, it could be successful. Art was an exceptional Foreign Service officer, well trained in economics as well as diplomacy, who understandably was hesitant about the possibility of breathing life into the SIG. I promised him all the help I could deliver, and he took the job and performed beyond any expectation anyone could have had. Happily, it helped rather than hurt a brilliant career. Later he became assistant secretary for European affairs, ambassador to France, and then ambassador to the Soviet Union, performing each assignment with distinction.

His character and integrity were tested after I left the department, when he was the only other person with the combination to my safe. In it was a copy of the Pentagon Papers, the only copy apparently in State. When the study, a history of our mistakes in Vietnam, was leaked to the *New York Times* by Dr. Daniel Ellsberg, Secretary Rogers, desperate to know what it was and what it contained, ordered Arthur to open the safe. Arthur refused to do so without my permission. Rogers called me and got my permission. Frustrated as he was by the delay, he nevertheless respected Arthur for his principled stand.

Reactivating the SIG was a far call from reforming the department, but it proved extremely useful under Hartman's careful guidance. The group's value was less in what it did itself than in what it forced the various regional groups to do. To take one important example, it focused on the AID budget at different appropriation levels and forced decisions as to expenditure priorities. All the participants, as well as the various assistant secretaries of state, had differently motivated interests in how much assistance went to various countries. By forcing decisions at low expenditure levels, the SIG forced all the various agency participants to abandon their parochial views—AID was not a Christmas tree to fund their preferences—and look at the problem from a national viewpoint, as the president would look at it. Thus an order of priorities was established. The exercise resolved virtually every problem that had arisen in prior years and greatly speeded up the allocation process once the actual figures were known. While final responsibility rested with AID and the various assistant secretaries, they had the advantage of hearing and recording the views and support of Defense, CIA, USIA, Agriculture, the joint chiefs, and so forth. Matters came to the principals whether there was or was not agreement, so it was relatively easy to sort out disputes, which in fact rarely existed once they had been thoroughly vetted below.

The groups also did contingency planning, which is never popular, because the contingency seldom occurs and a lot of work is involved. But the value of the work is often not the contingency itself but the light that considering it throws on present decisions and policies. And sometimes the contingency does occur, as it did when the Czechoslovakian protest against the Soviet Union began to heat up. The president wanted a paper on the problem. I not only had a paper, I had 200 pages of backup materials and draft cables and press releases. When the actual invasion of Czechoslovakia occurred, we were able to make diplomatic responses in a couple of hours that otherwise would have taken a week or more to prepare. So it is possible to be responsive.

By the time I got to the State Department, virtually everything except possibly Israel and the Middle East was dominated by the war in Vietnam. Walt Rostow, the younger brother of Eugene Rostow and a former head of intelligence in the department, had succeeded McGeorge Bundy as national security adviser on Rusk's recommendation. As I learned to my regret, Walt was absolutely dedicated to a military solution in Vietnam, and his position made contrary positions difficult to maintain without strong support from the secretary. There was no doubt in my mind that LBJ was anxious to get out of Vietnam; it was slowly killing his greatest love, the Great Society program. At the same time, neither he nor any of his advisers was willing to consider unilateral withdrawal. Indeed, even the growing protests in and out of Congress never suggested unilateral withdrawal. Those involved protested what they saw as our unwillingness to negotiate, protesting bombing in particular as an obstacle to settlement. It is curious in retrospect to realize that even those most strongly opposed to the war felt that a settlement, as in Korea, was possible if only we tried hard enough to get it.

In a sense, there was not a big difference in what the government and the public wanted. At a minimum there had to be some kind of negotiation and political settlement that bought time before the Communists could prevail. I think there was general agreement that the north would have to stop its attacks on the south and accept two Vietnams. In the south it would have been possible to give the Vietcong a role in the government if they had stopped their efforts to overthrow it. Those terms would have been as difficult to negotiate within the U.S. government as with the South Vietnamese government, the Vietcong, and the North Vietnamese. There was not a lot of room, and the issues were too narrow.

Nonetheless, I thought it might be possible to come to agreement if we could get the other side to negotiate. And my principal reason for that probably too-optimistic view was my conviction that if LBJ ever saw a way out, he would seize on it. The problem was how on earth to get negotiations started. There were people on our side who believed a military solution was possible and who therefore had no great desire to make negotiations appear attractive to the other side. The same was true of the North Vietnamese.

If I was to have any success with respect to Vietnam, it was important that I try to learn as much as I could about the situation there. When John Campbell left my staff for an assignment in Asmara, Ethiopia, I got Jack Rosenthal to look for a person with Vietnamese experience. He recommended Anthony Lake, a young Foreign Service officer who had spent two years in Vietnam and even spoke the language. (Tony went on to become President Clinton's national security adviser.) When he joined my staff, Tony was most helpful because of his time spent in Vietnam, and was also very pessimistic about any solution that gave our efforts much reward. I think it was his suggestion that I get educated by the CIA experts. I asked Dick Helms, who now headed the agency, if it would be possible for me and a couple of members of my staff to meet one afternoon with people at CIA's Langley headquarters who were working on Vietnam and get briefed in this unusual fashion. I told him that I did not want him or George Carver, who headed the Vietnam team and did the presidential briefings, to be present, but that I wanted him to tell the team to speak their opinions frankly. In return I would promise him that I would never use any of the intelligence gained in any formal way or to support a position contrary to that put forward formally by the agency. It was purely for my own education and information, so I could evaluate news and ask questions. Somewhat to my surprise, Dick agreed.

When, on the appointed day, I arrived with my team at Langley, Dick met me with a bottle of vintage champagne.

"Why this?" I asked.

"Because you are the highest official from the State Department ever to visit CIA headquarters," he responded.

Along with Jack Rosenthal and Tony Lake, I spent the next four or five hours with perhaps twenty CIA experts, who, true to my request, were utterly candid and in frequent and quite basic disagreement with one another. What I learned was what I guess I should have known in the first place. The daily intelligence reports were a synthesis of many views and facts, often conflicting and inconclusive, reflecting the best judgment of the senior officials. What I now knew was that a number of informed and intelligent experts had both large and small doubts about that synthesis. The naiveté with which I had been reading the daily briefing was replaced by a certain amount of skepticism about how much weight one could safely put on intelligence and why it was important to ask questions about sources. To say this is not, of course, to question the good faith of senior officials. As in any report, they have to make judgments and eliminate details, and the effort to do so as objectively as possible and with awareness of the problems often present is of great importance. The danger, of course, is that a desire to please the president can lead to a loss of objectivity—the greatest sin and disservice to national security possible.

I think it is fair to say that from the time I went to State until the end of his administration, LBJ desperately wanted to get out of Vietnam but was unwilling to just cut and run. He looked, as did most people, at Korea and wanted a two-Vietnams solution. We looked at the intelligence to see if there was anything there that would suggest a willingness of the North Vietnamese and Vietcong to negotiate. That would be some indication that they were suffering unbearable losses, that they were getting discouraged and wanted some settlement. Or, alternatively, that we were doing well, that the country was becoming pacified, that the South

Vietnamese government was growing in strength and the Vietcong were losing popular support. Without clear and unequivocal evidence of this nature, there is a tendency to pick and choose and see what one wants to see. The challenge to the intelligence experts is to avoid the temptation to tell their clients what they want to hear.

If, as I believe was the case, the option of simply leaving Vietnam was not on the table, then the problem of persuading the other side to begin negotiations tended to become a debate as to how best to persuade them that it was in their interest to do so. The interest of North Vietnam was to consolidate north and south into a single Communist state. Unless they could see this result as probable in the near future, they were unlikely to come to the table. Preventing this result was the basis for our being in Vietnam. Thus we had two problems—one, convincing government hawks that we could not achieve our objective militarily, and two, communicating to North Vietnam in a convincing manner that we were no longer committed to their defeat and that a negotiation could achieve their objective for them over time—all without totally destroying our ongoing efforts in South Vietnam in the event there were no talks or they did not succeed.

The growing protests and demonstrations against the war were another problem. Clearly the participants wanted us out of Vietnam, but it was by no means clear in 1967 that a majority of the American people and certainly not a majority of Congress wanted us out on any terms. They wanted an end to the fighting, not unilateral withdrawal. We had fought in Korea and stopped the war on honorable terms, and even those of us who were most anxious to negotiate an end to the war in Vietnam thought we needed a fairly substantial fig leaf to cover our withdrawal. The truth is that both within and outside the administration, there was nothing approaching agreement as to what the terms of our withdrawal should be. Those of us who wanted out made a virtue of ambiguity in the hope that negotiations would clarify the possibilities.

It was a situation that cried out for honest public discussion, but this never took place. Whenever foreign policy objectives require the use of troops and those soldiers suffer casualties, the president needs the support of Congress and the public. If that is not forthcoming in an overwhelming manner, the policy is almost certain to fail if it has to be sustained for any length of time. Americans will rally around the flag, but they will not stay there if they view substantial casualties in a war they simply do not understand. There is a huge difference between the attack on Pearl Harbor and the so-called domino theory.

Perhaps the biggest mistake LBJ made was the Tonkin Gulf Resolution. In 1964, essentially as part of the campaign against Senator Barry Goldwater, President Johnson had used what appeared to be two attacks on U.S. destroyers in international waters as an excuse for persuading Congress to give him the broadest possible authority to use military force against the North Vietnamese and even their allies. The resolution was so broadly written that technically it would have permitted the president to invade North Vietnam and even China or the Soviet Union if he found it necessary. The floor manager of the resolution, Senator William Fulbright, admitted as much during debate, but no one worried, because in the fall of 1964 they saw the whole matter through domestic political glasses. President Johnson could be as tough as anyone with that power, but no one, including LBJ, anticipated that he would use it even to the extent he did. It is, of course, ironic that Senator Fulbright became the leading critic of the war in Vietnam.

The Tonkin Gulf Resolution put the whole burden of the war on the president. Whenever he wanted the support of Congress, or even its sense of policy, he had no vehicle to secure it. The leadership pointed to the resolution and said he had the authority to do what he thought best. What he wanted was not that lonely authority but support, and the resolution had put that beyond reach. He could, and did, tell them that they could withdraw the resolution if they did not approve of his actions. But he knew and they knew that that was not going to happen. Congress preferred to talk rather than act in such a drastic fashion. And the president would have been far better off if he had had a means of measuring both his support and his critics on the Hill in a serious fashion. Oddly, the resolution was quite contrary to his own approach to Congress and his understanding that success in the White House can be very dependent on Capitol Hill. "If you want someone in on the landing," he used to say, "you'd better be sure they are on board at the takeoff."

In the case of Vietnam, neither the Congress nor the public was ever really on board. Whether or not it would have made a difference is hard to say, but a prudent president would have welcomed congressional approval and support of the major escalation in numbers of American troops that took place in 1965, which virtually transformed the war from a civil war in which America helped Vietnam into an American war. That was a crucial difference. The fact that the Tonkin Gulf Resolution made this in effect a presidential decision rather than a new legislative proposal made testing congressional support virtually impossible. And as our position deteriorated, members of Congress were able to distance themselves from that decision. The resolution made it Lyndon Johnson's war.

In August 1967, Senator Fulbright, who chaired the Senate Foreign

Relations Committee, asked me to testify before it. I told him I was far too green at the job to do so, that the questions would all be about Vietnam and I simply was not that well informed yet. He was insistent, saying only that the hearing would not involve policy in Vietnam and he would assure me he would prevent that. I reluctantly agreed. I guess he forgot his assurance, since the hearing, and indeed his own questions, all involved Vietnam.

What the committee, including the chairman, wanted to do was attack the Tonkin Gulf Resolution. They took the position that we were at war in Vietnam but Congress had never declared war. Therefore the president was acting unconstitutionally. I could understand why Democratic members in particular were unhappy with the war and wanted to distance themselves from it, but as a legal and constitutional argument, their position was close to absurd. I pointed out that since the establishment of the UN Charter, which limited wars to those of self-defense, declarations of war were something of an anachronism, as was all the international law doctrine with respect to the consequences of a declaration, such as rights of neutrals and so forth. Aiding a government involved in a civil war at its request, as we were doing in Vietnam, was permissible under the self-defense provisons of the charter. From a constitutional point of view, the Tonkin Gulf Resolution gave the president the powers there specified (which in fact were broader than a declaration of war would probably have specified) in aid of the South Vietnamese government, and legislatively the Congress had followed exactly the same procedure authorizing the use of military force—a joint resolution requiring a two-thirds majority—that a declaration of war would have involved. Consequently, the resolution was, in my view, constitutionally the "functional equivalent" of a declaration of war.

My testimony, which I believe was correct and which is today vindicated by almost all scholars examining the problem, infuriated many members of the committee. Nor was I as patient as I should have been, since I felt the chairman had intentionally set me up and I was irritated. To be attacked by many Democrats I respected and admired, who had supported me on civil rights, for giving what I thought was a pretty clearly correct legal opinion was a new experience for me, and one I certainly did not enjoy. Senator Eugene McCarthy was so angry that he said my testimony was the determining factor in his decision to run against LBJ for the Democratic presidential nomination in 1968. Even my friends and neighbors on Martha's Vineyard got into the act, denouncing my testimony. Since I suspect that none of the distinguished authors and artists who signed a full-page ad in the *Vineyard Gazette* strongly criticizing me had read my testimony, I thought this a low blow.

It had its amusing moments. Senator Wayne Morse, who a few months before had praised me as a great constitutional scholar, changed his mind and pointedly criticized my testimony on the floor of the Senate as uninformed and ignorant, particularly my statement that I thought declarations of war (not, please note, congressional authorization of the use of armed forces on any substantial scale) an anachronism. No provision of our beloved Constitution could be called an anachronism in his view. I wrote him a short note, tongue in cheek, pointing out that in the same sentence that gives Congress the power to declare war, the Constitution also gives it (not the president) the power to issue "letters of marque and reprisal" and inquiring if he had any in mind. Such letters were issued in colonial days to private parties (often called "privateers") with vessels on the high seas, authorizing them to attack and loot enemy merchant vessels. He telephoned me to say he was working on it and would let me know.

The reaction was also instructive because it demonstrated how deeply some in Congress felt about the war in Vietnam and how divided the country (and the Congress) was. Dissidents understandably felt that their approval of presidential authority in the Tonkin Gulf Resolution was being used to involve them in a war they had never seriously intended to happen. They were looking for reasons that the resolution did not really mean what it unfortunately said. That reaction was understandable. In context—during an election year, with the adversary Republican, Barry Goldwater, talking far more aggressively than LBJ—the resolution had been seen, and to a substantial extent marketed, as a meaningless political ploy. Now its very broad language had risen to bite them. But it seems to me that the president was the real victim. He got what he asked for, and it was far too much. He had to bear the burden of an increasingly unpopular war alone.

Perhaps it is always thus and the president has to pull the laboring oar. But if he can involve the Congress, it either provides much-needed support or demonstrates the need to cut his losses. The president alone, despite his bully pulpit, simply cannot hold the overwhelming public support he needs for any length of time without the strong support of Congress. It is not, as it is often made to appear, a constitutional problem nearly as much as a practical political one.

XXII

I TOOK MY FIRST TRIP TO VIETNAM IN OCTOBER 1966 WITH SECRETARY McNamara. I was accompanied by Jack Rosenthal. I knew that I would be tied up in official military briefings and other show-and-tell activities, so I thought Jack might be able to get facts I would not from his extensive contacts with reporters covering the war. In addition, Jack made the interesting suggestion that we take along Daniel Ellsberg (of later notoriety during the Nixon administration because of the Pentagon Papers), whom he had run into while lunching at the State Department cafeteria. He knew Ellsberg slightly from Harvard, where Ellsberg, a doctoral candidate, had sometimes hung around the offices of the *Crimson* when Jack was its editor. Both of us were aware of Ellsberg's work with Colonel Edward Lansdale, an administration expert on insurgency. Lansdale was something of a mysterious figure who had been in the OSS during World War II, then in the CIA in the Far East. He had been a political adviser to Ngo Dinh Diem (the president of South Vietnam, assassinated by Vietnamese generals in 1963), had managed some unsuccessful undercover operations against North Vietnam, and was currently a Pentagon official advising on Vietnam.

Ellsberg was a political scientist with a Ph.D. from Harvard who had served for two years in the Marine Corps in Vietnam, then with the Rand Corporation, and was currently working for Lansdale in the Pentagon. He was somewhat reluctant to go back to Vietnam, but I think he saw the possibility of face-to-face discussions with McNamara as too good to turn down. Neither he nor Dr. Henry Kissinger, whom McNamara had invited, was particularly modest about his knowledge.

We traveled in one of McNamara's converted Boeing 707 tankers. Bob had redesigned these planes for executive travel to places like Vietnam. They were gloomy but efficient. There were a few seats up front for additional air crew and occasionally reporters, then a series of perhaps twelve or so bunks, like those in a railway sleeping car, for passengers. The rear had comfortable seats and tables for working or eating and a galley. There were virtually no windows, just a few tiny ones that let in little light and provided little view. The plane had substantial range, making Vietnam with a single refueling stop, normally Manila or Alaska.

On the trip over, in addition to sleeping and eating, I got to know Kissinger and Ellsberg a little. I shall never forget Dr. Kissinger, dressed in a bright orange jumpsuit, lecturing on the Soviet Union, the cold war, and related matters. Both men impressed me in different ways. I made a mental note that Kissinger could be a most useful person in carrying confidential messages to the other side, because of his broad acquaintances in professional and academic circles in Europe and his own thoroughly professional demeanor. Ellsberg I found interesting for his knowledge of Vietnam and our presence there. He was highly critical of the way we were conducting the war and extremely pessimistic about its outcome. I thought he might well be right, but I wondered if we were capable of doing it differently. Both McNamara and I listened with interest to both men.

The long flight, coupled with the roughly twelve-hour time difference, made me grateful for McNamara's Pullman bunks. One thing Bobby Kennedy and Bob McNamara had in common was the idea that travel was a waste of valuable time. Therefore one should work as hard as possible on a flight, get some sleep, and arrive at one's destination ready to go to work some more. The converted 707s made this possible.

We arrived at Ton Son Nut Airport in Saigon in midmorning and were met by the top civilian and military brass. A line of khaki army sedans drove out to the plane to escort us to our destinations, one passenger with escort per vehicle. Ambassador Henry Cabot Lodge escorted Bob McNamara, and the deputy chief of mission, Philip Habib, took me to the ambassador's residence where we were staying. I had never met Habib and was instantly impressed with both his knowledge and his candor. As I got to know him better over the next several months, I realized what a really able diplomat he was. He was the best of the Foreign Service.

After a brief opportunity to freshen up, we went to headquarters for our briefings from General William Westmoreland, the commanding officer in Vietnam, and his staff. Army briefings for visiting brass are extremely well organized and informative, but it is difficult to avoid feeling that the information you get is the information the army wants you to have. I do not mean that it is intentionally deceptive or that you are not being told what the army believes is important. But the discussion was in startling contrast to Ellsberg's views on the difficulties of restoring peace to the south. Here there were slides and charts and facts and figures, all carefully rehearsed and delivered with military precision. While, to be sure, problems were mentioned, the war was going very well indeed. At the same time, nothing very encouraging was said about political developments, the support of the people for the South Vietnamese government, or the ability of its army to keep the peace, now or in the foreseeable future. Although the briefings were designedly upbeat, I did not feel particularly encouraged.

I think it is important for government officials and members of Congress to visit trouble spots to get a firsthand impression of how things are going. It is important for those on the scene to have the opportunity to talk with people from Washington, and even to register concerns they may have about some aspects of a problem. But at the same time it is very difficult to get a balanced picture, particularly in a group discussion. To some extent those on the spot have to believe that they are making progress, that things are not going badly, just to keep up their morale. You can only get a rounded picture if people are willing to talk candidly about problems, something neither military personnel nor bureaucrats will do if they are concerned about what their superiors, or even some of their colleagues, will think of their assessment. And even then it is hard to know if the pessimism is justified or just some fatigue speaking.

Vietnam was a new experience for the United States, evolving as it did from the familiar task of providing military and economic aid to bolster a friendly government in a struggle with dissident Communist revolutionary activities. If the government we are aiding cannot cope with its internal civil strife with our help, we have essentially two choices: first, provide more assistance in the form of combat troops, not simply weapons and American advisers, or, second, withdraw. Withdrawal carries the stigma of defeat and is unlikely to be a popular political choice even among those concerned about the cost of war in human lives and money. Surely there must be a third way—a negotiated stalemate perhaps, as in Korea. But Vietnam was not Korea, where Chinese intervention had made the military situation resemble traditional warfare, not the hit-or-miss tactics of a civil uprising. In Vietnam there was some of both, in part because for political reasons, the military was limited in its tactical options. It could not invade North Vietnam, or Laos or Cambodia, which were supply points and havens for the enemy from which it could launch attacks and then retreat.

President Johnson, who thought most often in domestic political terms, saw Vietnam as a second China. We had "lost" China because we had failed to give Chiang Kai-shek enough aid to prevent the Communist takeover under Mao Tse-tung. That had led to large domestic consequences in the United States, with the anti-Communist activities of Senator Joseph McCarthy and similar right-wing extremists. Given the size of China and its potential importance in world politics, the analogy was something less than perfect. But it was the way LBJ saw it from the outset, and once the huge commitment of troops had been made, it was that much more difficult to change course. In a very real sense we were no longer simply assisting the South Vietnamese government but were committed to its survival whatever the cost.

That evening Bob McNamara and I had dinner with Ambassador Lodge at his residence. Lodge had served two difficult years in the post and was retiring. He too was optimistic that progress was being made, although just what that meant was hard to measure. The only way to measure political progress that I could see was the number of attacks, incidents, and acts of violence against the South Vietnamese and ourselves. These continued apace, although the Vietcong, and perhaps to a lesser extent the regular North Vietnamese army, were suffering heavy casualties. Westmoreland and Lodge took satisfaction in this fact, presumably on the theory that heavy casualties would eventually cool our opponents' ardor and their capacity to unite Vietnam under Communist rule. Nobody knew how many losses were too many losses or when any break in will might come.

One observation was that once the military arrives in substantial force, the role of our political representatives is inevitably diminished. This is not because the military necessarily wishes this result. It simply occurs because the power is with the army, the money is with the army, the crucial decisions are the army's to make. One result is that ambassadors almost always support the recommendations to Washington that come from the military commanders.

I must say I was more impressed with the fish at dinner, which came from the Saigon River, than I was with the discussion. It was amazing to me that such a delicious fish could come from a river that was little more than an open sewer.

The next morning we took a helicopter ride north over the so-called Demilitarized Zone, or DMZ. The helicopter flew close to 10,000 feet to avoid any enemy fire, and I was uncomfortable all the way, though I struggled not to show it. The chopper had six or so seats facing out on each side, and the sides were completely open so troops could jump quickly onto the ground and the helicopter take off again. The last seat on each side was occupied by a soldier with a machine gun. My problem, for no reason at all, was a lack of confidence in the seat belt as I looked at the ground, two miles beneath me, and throughout I kept holding on tightly to the seat itself. I envied the soldier, who swung his feet casually out in the air as he turned to look around.

General Westmoreland sat between McNamara and me and kept up a running monologue of explanation about what we were seeing on the ground—mostly supply routes of one kind or another down from the north. I have no idea what the purpose of the trip was, except perhaps to demonstrate the difficulties the general was up against and perhaps to test us a little on whether the rules of engagement might be modified. While that did not seem to me likely without real risk of widening the war, as had happened in Korea, I did feel genuine sympathy for the soldiers. They could not pursue the enemy and its source of supplies, as they had been trained to do, and yet were expected to produce quick results, fighting a war for which they had not been trained, in a country in which they could not speak the language, a war without fronts and battle lines, where it was often impossible to tell who was on which side. It is difficult when you find that your friendly guide is actually a spy for the Vietcong.

The next day McNamara spent going over military requests and budget with Westmoreland and his staff, and I joined up with Jack Rosenthal. I wanted to get out of Saigon and get a sense of the countryside. So we got hold of a jeep and were joined by Ward Just, at that time a correspondent for the *Washington Post*, who had been in Vietnam for almost two years. I cannot say I learned much about Vietnam by looking out on the deceptively peaceful countryside, with men and women laboring in the fields and rice paddies, but I learned a good deal from Ward. He simply did not think our war of attrition was going to work, and I began to suspect he might well be right. Not only was it unlikely to stop the Communist revolution to unite Vietnam, but it was a policy that was extremely distasteful to much of the American public.

The final morning of our visit, Ambassador Lodge took McNamara and me to pay a courtesy call on South Vietnam's prime minister, Nguyen Cao Ky. The conversation was courteous and generally upbeat, but I did not learn much of interest. The problem, as it always was, concerned time, not progress. Progress was difficult to measure. When could the South Vietnamese create a government sufficiently supported by the people to discourage the Vietcong from taking over and the north from seeking to consolidate Vietnam under a Communist government? Progress was measured in numbers and seriousness of incidents, in casualties, in isolated examples of success. But those numbers, often questionable in themselves, never answered the fundamental question of how long this would go on before some kind of normal life returned to the country. It was obviously going to take time, and time at home appeared a diminishing asset. When one tried to measure progress in terms of time, there was never a good answer. It always came out in years, not weeks or months.

Our trip back to Washington was uneventful. Discussions on the airplane indicated that no one was particularly happy about the situation in Vietnam, although some of us were more pessimistic than others. Was there any way, I wondered, that the North Vietnamese could be brought to negotiate? No one was very optimistic, but Kissinger thought it might be possible through some of the French Communists he knew and promised to keep in touch with them and us.

XXIII

SHORTLY AFTER THE BEGINNING OF 1967, I BEGAN MAKING PLANS FOR an African trip. The Kennedy administration had begun with high hopes for developing viable nations in Africa from the former British, French, and Belgium colonies. Part of the emphasis was due to the fact that these countries were obvious targets for Communist expansion, particularly by the Chinese. I think part of our interest simply stemmed from our own colonial past and our dislike of colonial systems generally. Perhaps part was the desire to demonstrate that black Africa could be successful in the world.

In any event, Kennedy had made African aid and development a priority, and one of his very early appointments, with great fanfare, had been G. Mennen ("Soapy") Williams, the former governor of Michigan, to be assistant secretary for African affairs—only the second in the department's history, and Kennedy's first appointment to the State Department. The job of nation-building in Africa obviously required time, so these nations could begin to catch up with the industrial powers of Europe and Asia, and while the interest continued, the crises of the cold war occupied the immediate attention of both the public and the government. Indeed, it was because we wanted to reassure African nations of our continuing interest in their welfare that my trip had some modest significance. It was not designed to open new initiatives or to make new proposals. It was simply a showing of the flag, an indication of support and friendship, despite our preoccupation with Vietnam and its problems. It hardly seems credible, but I was the highest-ranking American official ever to visit black Africa. While we were enthusiastic about the exit of the French, British, and Belgium governments, we had the problem of Portugal (a NATO ally) and Spain continuing to have colonies there and the ongoing civil war in Rhodesia (now Zimbabwe) between the white government of Prime Minister Ian Smith and Marxist black revolutionaries led by Robert Mugabe, which eventually overthrew Smith.

The planning for our trip was done by Wayne Fredericks, the acting assistant secretary for Africa. Williams, who had left the department soon after President Kennedy's death, had brought Wayne in as his deputy from the Ford Foundation, where he had set up an African program. Wayne was a remarkable man. One of the first B-17 pilots to go to Europe in World War II, he had completed fifty missions, had a Distinguished Flying Cross with several clusters, a Bronze Star, and a Croix de Guerre for his service as a liaison officer with the Free French forces. After the war he had worked setting up a manufacturing plant in South Africa for the Kellogg Company. There he encountered South African racial laws, which made him a passionate supporter of rights for blacks in all of Africa. He got to know many of the revolutionary black leaders, including Nelson Mandela and Eduardo Mondlane. Mondlane was to Portuguese Mozambique what Mandela was early on to South Africa. In 1961, Wayne had had his picture taken with Mondlane, and Rusk threatened to fire him on the grounds that it would offend the Portuguese government, but repented. Wayne had been trying unsuccessfully to promote a high-level American visit for six years and was delighted that I was an enthusiastic volunteer.

I had no trouble accepting Wayne's judgment as to what countries we should visit, a decision determined by both political factors and the length of an available runway. It was a mix of former British, French, and Belgian colonies with varying political views. By and large our ambassadors were very enthusiastic, although arrangements for our visit involved a lot of work for them and their staffs. I arranged with Bob McNamara to use one of his converted 707 tankers and spoke to the commanding general of the Special Air Mission about the need for an integrated crew, including pilots. He assured me that he understood and that it would be no problem. I got up early each morning to bone up on my French with an instructor furnished by the department.

We were planning a trip for early March, but unfortunately other matters came up and I had to postpone. I assured the embassies that it was simply a short postponement, not a cancellation, and that the trip would take place in the spring. Given the history of no trips by high government officials in the past, the postponement was met with some skepticism by both the countries involved and our ambassadors.

One of the reasons for the postponement was an article in *Ramparts* magazine about the CIA's dirty tricks. It focused on how the agency secretly paid for American youth leaders to attend meetings with foreign students abroad. Coming as it did in the midst of youth demonstrations in this country against the war in Vietnam, it created an enormous stir, especially since its facts were essentially accurate. Young people saw CIA involvement as an effort to distort their views. LBJ was extremely angry, and so was the secretary of health, education, and welfare, John Gardner, who was so upset he threatened to resign. In an effort to stem the tide of criticism, LBJ appointed me chair of a three-person committee to investigate and make recommendations. The other members were Gardner and the head of the CIA, Dick Helms. Obviously I had to bring Helms and Gardner into agreement, and I was not sure that was possible.

I asked Jack Rosenthal to dig out all the facts. Responsible for the CIA program involved (as well as many others) was Cord Meyer, a very able and very dedicated official whom I thought of as an idealist because of his postwar activities for world government. I had known Cord slightly from high school days, when he was the ice hockey goaltender for Saint Paul's School and I played the same position for Exeter. I knew that his twin brother, Monk, had been killed on Okinawa and Cord had devoted himself to efforts for world peace ever since.

Both Helms and Meyer were totally cooperative, which was most helpful. It was obvious from the start that the particular youth program would have to go, even though Cord assured Jack and me that the agency did not tell the youth leaders it financed what to say. I was inclined to believe that, simply because it was obviously easier to pick a reliable young man or woman than to try to control the person. The problem was how to kill this program publicly by stating principles that did not kill other programs outside the scope of our inquiry. After considerable struggle, Jack came up with a report that reflected our discussions, saying that the CIA had no authority to operate with students in this country as distinguished from abroad, which Helms and Meyer said they could live with. Jack took it to Gardner, who wanted to bar all CIA involvement with private domestic organizations. Helms insisted that we could not say that without killing such organizations as Radio Free Europe and Radio Liberty. Gardner was willing to modify the ban by reference to rare classified exceptions. His agreement and Jack's skill with words helped create a report that was generally well accepted publicly despite punting on certain issues, and another public relations crisis was put behind us. LBJ was pleased with the outcome, perhaps more than either Jack or I.

Covert activities by definition get little scrutiny and therefore are subject to little accountability. They run counter to every governmental principle we proclaim, because it is always the end that justifies the means. We pride ourselves on a government in which the means—the processes of government—are the important determinant of the ends. If we feel free to interfere covertly with governmental processes elsewhere—to do things we would be horrified to find being done here at home—we run the risk not simply that others may do them to us, but that they will begin to assume a legitimacy as political actions. To some degree that is what happened in the financing of youth activities by Americans abroad. It was far more obvious in other activities by the agency with respect to supporting revolutionary groups and activities. We cannot always count on people as moral as Cord Meyer to be selected as the responsible officials, and even if we could, the covert nature of the political activities runs counter to our fundamental political principles.

After I left government, I wrote a piece for *Foreign Affairs* in which I suggested that we put an end to all covert activities. I still feel that way. But the temptation to accomplish a goal one thinks important by secret means is always enormous, particularly if the opponents are regarded as evil. The temptation is enhanced by the secrecy, by the lack of accountability, and by the fact that other countries are engaged in similar activities. But every time we do so we weaken our own principles at home and our moral image abroad and damage the leadership, in which rigorous adherence to what is right and decent is an important factor. I find it hard to ignore the fact that it was former CIA agents who broke into the offices of Democratic headquarters and of Dr. Ellsberg's psychiatrist under President Nixon, leading to Watergate. I find it difficult to accept that we can interfere with elections abroad to help a candidate friendly to the United States or, even worse, that we can help revolutionaries we like and help assassinate those we do not. If it is moral to use such means to achieve an end we desire abroad, why not here?

At the time I wrote that "we should abandon publicly all covert operations designed to influence political results in foreign countries. Specifically, there should be no secret subsidies or police or counterinsurgency forces, no efforts to influence elections, no secret monetary subsidies of groups sympathetic to the United States, whether governmental, nongovernmental or revolutionary. We should confine our covert activities overseas to the gathering of intelligence information."

The essence of our democratic government is openness and accountability, and this applies as much to foreign policy as it does to domestic policy. In a sense it is more important to insist on openness in foreign policy, simply because it is there that presidents lead, and when, as in Vietnam, they lose public support, it is precisely because they never made clear the risks and potential consequences and covered up problems with unjustified optimism and invocations of the enormous cloak of "national security." We cannot give the president the power to lead us astray abroad any more than we would delegate to him the power to determine our policy at home. Unhappily, it is easier to lie about success abroad. Secrecy, here or abroad, is the enemy of a free democratic society. It cannot always be avoided, but it can be minimized, and we can insist on standards of conduct wherever they take place.

After completing the CIA inquiry and some other less important chores, I returned to planning a two-week African trip in May. From the department I decided to take only Wayne Fredericks and Jack Rosenthal. The department insisted on two bodyguards, and I was adamant in my refusal. The administration also insisted on an accompanying doctor. Again I refused, unless, I said, he was black. Here administrators trumped me, coming up with a professor from Howard Medical School, Dr. John Kenney, a dermatology specialist. While we had no need of his services, he was a fine traveling companion, and he visited and reported on hospital care in the various capitals on our itinerary and told me that the whole trip was more than worthwhile for him because he saw his first and only case of smallpox at one of our stops.

We had three reporters on the trip: Benjamin Welles of the *New York Times*, Richard Rovere from *The New Yorker*, and Bruce Oudes, a freelance reporter working on assignment from the *Chicago Daily News*. Welles was a foreign affairs reporter whose father, Sumner Welles, had been an important undersecretary of state for FDR. Rovere was a surprise, although he wrote on foreign affairs for the magazine. Oudes was a former USIA official in Africa and knew the continent and its leaders well. Obviously my trip was not about to crowd Vietnam off the front pages of the nation's newspapers, but it was undertaken with a congenial group from whom I could learn much.

I arranged for our 707 again, and the commanding general told me he was thankful for the delay. It seems he had been mistaken about having a black pilot available, so he had used the time to find one and bring him to Washington to train with Special Air Mission colleagues. The pilot he found, Captain Henderson, was flying 707 tankers out of Guam to refuel B-52 bombers on their way to North Vietnam. I have always pictured Henderson being plucked from the ranks in Guam and told that he was being selected to fly with the elite Special Air Mission Command and that his first trip was a two-week tour of black Africa.

Apart from this dream-come-true quality, Henderson was an ideal addition to the crew. Not only was he a fine pilot, but he was over six feet tall, heavyset, with very black skin. When he flew in the first pilot seat (the commanding colonel alternated himself and the other two pilots), he created a bigger sensation on arrival than I did. Africa had its airlines, but all had white pilots.

The commanding general was as good as his word: three pilots, one black; a black crew chief; a black chief steward with two white assistants—an integrated crew with blacks in important positions. The colonel commanding our flight was scrupulous about insuring that all military personnel were treated equally and made Henderson, the new man, his personal responsibility.

Wayne put together a lot of reading for both Lydia and me, and we did our homework faithfully. It was not just the usual information about each country and its history (which the department does quite well), but also some literature and background books so we could appreciate some of the sights we would see and people we would meet. For example, knowing that we would meet with President Senghor of Senegal, Wayne gave us two slim volumes of his poetry. Lydia knew he was a well-regarded poet. In my ignorance of Africa, I did not even know that.

At our final briefing, we were asked if we had any further questions about the trip arrangements. Lydia said, "Yes. I'd like to be paid seventy-five dollars a day."

Silence from the administrative types. But the point, not the price, was important. Married Foreign Service officers stationed abroad often had spouses who gave up jobs here to accompany them to their overseas post. Once there, more often than not, the embassy exploited their presence by using their unpaid services quite unscrupulously. It was a practice I wanted to change, and one that is handled today in a considerably more enlightened fashion.

On a trip of this sort there are many similarities, despite cultural and political differences, in the countries visited. We were almost always met by a military band, which played both national anthems, after which we were escorted from beside the plane by the country's chief of protocol, accompanied by the U.S. ambassador, and introduced to the foreign minister and other government officials. The foreign minister would make a welcoming speech, to which I would make a short response. We would then be escorted in a number of cars to our accommodations for the night. Lydia and I usually were put up by the ambassador at his residence. Depending on the length of the particular stay, there would usually be a state dinner or luncheon with the head of state and a number of his ministers. Then there would be visits to whatever officials of the country and the ambassador thought would be of particular interest to me: a dam, a factory, a university, the courts. At the universities the questions were mostly about Vietnam (why were we interfering in a civil war?) and Rhodesia (why were we not interfering in a civil war?), the clear implication being that we chose to interfere when whites were not involved but would not interfere with Ian Smith's white rule in Rhodesia. Lydia had her own separate program, usually art exhibits, schools, a dance group, or a clinic. There was almost always entertainment by a dance group, and they were always talented and interesting. We were on the go from the moment we arrived until we left and I had made my short departure speech, thanking my hosts for their hospitality and expressing my admiration for their country. It was exhausting but pleasant, and the ambassadors were right to make use of every minute. We could always rest on the plane.

While much of the trip followed this routine, there were many memorable moments, none particularly significant from a foreign policy viewpoint. The trip itself served that purpose. It began in Dakar, where Lydia and I were received warmly by Senghor. I am not sure any policy matters were discussed, but Lydia and President Senghor had an interesting discussion of poetry, and he read from several of his poems. I think he enjoyed the meeting. Of such stuff are international relations made.

Our stop in Ghana was quite different. Our visit came a year after the military coup that unseated Kwame Nkrumah, its first president, who was now in exile in neighboring Guinea. Nkrumah, a dedicated Marxist, had been elected prime minister by an overwhelming vote while in jail and had then become president on Ghana's independence from British rule in 1960. His efforts to modernize Ghana rapidly on a socialist model were initially successful, but his forceful and somewhat arbitrary methods alienated a number of the industrial and commercial interests, as well as virtually bankrupting the country, and led to a bloodless coup when he was visiting China. His successor, General Joseph Ankrah, now ran the country and was not, to put it mildly, interested in what he disparagingly called "politics."

There was much in Ghana I found impressive, despite Nkrumah's overambitious efforts. The university was first-rate, under the tutelage of a president who had a doctorate from my alma mater, Princeton, and the offer of a full professorship there whenever he was willing to come. Further, the government was able to operate effectively with almost no expatriates in governmental roles—I think six or seven in the whole administration, very unusual for a black African country coming out of colonial rule. While in general natives in the former British colonies were far better trained in governmental administration than those in the French- or Belgian-dominated areas, the small number in Ghana showed a real determination by the black government to row their own boat. The country still mined and exported gold (in colonial days the area was known as the Gold Coast), but its principal export was cocoa. Obviously the government's greatest interest was the price of cocoa.

There was a beautiful state dinner in the evening (to which the American reporters were invited), set in an old Danish castle whose dungeon at one time had been used as a prison. I know this because General Ankrah demonstrated how he had escaped from it and jumped into the moat, although this time he was restrained from making the jump into the water. He told me he was a great admirer of LBJ and his conduct of the war in Vietnam (a fact I am sure Ambassador Franklin Williams faithfully reported to Washington), but told me there was one aspect of that war that puzzled him.

"What is that?" I politely inquired.

"Why," he asked, "haven't you dropped the bomb?"

Slightly taken aback, I made what I thought was a diplomatic response. "Spoken like the general you are," I replied.

The table was a beautiful long mahogany one with sterling silver bowls and candlesticks as well as place settings. We were served a sumptuous meal. Not only was it pleasant, but our host had taken into account American tastes: on the beautiful table were several unopened bottles of Heinz tomato catsup. Ankrah was a pleasant man and proud of his military prowess. He spent much of the meal explaining to Lydia the best ways to kill a man in hand-to-hand combat. He was anxious to come to the States to meet LBJ but was, I think, a little nervous about leaving Accra for long. He did not want to repeat Nkrumah's mistake.

The ouster of Nkrumah was but one instance of the effect of the cold war on African politics. Our visit to the Democratic Republic of the Congo provided another, more dramatic one, because of all the machinations among Belgium, the United States, the United Nations, and the various leaders in the Congo with respect to Patrice Lumumba. Like Nkrumah, Lumumba had been an active black leader for independence and was jailed for his activities by the Belgians. Nonetheless, he was elected prime minister under President Kasavubu. His activities were far too radical for the Belgian government, and there was a revolt in the province of Katanga (perhaps encouraged secretly by Belgian intelligence services), leading to a civil war in which Lumumba was dismissed as prime minister and put under house arrest, where he was protected by UN troops. He attempted to escape and was recaptured by government and Belgian troops, put in jail, and then executed; the UN claimed that his escape had ended its responsibility for his protection. At this point another coup took place, under Colonel Joseph Mobutu, who got rid of President Kasavubu and Prime Minister Moise Tshombe and declared himself president. A more appropriate title would have been dictator. He too had no use for "politics" and demonstrated his dislike by a number of public beheadings of former ministers. He had been in office almost two years when we arrived. Because of his overthrow of the leftist government with Soviet ties, he was a Belgian (and U.S.) favorite.

We had the usual ceremonies at the airport plus some excellent dancers, and I met with a large number of tribal chiefs, who had been brought in from the countryside for the occasion. The high point for me was not the large breakfast with the president and his aides, followed by about an hour's private discussion. Mobutu was very cordial, which was not surprising, and very grateful for the promptness of U.S. aid, which he slyly suggested was faster in a crisis than that of the Belgian government. The high point for me came after the private meeting. Apparently my newly learned diplomacy, even when conducted in French, was so effective with the president that he determined that I was eligible to stroke his pet leopard as a mark of esteem. The leopard was a beautiful creature, caged in a large, round steel cage outside his office. The president stuck his arm between the bars and gently stroked the enormous cat, inviting me to do the same. Fond as I am of animals, it was an honor I would willingly have forgone. But having dutifully stroked the dictator for two hours, I put my arm through the bars and followed his example. After a few seconds, I gratefully removed my arm—intact.

Back on our plane flying to our next stop, I found Ben Welles and Dick Rovere hard at work, huddled over Ben's typewriter.

"I hope you're writing a favorable story about my extraordinary courage," I commented.

"Oh, no," said Dick. "Much better than that. We are doing you a favor. We are composing an arrival speech for you, in French and English, which is the same for all countries. All you have to do is remember the name of the country and its president."

"That's very kind of you," I said. "But what do I do when I'm departing?"

"We're working on that," said Ben. "I think you can give the same speech, but Dick thinks that might be inelegant. I doubt anyone would notice, particularly if you are speaking French."

Later, with simulated fanfare, they delivered their product. It was a hilarious takeoff on my airport speeches, cleverly repeating some of my favorite phrases and sounding at times like one of those old-fashioned travelogues we used to see at the movies. Thereafter I had to avoid looking at either reporter when we were in the airport for fear I would break down laughing.

One of the more challenging visits was to Guinea. President Sékou Touré was well to the left of center, a fiery African nationalist with prickly relations with the United States. He did not wish to meet with me in the capital, Conakry, but at his country residence, to which he offered to fly me in a Soviet plane that could land on the short dirt runway. That did not seem to be the best press image for my visit, so we arranged to get an old DC-3 from the air attaché at another U.S. embassy for the trip. At Conakry, Touré put us all up at rather lavish VIP quarters. We were met in the usual fashion at the airport and taken by motorcade to our quarters. Since the president was in the country, not Conakry, Ambassador Robinson McIlvaine had arranged a dinner with some foreign ambassadors and his senior staff, which of course Touré knew about. Nonetheless, as we prepared to leave for the ambassador's residence, we came across a banquet table set up for all of us with gold plates and champagne and a fancy dinner. We explained that we would not be having dinner there and left. When we returned about midnight, the waiters were still in place and the kitchen chefs prepared. Explanations did no good. When we arose in the morning to find everything still awaiting us, I gave up. Before catching our DC-3 to the country, we had a champagne dinner for breakfast. It seemed the only decent thing to do.

We used our borrowed DC-3 to fly to Labé, in the hill country, to visit President Touré. Labé was a small resort used by the French to get away from the heat of Conakry and now used for similar recreation or meetings by the Guinean government—a sort of African Camp David. We landed on the dirt runway and made our way up a hill to the assorted buildings. The street was lined by people in colorful dress, with signs welcoming us and proclaiming African nationalism and freedom from colonial rule. Groups of African dancers performed briefly along the road, and Lydia from time to time would join them, to their joy and amusement. At the top of the hill, President Touré greeted us cordially. He cut a handsome figure, dressed all in white with a flowing short-sleeved white shirt and a white lambskin hat. He escorted us into a building with a long table, past guards in elaborate dress with long curved sabers. Our party (including the reporters) sat on one side of the table and Touré, surrounded by his ministers, on the other.

The president then began a long speech without any notes in beautiful French, largely devoted to criticizing the United States for its failure to support African nationalism in Portuguese Martinique, for its support of British tolerance of Ian Smith's white government in Rhodesia, for Vietnam, for too little aid to his country, for multilateral rather than unilateral aid programs, and so forth. When I say long, I mean long—almost two hours, during which I only occasionally, and somewhat haltingly, interrupted with a question in French. Despite all these often harsh words, President Touré remained friendly, and it was difficult not to like him. When he was finished, he gave me warmly autographed copies of two books he had written so I would have the opportunity to know his political philosophy better. One could question his judgment, but it was easy to see his charismatic appeal. I had little doubt he could be brutal when he felt the occasion called for it. I was glad we had had that breakfast, and hopefully, as a result there would be no retribution to the staff for their failure to serve his guests.

Our visit to Nairobi, Kenya, was on a Friday and Saturday. We had dinner at the president's residence, and it was interesting to meet and talk with President Jomo Kenyatta, one of the real heroes of African independence. He was, of course, getting old and not in good health, so there was much speculation about his successor. I was impressed with his attorney general, Daniel arap Moi, but our intelligence held that he was a very unlikely successor because he came from a small tribe. As it turned out, Kenyatta continued in office for several years and was in fact succeeded by Moi. Our intelligence was wrong, and so was my judgment about Moi. He turned out to be a brutal dictator.

We had most of the weekend off and visited a game preserve about 170 miles southwest of Nairobi, staying at the Keekorok Lodge on the Masai Mara Reserve. We flew down in two small planes. When Lydia and I got to the Nairobi airport, I suddenly felt right at home. Our pilot greeted me with a broad smile. He was the same Border Patrol pilot who had flown me to the University of Alabama when I confronted Governor Wallace. Kenya was having border problems with Somalia, and the United States, as part of its AID program, was providing instruction and help in setting up an effective border patrol system.

Our Sunday at the lodge was fascinating. The lodge was run by an English couple who had lived in Kenya all their lives and were assisted by many efficient and cheerful Kenyans. The food and drink were excellent. We were driven around the reserve in an open Land Rover on rough trails and through waist-high grass and saw a large pride of lions at close hand, elephants, giraffes, water buffalo, all manner of wild African animals in their native habitat. Our driver was a large, bearded man who proudly told us he was the first black head gamekeeper in Kenya. He knew his business thoroughly and had no trouble locating the animals and going surprisingly near them. Sadly, he told us of the huge problems with poachers and their high-powered rifles; they were seeking elephant tusks, lions' teeth, and so forth for sale. Still, it was exhilarating, even if it had its depressing moments. We returned Monday morning to Nairobi refreshed from our visit, the absence of pressure to behave like a diplomat, and the excellent attention of our hosts.

I looked forward to our visits to East Africa and former British colonies, where I would meet political leaders who, like Kenyatta and Nkrumah, had gone from jail to prime minister to president. In Tanzania there was Julius Nyerere and in Zambia Kenneth Kaunda, both trying to maintain an unaligned status in the cold war while vigorously pushing socialism and one-party rule at home. Their problems were real. Most of the wealth was still owned by foreigners, and they wanted to modernize and expand industry, education, health care, and the other benefits of the industrial age. They had fought for independence largely through union movements, strikes, and efforts at collective bargaining, so the movement toward a socialist state was understandable. Given past exploitation by whites, you could even be sympathetic. But the pace they set was too fast, too uncompromising, and, after promising beginnings in the 1960s, much too aggressive to survive. Their governments were clearly influenced by a Soviet model and rapidly became intolerant of dissent or opposition, despite the good intentions of both men. They did maintain their neutrality, having warm relations with both East and West, but we—unfortunately, in my view—were not as responsive to the government objectives as we might have been. Had we been more responsive, we might have moderated their ardent socialism.

Both men were intelligent and interesting, with enormous problems and enormous desire to resolve them with their three-year, four-year, and five-year plans. But I found the lack of political debate or discussion discouraging. While I was in Dar, the port and then capital of Tanzania, Wayne arranged for me to have an off-the-record, secret meeting with another revolutionary, his friend Eduardo Mondlane. Mondlane was a handsome and well-educated man who had started life in poverty, herding sheep, and had been unable to get an education in Mozambique or later in South Africa. He eventually got to a Swiss school in South Africa and, at age thirty, to the States, where he graduated from Oberlin College. He had then taken a Ph.D. in sociology at Northwestern University, where he met and married his American wife, Janet Johnson. I was greatly impressed by him, and I think the fact that I was willing to meet with him, even though secretly, was encouraging to him and his anticolonial movement. At the time he was head of FRELIMO, a liberation movement to free Mozambique from Portuguese rule that had its headquarters in Dar. Unhappily, he was assassinated two years after I met him, but his movement succeeded and he is honored today in Mozambique, where the university is named after him.

As we were concluding our trip, the Egyptian government of Abdel Nasser decided to close the Straits of Tiran and the Gulf of Aqaba to Israeli shipping, and Nasser and his Syrian allies stationed troops on the Israeli border. There was a real threat of war, but not enough to lead me to conclude my trip early, particularly since what was left—Somalia and Ethiopia—had strong ties to Egypt. To have canceled would have been more disturbing than simply to continue, but recent events in the Middle East tended to dominate the discussion, and I felt less informed than perhaps I should have been. I wished that I were back in the center of things. It is always disappointing to have a crisis occurring in which you would in other circumstances have been an important actor.

After a gala reception and entertainment by President Milton Obote in Uganda, we went on to a luncheon in Somalia and then a state dinner in Ethiopia. Emperor Haile Selassie received us first in his palace reception room, where he sat on his throne, surrounded by his ministers. I was told by our ambassador, Ed Korry, that one had to approach and leave the emperor always facing him. That was not so hard. The more amusing test was his little chihuahua, obviously not subject to the same protocol. The ministers all sought to attract the attention of the little dog, which, I assumed, was a way into the emperor's favor. After we had made our entrance and Lydia and I had been seated on either side of the emperor, the dog made his choice—a wise one, I thought—and jumped into Lydia's lap. The emperor was delighted, the ministers disappointed, and the ambassador amazed. He was, I think, unaware that as a young girl my wife had earned money training dogs.

The emperor was so pleased that he invited Lydia to go horseback riding with him in the morning. She politely declined, on the ground that she had not brought her riding clothes with her, which was true enough. Still he expressed disappointment, saying that the only other lady he had ever invited was England's Queen Elizabeth, and she had accepted. Apparently she traveled with a more extensive wardrobe than Lydia, which on the whole I did not find surprising. Lydia too was disappointed, because she was sure his stable included some beautiful Arabians that would have given her pleasure to ride.

I remembered Haile Selassie from pre–World War II days, when he had bravely resisted the invasion of Mussolini's Italian troops. He was a tiny man, heavily bearded, and seemingly quite fit despite advancing years. Predictably, he was interested in what was happening in Egypt and Israel and what the U.S. view was. Much of our talk centered on Nasser's actions and what the United States would do. He had no love for Israel, but he was concerned, rightly, about Nasser's aggressive actions.

The next morning we visited an American-sponsored effort to codify Ethiopian laws, and I spent quite some time with the American professors (some of whom I knew) and students working on the enormous project. I felt at home, since it was the kind of academic work that interested me.

Our trip finished in Ethiopia, and we headed for Washington after a brief stop in France for fuel and food. I had enjoyed every minute of the trip and found Africa fascinating. It was obvious that the countries we had visited had a long way to go and that any real democracy as we knew it was some distance off. But most of the leaders I met were serious people who wanted to emerge from colonialism to take a place in the world. To me, it appeared that the predominant interest in socialism stemmed more from tribal values contrasted with colonial rule than any great Russian, or even Chinese, model. Since the United States, despite our capitalist ideology, had an anticolonial history, we were much admired. They were well aware of our progress in civil rights, of Martin Luther King and his demonstrations, and of the Kennedys' interest in Africa. Bobby, as senator, had visited many of these countries a few months before our trip. The African leaders obviously appreciated the official trip and, irrespective of socialist politics, had great admiration for the United States. All we ever had in mind to do was to enhance that view, and in that I think we succeeded. But bringing Africa into the modern world was going to take a lot more than smiles, handshakes, speeches, and state dinners.

XXIV

BACK IN WASHINGTON, I WAS BRIEFED ON THE MIDEAST CRISIS BY BEN Read and Larry Eagleburger and read a bunch of cables and intelligence memos. There was a real risk of war breaking out, although all the intelligence assessments concluded that Nasser and his Syrian allies would be no match for the Israelis (even with the help of a reluctant Jordan) should the Arabs launch an attack. The other possibility was that Israel would use the buildup of troops on its borders as a reason to attack first in alleged self-defense. The secretary was seeking to mediate, and with the Egyptian vice president coming to Washington at LBJ's request, he was fairly optimistic about getting an agreement. The Israeli foreign minister, Abba Eban, was already in Washington, seeking American support to open up the Gulf of Aqaba as, he urged, we and the British were obligated to do by treaty. Nasser, having gotten the UN forces out of the Sinai, continued to mass his troops and threaten to eliminate Israel, though nobody thought he really wanted a war he was unlikely to win.

I went to Gene Rostow's office, where, in my absence, he had been working to persuade various NATO nations to send warships through the straits and open up the gulf to shipping. At this point only the British had agreed to join us. It was clear the Israelis wanted us to act on their behalf, just as it was clear that the Arabs would resent it. Gene had put together a crisis team, and it was obvious that he was thoroughly enjoying working with his brother Walt, the national security adviser, in the White House. My role would clearly be marginal.

Given the optimism over settlement, coupled with the intelligence about Israeli strength, LBJ was reluctant to send warships into the gulf.

President Johnson used the hot line to the Soviet Union to insure that the Russians were not pressing for an attack on Israel. The Egyptian vice president arrived in Washington, but before any mediation could take place, the Israelis attacked as a matter of self-defense. Rusk was furious, and so, perhaps to a lesser degree, was LBJ. The Israeli attack was brilliantly conceived and carried out by Defense Minister Moshe Dayan and Chief of Staff Yitzhak Rabin. Air attacks neutralized the Egyptian air force from day one. With absolute air superiority, Israeli ground forces were punishing the Jordanian, Egyptian, and Syrian armies mercilessly. Thus began the Six-Day War.

Apart from the war itself, which the United States would have liked to avoid despite Nasser's inexcusable provocation, there were two unfortunate incidents. First, the State Department issued a statement of neutrality that was both unnecessary and unwise. It irritated the Israelis and angered the American Jewish community, including some of LBJ's most loyal supporters. How it happened, I have no idea. Second, the Israelis attacked and sank an American naval intelligence vessel, the USS *Liberty*, in international waters, killing more than thirty sailors and wounding more than a hundred. The Israeli government quickly apologized and said it was an accident, a case of mistaken identity. That explanation was hard to accept, given the fine weather, the large American flag, and the clearly visible ship's markings. The navy did not believe it, nor did most American officials, but it seemed inconceivable that such an attack would have been ordered by senior Israeli officials.

LBJ demonstrated his political finesse by accepting the Israelis' apology but insisting that they do more than simply say it was a mistake. He called me and told me to tell the Israelis that they should not only pay for the *Liberty* but should offer generous compensation to the families of the victims. I spoke to the minister in charge at the Israeli embassy and delivered the message, but the Israelis insisted that the whole thing was an unhappy accident and said that they did not wish to assume any additional responsibility. I pushed hard on them from the outset and on subsequent occasions, arguing that it was clearly in their best interest to do so. Eventually Israel came up with some $13 million in compensation. But the incident angered many, and to this day the Israeli explanation remains questionable in the view of many people, including me.

The controversy over the neutrality statement was probably the most important factor in LBJ's decision to make little effort to obtain a cease-fire for the first few days, other than in the UN, where the matter was bogged down in language about territorial lines. Having angered the Jewish community with the department's statement on neutrality, LBJ was not about to anger them further. The UN worked on the language of a ceasefire—what to do about the occupied territories—to no avail. Finally the president called us into the Situation Room—Rusk, McNamara, Helms, General Earl ("Bus") Wheeler, and Walt Rostow, among others—and said he thought it was time to act. The Soviets had been on the hot line in a small panic about the failure of their Mideast satellites, whose aggressive conduct they had no doubt encouraged. With Israeli tanks seemingly on the road to Damascus, there was no disagreement. LBJ said he wanted a ceasefire and he wanted it now—no dilly-dallying, no delays. Rusk said that he had a speech in Atlanta and that I should call in the Israeli chargé (Ambassador Avraham Harman was in Israel) and deliver the message.

I returned to the department and told Minister Ephraim Evron that I needed to see him urgently. Within minutes he was in my office, and it was clear that he knew what the message was. Indeed, I suspect he had expected it earlier.

"President Johnson says it is time for a ceasefire in place, and he is not prepared to tolerate delays," I said, or words to that effect.

"I understand," he responded. No protest. No argument.

"Do you want to inform your government, or do you want me to have our ambassador in Israel do so?" I inquired.

"Your communications may be faster. Let's both do it," he replied.

He was as good as his word, and the ceasefire took place within a couple of hours. A few months later, the UN did deal with the territorial problems by passing the somewhat ambiguous Resolution 242, "land for peace," which has been the basis for settlement discussions ever since.

I had spent relatively little time thinking about the Middle East prior to the Six-Day War, but even my small involvement sparked my interest in seeking answers to the difficult problems there. I worked with Joe Sisco, the assistant secretary for United Nations affairs, trying various schemes to make Resolution 242 work. What could provide Israel with the security it needed? What could persuade the Arab countries to accept its existence? How to deal with the refugees? With Jerusalem, in which Muslims, Jews, and Christians all have important religious interests? I did not think and I do not think the problems are insoluble, but it will take real leadership on all sides to accomplish peace in the region. Time is no longer on the side of peace, if it ever was. Failure to find some solution makes it even more difficult as circumstances change and bitterness festers. After the Six-Day War there had to be some delay, but I thought a settlement could be reached if we were willing to press hard on both sides. I think my major reason for some measure of optimism was Yitzhak

Rabin. When he became ambassador in Washington, we spent many hours discussing how the problems might be resolved. His openness and flexibility were a breath of fresh air. Unfortunately, the U.S. focus on Vietnam kept getting in the way. But I firmly believe that after Rabin became prime minister in 1992, he would have succeeded in bringing peace to the region. His assassination in 1995, like JFK's and Bobby's, was a tragedy for all of us; no one of similar stature has yet emerged in Israel, and the Palestinian leadership has continued to be both divided and weak.

One direct consequence of the Six-Day War was the meeting between President Johnson and Soviet premier Aleksey Kosygin in Glassboro, New Jersey. In retrospect it is hard to believe that three and a half years after becoming president, Johnson had never met the Soviet leader. Kosygin was coming to New York for a special UN meeting convened at the Soviet Union's request to urge Israeli withdrawal from occupied territories, and the moment seemed propitious. Given the Soviet embarrassment as a result of the Israeli victory, the threats that Kosygin had made toward the end of the Six-Day War, and the unfinished business on arms and nuclear proliferation, it seemed important to all of us that the two leaders meet before relations deteriorated further. In addition, Soviet relations with China were somewhat strained, and they feared that we might turn to China for an accommodation with respect to Vietnam. Ambassador Llewellyn Thompson, a truly great Soviet expert, thought discussions might be helpful in laying the groundwork for eventual settlement there.

While it was clear that LBJ welcomed the opportunity, he also was somewhat reluctant, for fear that public expectations might go well beyond anything that could possibly be achieved—which, he agreed with Ambassador Thompson, was likely to be nothing concrete. At the same time, all of us thought the meeting important and that not having a meeting could lead to a further deterioration of relations.

If there is any one thing that LBJ did superbly, it was measuring a man. He knew how to flatter, to cajole, to bully, to pursue an issue, and to change the subject—and, perhaps more important, when to do each. He had honed those political skills all his life, and more than anything else, they had led to his success. LBJ has often been accused of insensitivity, but in his meetings with other political leaders, his personal radar as to when to press and when to back off was virtually infallible. In a very real sense, it was no different dealing with Senator Dirksen on Senate bills and Aleksey Kosygin on Soviet-American relations.

I did not accompany Johnson to Glassboro, and my knowledge of the talks is all secondhand. The president had not expected to get agreement on anything concrete and did not—but it was typical of LBJ that he was nonetheless somewhat disappointed. I think he was particularly unhappy that all he got on Vietnam was regurgitation of the North Vietnamese line that the bombing must stop unconditionally before any talks would be possible. LBJ put this down to the fact that Kosygin had no authority from his colleagues in the Kremlin to go any further, but it nonetheless frustrated the president. Apart from a general unhappiness that more could not be accomplished, I think he felt, correctly, that the talks had gone well and that tensions had relaxed somewhat. The only other complaint he had was that the Russian translator was better than ours. We flew in a second translator from Moscow, but although both our people were excellent, I doubt any country had a translator as good as the Russians'. When he translated here, he had an American accent; when in Great Britain, he had a British one.

I had some changes in my own immediate staff. Jack Rosenthal left on a Kennedy Fellowship to study urban affairs at the new Institute of Politics at Harvard. He later went to *Life* magazine and then to the *New York Times*, where he won a Pulitzer Prize for his editorials. Tony Lake was so discouraged with the stalemate in Vietnam that he wanted to resign from the Foreign Service. I felt he was far too valuable a young officer to let go, so with Larry Eagleburger's help, I got him a leave of absence and a scholarship to work for a doctorate at Princeton. To succeed Jack as my designated troubleshooter, I got Philip Heymann, who had worked at Justice in the solicitor general's office and had teaching offers from virtually every law school in the country, but who was willing to spend a year in a new job in Washington. To my disappointment, he eventually chose Harvard over Yale, but he later returned for brief tours as an assistant attorney general heading the Criminal Division and, in the Clinton administration, as deputy attorney general. To replace Tony, I got Richard Holbrooke, a friend of Tony's and another outstanding young officer with Vietnamese experience. Art Hartman continued to work with the SIG and provide intelligent counsel on a variety of economic matters. Once again I had an exceptional staff who worked well together and had no trouble speaking their minds. The only problem I can recall was that Art thought Dick Holbrooke's ties were too loud.

XXV

Vietnam, Vietnam, Vietnam—it got in the way of everything: LBJ's Great Society programs, our African initiatives, the Middle East, everything. The protests were increasing, dissent in Congress was more serious, and there simply were not any good answers. "Victory" in Vietnam, if it meant anything, meant the emergence in the south of a stable government supported by a sufficient majority of the populace to stabilize a South Vietnam not wishing to unite with Communist North Vietnam. This stability could only be established, it was thought, if the rebel Vietcong, supplied by the North Vietnamese, could be diminished through a combination of military force in South Vietnam and some kind of destruction of the supplies and troops provided by the north. Given the restraints put on the military with respect to North Vietnam and the safe havens for both the North Vietnamese troops and the Vietcong in neighboring Cambodia and Laos, it was by no means clear that this could be accomplished in the foreseeable future, if indeed it could be accomplished at all.

The hawks thought it might be accomplished through negotiation if both North Vietnam and the Vietcong suffered enough losses. The doves believed a negotiated peace might be possible, because once American troops were withdrawn, through negotiation the Communists would see the chances of an eventual victory sufficiently enhanced to make some delay worthwhile. They believed that the Russians, and perhaps even the Chinese, would encourage compromise because of the dangers that the war would spread.

The president was increasingly distressed and frustrated. With the "loss" of China to the Communists after World War II, he may have exaggerated the power of the political right should South Vietnam go the same way. Since China and the McCarthy aftermath, no president in fact had been politically willing to question the basic objective of preventing Communist expansion anywhere. We saw dominoes everywhere we looked—Southeast Asia, Greece, Turkey, the Middle East, Africa, Latin America—and the whole of our aid program, our system of alliances, and our covert activities was based on the proposition that we could not lose territory to the Communists. I do not suggest that the threat of communism, backed by the Soviet Union and China, was not real. But I do suggest that the war was motivated as much by fear of domestic political consequences if territory was lost to the Communists as it was by any serious calculations about the consequences of the loss in terms of national security.

Between 1960 and 1964, our military operations in Vietnam through "military advisers" were both modest in numbers and at least partially covert. The fact of their numbers was known and their activities at most were only partially concealed. I do not believe either President Kennedy or President Johnson had seriously considered what actions would be taken in worst-case scenarios. As the possibility of more significant action became clearer—but long before any decision had been taken as to how far or in what circumstances he would intervene—President Johnson did go to Congress with the Tonkin Gulf Resolution, preserving in a sense the form but certainly not the substance of public knowledge and congressional participation. Worse than that, because of its political purpose, it was at best misleading to both Congress and the people. Despite the broad language of the resolution, no one—and I include the president and his advisers—really contemplated at the time the extent of our possible military intervention in Vietnam or its consequences.

When President Johnson was faced with the choice of greatly increasing our military presence and function or turning Vietnam over to the Communists, he clearly had the formal power to make that decision without any need to claim presidential constitutional prerogatives. What he did not do, and what was never done, was lay out fairly for Congress and the public the pros and cons of massive intervention, the risks involved, and the potential costs. Could this have been done? I have serious doubts, for the simple reason that if the president thought massive military intervention the best course of action, it would be because he probably underestimated the risks and the dangers of failure. Even if that were not the case, his interest would be to gain public support for intervention and unite the people and Congress behind his decision. It would be counterproductive to emphasize the downside, particularly if he was not himself convinced of its merits and thought the risks worth taking. Thus, there is a strong likelihood that any president will tend to exaggerate the national security threat, to minimize the risks, to use fear and patriotism as uniting forces, and, worst of all, to use secrecy to support expert conclusions. Even if the president were to make every effort to give a fair and candid presentation of the important considerations, it might well not appear fair and candid if things went wrong. Making predictions is full of pitfalls. Just as one can cherry-pick intelligence to support a decision, critics after the fact can almost always find evidence that should have led to a different risk assessment.

By and large, the Congress is not much help to a president in matters of foreign policy. There is little political profit, particularly in the House, with its two-year terms, in taking positions on foreign affairs before a presidential decision and little political gain in getting involved as a critic at the outset. While the Constitution does not make clear political distinctions between the respective roles of Congress and the president in domestic and foreign affairs, practice has tended to give the president a far greater power of leadership in foreign policy than in domestic policy. In a dangerous and complex world, most of the public tends simply to place its trust in the president, our nationally elected leader and our "sole voice" in foreign affairs, and for the most part the Congress simply goes along with that trust. Unfortunately, presidents are inclined to think this blind faith in their wisdom is justified, and in recent years have become increasingly enamored of their role on the stage of foreign affairs. It can be a heady business. I think of President Kennedy and the Cuban missile crisis or, for that matter, the earlier disaster of the Bay of Pigs. That American-supported invasion was totally an executive action, and JFK's public apology was an apology for its failure, not for its secret undertaking. And I think virtually every president after LBJ has sought to exploit foreign affairs for political gain at home, a mark of leadership in a dangerous world.

The more interesting question is whether, had the president decided (as the French had a decade earlier with respect to their own role) that the United States could not effectively rescue Vietnam from eventual unification under Communist control, he could have persuaded the Congress and the public that it would be wise to withdraw our advisers. Even without the Tonkin Gulf Resolution, it would be a largely presidential decision, and he would bear the onus. In 1965 it was certain to be controversial and extremely divisive, particularly after Goldwater's campaign. Goldwater was a very conservative candidate, a veteran of World

War II, and a strong supporter of the military. He would have ridiculed any withdrawal as unnecessary and cowardly. President Johnson obviously thought it both politically disastrous and unnecessary, since we could prevail. To make it possible to prevail was to increase our military presence greatly and to take over much, even most, of the responsibility for preserving South Vietnam's independence. From a domestic political viewpoint, the option of unilateral withdrawal then became, if not impossible, many times more politically costly. It was now the United States, not South Vietnam, that would "lose" the war.

Ironically, I do not think LBJ's Vietnam war was the result of an exaggerated view of presidential prerogatives or power, although largely as a result of power delegated to him in the Tonkin Gulf Resolution, the crucial decisions were his and the war was his responsibility. Because he saw foreign affairs in domestic political terms rather than as a field of particular presidential expertise, he was convinced not of the strategic importance of South Vietnam but of the fact that the American public, and the Congress, would not tolerate our "losing" it to the Communists by failing to provide enough military support, whatever that might amount to. He wanted to get Congress on board, but the Democratic leadership pointed to the resolution and said that Congress had already given him all the authority he needed. So it became Lyndon Johnson's decision and Lyndon Johnson's war.

I think there is very little doubt that in 1965 the Congress would have supported Johnson's decision had there been hearings and a vote. He was correct, as he usually was, in assessing the mood of the Congress. But the absence of any serious public discussion or congressional hearings exploring our reasons, our objectives, potential problems, the dangers of escalation, and the costs made it difficult later on to explain those objectives, their importance, and how to measure progress in their achievement. Whether hearings would in fact have sufficiently explored all those important considerations is doubtful, because we had not then, and have not since, learned how to put foreign policy on a par with domestic policy and invite the participation and debate necessary in a democracy to give it a solid footing over time. People seem to prefer to put trust in presidential wisdom, and Congress prefers the role of Monday morning quarterback. Thus, when things go wrong or something that passes for "victory" is not achieved relatively quickly or painlessly, trust in the president erodes. The president, in turn, is unlikely to admit failure and, without a fair public discussion to fall back on, tends to defend failure as if it were simply a bump on the road to success. If criticism mounts, the president's credibility is almost certainly brought into issue, and the country is weakened at home and abroad as a result. That, of course, is what happened with Vietnam, but it has not yet discouraged presidents from acting without informed public support and either basking in the popularity of a successful war or suffering the consequences of unforeseen difficulties. Trust in the wisdom of presidential leadership continues as long as that leadership is successful but disappears rapidly when it is not supported by public understanding.

There often are legitimate problems of secrecy stemming both from efforts to protect intelligence sources and from the fact that candor may actually jeopardize a legitimate objective; it may, for example, be difficult to give a frank analysis of a political situation abroad without doing damage to a friendly government. But there is little doubt that secrecy has been used as an excuse for insufficient evidence or poorly reasoned analysis and that in almost every situation it is possible to give a fair and balanced argument for a foreign policy. If there is the possibility of significant military action and casualties, I cannot see how a democratic society is justified in failing to do so. Secrecy and national security simply cannot be allowed to substitute for facts and reasoned action, and appeals to the flag cannot take the place of thought and analysis based on a fair presentation of the facts.

I do not mean that it is always easy for a president to do so. Foreign policy is, after all, a series of acts with future consequences, and its success is determined by the accuracy of prediction about future events. What we call "facts" are rarely facts and far more likely estimates of probabilities based on the best usually imperfect information available. The consequences of being mistaken can be severe. A reasonable understanding of the problems and risks might lead to a more cautious policy and might even include missed opportunities. But surely that is part of the price we pay for an open and free society. If the question were put again, as it was to the founding fathers, we would once again vote for constitutional restraints on presidential power to use force, whether here or abroad.

What was missing in Vietnam was a public understanding of the risks of intervention to preserve a non-Communist South Vietnam. When JFK sent military "advisers" to assist President Diem against the Communist insurgent Vietcong, the risks seemed minor. We had done similar things in a number of instances to shore up existing governments—usually right-wing, like that of Diem—against Communist-aided rebellion. But with the assassination of Diem and the disintegration of the South Vietnamese government, the problem became much more difficult, and our acquiescence in Diem's assassination gave us a moral responsibility as well.

LBJ was right in thinking that it would be risky domestic politics simply to let the Vietcong triumph in South Vietnam and create a unified, Communist Vietnam. What was not understood by the Congress, the public or, in my opinion, the administration was the potential cost of preventing that result. The domino theory, which saw preserving a non-Communist South Vietnam as the key to preventing Laos, Cambodia, and all of Southeast Asia from falling into the Russian-Chinese sphere of influence, undoubtedly inflated the value of South Vietnam. But it was less that theory than the conviction that the result could be accomplished expeditiously, at relatively small cost, that made intervention a popular decision, and I believe that assumption was shared by most people, even within the administration. There was concern that China or North Korea, or even the Soviet Union, might get involved, but it was also clear that LBJ would be careful to avoid that contingency. There were some who questioned the domino theory itself and the importance to our national security, or that of the free world, of South Vietnam. Nevertheless, if the problems and risks had been fully aired, I believe the decision would probably have been the same, as long as the president supported it. Still, the process is important, because there are future decisions to be made and a public to be informed and educated in a democracy if government is to be responsible to the people.

The unstated problem is that if the president wants to commit large numbers of American troops to a war or insurgency abroad, he needs the support of the American people. He is more likely to get that support by emphasizing success than by encouraging honest assessment of risk, which may well prove divisive. Congress has the capacity to explore domestic legislation thoroughly, but it has never developed a similar capacity with respect to foreign affairs. Presidents have enjoyed their relatively free hand, especially as foreign affairs have become increasingly important. Today it is far less likely that the Congress will take on its constitutional role in foreign policy than that the president's leadership in foreign affairs will spill over into domestic matters and make Congress into a rubber stamp, especially if it is controlled by the president's party.

In any event, the continuing failure of the South Vietnamese to gain control of the countryside and our acceptance of increasing responsibility for success or failure eroded confidence in the administration. There was less and less support for a war in a far-off place when it was difficult to explain our objective and even more difficult to explain how it was going to be achieved. As I think must almost always be the case, an administration under some attack began to seek evidence of progress to calm a critical populace. Since whatever progress existed was minuscule, particularly when measured against any acceptable timeline, administration optimism just served to escalate criticism and charges of deceit.

That LBJ wanted out of Vietnam as ardently as any of his critics, I have no doubt. He, like they, saw negotiation as the way to a peaceful withdrawal. He did not have confidence in the possibility of "victory," though he did not entirely reject it. Generally he saw military action as the means of pressing the Communists to negotiate. He was unwilling to withdraw unilaterally, but so too were virtually all his critics. Among the politicians, only Senator George Aiken of Vermont suggested declaring victory and getting out, and no one took him seriously. Eugene McCarthy and Bobby Kennedy, for all their outspoken criticism of the war, did not suggest unilateral withdrawal. Rather they, like most of the others, suggested that LBJ was not serious about peace through negotiation. They were convinced that if the bombing stopped, negotiations leading to a reasonable settlement could be achieved. Like so many critics, they thought President Johnson was committed to a military solution.

I had been in the State Department only a few months when, in early 1967, matters of difference on Vietnam policy between the president and Bobby came to a head. There was no way the president and Bobby were ever going to be friendly as people, even when they shared the same objectives. LBJ thought Bobby regarded him as an illegitimate usurper of his brother's presidency, and to some extent that was true. I think Bobby's criticisms of the president hurt LBJ far more than the same ones from others, and angered him as well. In January, Bobby was in Europe meeting with various government leaders—as JFK's brother, he had unusual access even for a senator—and President Johnson seethed. Bobby was quite scrupulous about not publicly criticizing American policy in Vietnam even when he spoke to the Oxford Union or met with Prime Minister Harold Wilson in London or President Charles de Gaulle in Paris or government leaders in Bonn and Rome, all of whom were critical of the war in Vietnam. In Paris he met with the French foreign expert on the Far East, Etienne Manac'h, accompanied by John Gunther Dean, an Asian expert from the American embassy. Bobby heard nothing at the meeting that he thought new or significant about Vietnam, but Dean apparently thought otherwise and cabled Washington. Manac'h had said that the one indispensable condition for peace was to stop the bombing—a familiar theme. But Dean interpreted it as having some significance, and said so in his cable. I find it hard to believe he thought it very significant, since he classified the cable "confidential" and must have known it was unlikely to get the secretary's attention or, for that matter, that of any of the senior officials who occupied offices on the seventh floor in Washington. However, someone in the bowels of the department thought it interesting and showed it to *Newsweek*'s diplomatic correspondent. Because it involved Bobby Kennedy, it became a front-page story everywhere that Bobby had received a "peace feeler" with respect to Vietnam. When LBJ saw the newspapers, he hit the ceiling.

Bobby was still in Europe, and none of us in the department knew what was going on, since we had never seen Dean's cable. We searched through department files and found nothing (the cable had apparently been misfiled). Our failure to locate the cable further convinced LBJ that Bobby had intentionally leaked the story to embarrass him. Actually Bobby was as mystified as any of us, and no one in the department came forward with any explanation.

Upon Bobby's return a couple of days later, I got a call from the president asking me to see Bobby and talk about the story. I called Bobby and we met shortly thereafter. I had avoided being LBJ's emissary to Bobby; I felt uncomfortable, and I told Bobby so. He told me not to worry, that he had no idea what the story was all about, and that to his knowledge he had never received a "peace feeler." He went on to say that he thought President Johnson was seeking victory in Vietnam and that victory was not possible. What we needed was to negotiate our way out in an honorable settlement, and that meant stopping the bombing. He then surprised me by saying he could not fault LBJ on his domestic programs, but if we could not find a way out of Vietnam, the Great Society would come a cropper.

It was at that moment that his secretary, Angie Novello, buzzed him to say that the president wanted me on the phone. The president asked me if Bobby would come over to the White House now, and if so, would I accompany him. Bobby was willing, and so we headed for 1600 Pennsylvania Avenue.

Bobby and I were escorted into the Oval Office, where an obviously angry president was waiting with Walt Rostow. LBJ began by accusing Bobby in a loud and rising voice of leaking the "peace feeler" story to embarrass him. Bobby, while clearly offended, said, as he had said to me earlier, that he had not leaked the story and was not even aware of any "peace feeler," if one existed. The leak, he suggested, had more likely come from President Johnson's State Department. Since we had not yet located the Dean cable, Bobby's response simply angered the president more.

"It's not *my* State Department," he shouted. "It's your goddamn State Department!" which I took to be a crack at me, since LBJ knew my views on Vietnam were pretty close to Bobby's.

There was no calming the president. Bobby tried to explain his thoughts on Vietnam, but the president was not interested. I had never seen him like this, almost totally out of control, and it was not a pleasant sight. As Bobby talked about stopping the bombing and seeking a negotiated peace—thoughts I knew LBJ had entertained in his own mind from time to time—he responded by accusing Bobby and his friends of prolonging the war and causing American soldiers to die as a result.

"You have blood on your hands," he shouted.

Bobby, pale with repressed anger, stood up and said simply and with some dignity, "I don't have to listen to this. I'm leaving."

I got up with him and we both left. Outside was a mob of cameras and reporters. Bobby turned to me and said, "What shall I say?"

I felt conflicted and worried. I had no idea what the president in his anger might do or say. I did not want Bobby hurt, and I had no doubt he was telling the truth. I suggested that he simply tell the press what he had told the president—that he was unaware of receiving any "peace feeler" with respect to Vietnam. That is what he did.

That was the only occasion on which I ever saw President Johnson behave in an angry and irrational way. I saw him angry more than once, but it was an anger he had under control. On that occasion he simply did not, and it worried me for a long time. It was, of course, totally counterproductive. Bobby left the office feeling that Johnson had no interest whatsoever in peace, that he was determined to secure a victory, and that his course was unalterable. In a saner moment, LBJ would have understood that that was a message he never should have delivered as he did.

Even in retrospect, I am not sure how to assess LBJ on Vietnam. He certainly did not want to see the United States defeated, and obviously what he wanted was, as in Korea, the continued existence of a divided Vietnam; a return to the status quo ante was sufficient. There were times when it was difficult to distinguish "peace" from "victory" as he saw it. While in fact he wanted negotiations, he was always concerned that negotiations would be seen by the enemy, and the right wing at home, as a sign of weakness. He would not, I think, have been adamantly opposed to seeing members of the Vietcong join the government (the South Vietnamese government might well have been), so long as it was not a Trojan horse to promote a quick Communist takeover. He was quite passionate about not turning Vietnam over to the Communists on his watch, primarily for domestic political reasons.

The president had charged me with seeking a way to peace in Vietnam. Perhaps some of my "Ivy League friends" had some bright ideas. Instead I put together, with his knowledge and approval, what I called the "Non-Group," a name designed to reflect that it did not exist for any purpose other than frank discussions of Vietnam. The rules I laid down were interesting: nothing said at a meeting could ever be quoted or used by any other member of the group to support a position; thus a member was theoretically free to say one thing at a meeting and a different thing to his boss or in a memo. I wanted open and candid discussion and did not plan to use the group for policy purposes, except indirectly and without mention. Any member was free to use an idea as a basis for a formal policy recommendation, but without attribution. The second rule was that if a member could not attend, he could send a superior but not a subordinate in his place. I did not expect superiors—in some cases that meant the president—but I did not want attendance delegated.

It was a surprisingly high-powered group. From Defense I invited the deputy secretary, Cyrus Vance (and later Paul Nitze), the assistant secretary for international security affairs (John McNaughton and then Paul Warnke), and the chairman of the Joint Chiefs of Staff, General Bus Wheeler; from the CIA, the director, Richard Helms; from the White House, the national security adviser, Walt Rostow; and from State, Ambassador Averell Harriman and Assistant Secretary for East Asian Affairs William Bundy. Larry Eagleburger and Tony Lake (later Richard Holbrooke) sat in but did not participate unless asked, as did Ben Read on occasion. I sometimes invited a guest with particular responsibilities to discuss them, such as Ambassador Robert Komer, a former high-ranking CIA agent now in charge of pacification in Vietnam.

We met most Thursday afternoons from five until six-thirty, and I served drinks. The attendance was almost perfect, and when one of the two Defense secretaries could not make a meeting, often Robert McNamara came in his place. It had the quality not of a debate but of a college bull session, and the discussion was both honest and friendly. I think it was John McNaughton who started things off on the right foot by declaring that the war in Vietnam was a huge mistake and absolutely unwinnable. To my surprise, this did not cause an explosion, but rather a discussion of why he felt that way, which engendered a surprising amount of agreement, though often for different reasons. Bus Wheeler thought the problem was that the restrictions on the military, while understandable from a political viewpoint, imposed an almost impossible problem of securing peace on General Westmoreland. Paul Nitze thought we were far too focused on Asia when we should be concerned with Europe. Helms did not feel intelligence gave any hope of a quick ending. Bundy was concerned about the fragility of the South Vietnamese government. Rostow was the only confirmed hawk in the group. I suspect he feared I was fostering a revolutionary cabal. I know he reported the discussions to LBJ, but I do not know what he said. I do know that on occasion there was a seemingly promising consensus for a modest initiative, but before anyone could initiate it, Rostow would nip it in the bud. To be honest, as decent a man as Rostow was, I was happy when he missed a meeting.

I kept no notes on the meetings, and it would be unfair after all these years to characterize in any detail the positions taken by those present. In a general way, after John McNaughton's unfortunate death in an airplane accident, Paul Warnke picked up his role with similar convictions. It would be fair to say that no one in the group except Rostow was in any way optimistic about Vietnam. I found it instructive to know that virtually no one saw any end to the war within any foreseeable time frame. We soldiered on because we could not agree on how to get into peace negotiations, and I think some were concerned that they would not be productive and could easily weaken the already fragile South Vietnamese government. We did discuss various approaches to the Soviet Union, and some were made. But it was never very clear how much influence Russia had, as compared to China and North Korea. We did discuss Robert Komer's plans for "Vietnamizing" the war, securing safe areas, and expanding them gradually. But that took time. Bob McNamara's expensive plan to expose the supply route to bombing was ingenious but inadequate. Native porters carrying heavy loads on their backs along the Ho Chi Minh trail trumped technology. Bus Wheeler repeatedly put forward the generals' case for loosening the rules of engagement to improve military performance, but most of us thought it too risky and the gain too speculative.

To put it bluntly, all saw a stalemate (although not all would have used that word), with neither "victory" nor "defeat" on the ground likely in the near future, if "victory" was defined as a return to the status quo of two Vietnams. The only hope for peace soon was a negotiated settlement, but even that was risky, because of the weakness of the South Vietnamese government. What would bring North Vietnam and the Vietcong to the table? Was it the carrot or the stick? Or some combination of the two? What settlement would we or they accept?

I found the Non-Group discussions helpful in bolstering my belief that negotiations, wherever they might lead, were the only way short of unilateral withdrawal to get us out of Vietnam. Whatever was said in response to presidential questions or opinions at Security Council meetings about progress on the ground, I felt confident I knew the difficulties of any other solution. The Communists were not about to give up, and violence, usually in the form of sneak hit-and-run attacks, was going to continue.

To the extent that there was division in the government, it revolved around the best way to get negotiations started. LBJ (and therefore a majority of his advisers) thought they would be the result of military pressure, primarily bombing of Hanoi and Haiphong. A minority of us—Bob McNamara and myself, for example—thought that the bombing damage done to the north's war effort, even assuming the targets were hit, was too insignificant to make a difference and too risky to boot. The risk most frequently discussed was accidentally hitting a Russian or Chinese freighter or some other noncombatant country's property. But the greater risk was the attitude at home to our bombing. The North Vietnamese rather cleverly said they would not negotiate as long as the bombing continued, without saying they would negotiate if it ceased. Much of the American public saw the continued bombing as our refusal to negotiate.

LBJ wanted to negotiate, but from a position of more strength than we were likely to achieve. We began to announce bombing pauses, in the hope that this would induce a positive response from the Communists. The pauses were opposed by the military, especially the navy and air force, who saw them as a sign of weakness on America's part. That concerned LBJ, as did the fact that Hanoi's failure to respond seemed to him and others simply to be giving them a free ride with nothing in return. The doves in Congress and the public welcomed the pauses but were never satisfied that they were long enough. Maybe a little longer would bring the north to the negotiating table. The hawks thought that the more determination to stay we showed and the higher the Communist losses were, the more incentive the north would have to negotiate a peace. LBJ, still concerned about the right wing domestically, was inclined to side with the hawks so long as we did not risk expanding the war.

I tended to favor longer bombing pauses, in part because I did not think the bombing put much pressure on the north and, more important, because it fed domestic dissent. Further, I doubted we could bring the Communists to the negotiating table unless they could see the possibility of achieving a united Communist Vietnam within a reasonable time (no longer than they thought they needed to do it forcibly). They were not going to agree to a permanently divided Vietnam. Indicating a willingness to negotiate could adversely affect their revolutionary efforts in the south in the same way it could weaken the South Vietnamese government.

There was somewhat more support for the hawk position, primarily because the military was never quite willing to face squarely the problems of fighting a guerrilla-type war and as a consequence gave mostly upbeat reports. Rusk, although he was critical of the military to me in private conversations, could not bring himself to believe that we would not succeed. Often he would say, "When we put our shoulder to the wheel, something will give." Rostow was the optimist, culling through intelligence for bits of good news about deterioration of enemy morale. McNamara was pessimistic, reflecting the views of his civilian subordinates rather than the military, as well as his own growing doubts about the prospect of success. There was never any intelligence that indicated the north was willing to enter into serious negotiations that would not lead to eventual unification under a Communist regime.

Security Council meetings really performed little function with respect to Vietnam other than giving people an opportunity to express their highly predictable views, and they were largely replaced by Tuesday lunches for principals only. I do remember vividly one meeting where at the outset LBJ said that he had determined to end the current bombing pause. He then said I would tell the group why he was wrong. I said that if the president had made up his mind, there was no reason for me to say anything. He was insistent, and I got increasingly annoyed. Finally, more in anger than in conviction, I did as he asked. When I had finished, he said, "All right. Let's take a vote. Who agrees with Nick and who agrees with me?" The vote was not surprising. I got one vote—my own.

A couple of minutes later LBJ rang for his secretary and whispered something to her. She went out and came back a few minutes later with a small package wrapped in white paper and tied with a ribbon. The president took it and passed it down the cabinet table past Rusk to me, indicating that I should open it. I did. It was a gold cigarette lighter with the presidential seal—the third one he had given me. It was, I think, about as far as LBJ could go in making an apology.

It was obvious in the fall of 1967 that the frustrations of the war in Vietnam were taking a toll not only on Bob McNamara but, even more important, on LBJ himself. He could not see an end, and his Great Society programs, which is where his New Deal heart lay, were suffering. Demonstrations against the war increased, public opinion became more and more critical, casualties increased. The military continued to report progress, mainly in the form of enemy combatants killed. But optimistic spin from the White House and the Pentagon did little to stem dissent and dissatisfaction. We pursued an approach to Hanoi through two French contacts of Henry Kissinger's, to no avail.

Convinced that we must persevere in Vietnam, Johnson sought the support of a distinguished bipartisan group of former public servants. The idea was Clark Clifford's (not yet defense secretary), and the group of "Wise Men" LBJ convened was indeed impressive: Dean Acheson, General Omar Bradley, George Ball, McGeorge Bundy, Arthur Dean, Douglas Dillon, Robert Murphy, Justice Abe Fortas, Ambassador Henry Cabot Lodge, Cyrus Vance, and Clifford. These former statesmen were joined by senior officials still in the government: Averell Harriman and Maxwell Taylor. The group was given generally upbeat, optimistic briefings by General Wheeler and George Carver of the CIA. Meeting with the president the next morning, the group—not surprisingly, in view of the optimism of the briefers the night before—was unanimous in urging the president to stay the course. Even George Ball, to the president's pleasure, agreed generally, though with some reservations. LBJ's resolve was strengthened by the unanimity of this diverse, experienced group of statesmen.

Ironically, though no one but LBJ knew it, McNamara had written a long memorandum to the president the night before (November 1) concluding that our course of action in Vietnam was doomed to failure; even slow, steady progress would not achieve our goals in any reasonable time frame. He would stabilize our force levels, stop bombing, and press for negotiation. He also in effect offered his resignation, and LBJ realized that if he were to stay the course in Vietnam, he would have to have a new secretary of defense.

I did not know of Bob McNamara's letter at the time, or for that matter until much later, since the president scarcely thought it wise to circulate it. I was, of course, aware of Bob's increasingly pessimistic views of the war from my Non-Group meetings as well as from a close personal attachment to him and his family. I was distressed by the briefings given to the Wise Men, which I thought misleading, as did my staff. But LBJ had thought of them as a means of validating his decision, not as a source of advice. Accordingly, I had a memorandum prepared for the president at Dick Holbrooke's suggestion—a memo he wrote, based, I believe, on Non-Group discussions, our conversations, and his own strong views. I did only some minor editing of what I thought was a brilliantly written analysis which was to bear my signature and which I knew was contrary to Rusk's view and would in all probability upset LBJ. I was hesitant to sign it, but, not knowing that McNamara had already expressed many of the same views, I thought it important that the president be aware of the problems that staying the course involved. I signed it and sent it to the White House in mid-November, and immediately gave a copy to Rusk so he would not be embarrassed by a call from the president. I think it was the only time I ever did anything behind his back, but I feared if I showed it to him first, it would never reach its destination.

I expected an explosion from the White House but never heard a word about the memo from the president or Rostow, then or later. I did not circulate the memo in the State Department to anyone other than the secretary, who said I might be surprised by how much of it he in fact agreed with. The only other comment I recall was from White House counsel and speech writer Harry McPherson, who cryptically commented, "Well, Nick, you have guts." I assumed it was in relation to the memo.

I think Dick's memo was as good a description of the problem as I have seen, and I am proud to have signed it. It argued for shifting more weight to the Vietnamese as an effort to reduce American casualties and a bombing halt to induce negotiations. The most quoted paragraph by historians after the event was an analogy that was indeed prophetic: "Hanoi uses time the way the Russians used terrain before Napoleon's advance on Moscow, always retreating, losing every battle, but continually creating conditions in which the enemy can no longer function. For Napoleon it was his long supply lines and the cold Russian winter; Hanoi hopes for us it will be the mounting dissension, impatience, and frustration caused by a protracted war without fronts or other visible signs of success . . . Time is the crucial element at this stage of our involvement in Vietnam. Can the tortoise of progress in Vietnam stay ahead of the rabbit of dissent at home?"

This timing problem was always the major weakness in our Vietnam policy. Given the constraints put upon the military with respect to staying out of North Vietnam, Laos, and Cambodia, the policy became one of attrition almost by default. The military sought to slowly grind down the enemy until he would come to the table and negotiate a reasonable settlement. We tended to underestimate his tenacity, and nobody could say when he would cry "Enough." We could not measure progress toward that goal, and until it happened we could not know if we were close or far away.

It was that equation in the United States—more casualties, more costs, and no ability to measure progress as to where we were—that fueled opposition at home. The military was following its policy and claiming incremental progress with upbeat communiqués. But "progress" was meaningless if we had no idea of how far we had to go. Given the constraints, more troops could not resolve the problem. Arguably, fewer troops and more pressure on the Vietnamese to get their house in order, both politically and militarily, was a better alternative.

President Johnson nominated McNamara to be president of the World Bank, a post Bob had always coveted, though perhaps not under the current circumstances. There was an irony in that all the truly serious reforms he had made in running the Pentagon in an efficient, business-like way were coming apart under the strain of the demands—and inevitable waste—of a war. LBJ sought a new secretary of defense and was careful to select a loyal friend, who he was confident shared his views, in Clark Clifford. Accordingly, at the beginning of February, Clifford began what he has described as the worst year of his life. He and McNamara worked closely on a transition, and he kept Paul Nitze and others on his staff. Indeed, although confirmed by the Senate on January 30, he and LBJ asked McNamara to remain as secretary through March to oversee the complex budgetary process.

I knew Clifford only slightly. He had been helpful in the Cuban prisoner ransom and even more so when, at Bobby's request, I tried to help Jackie Kennedy preserve some of her restoration work in the White House after JFK's assassination. Clifford had represented the Johnsons but had shown a sympathetic understanding of Jackie's fears that her hard work of restoring authenticity would go for naught. I respected him as a careful lawyer who paid attention to the facts and as an experienced politician who had served Truman well. I assumed LBJ had selected him because he was sympathetic to the president's determination to stay the course in Vietnam. At that time he may have been, but it did not turn out that way.

Before he left for the World Bank, McNamara spoke to me about his plan to examine in depth the decisions with respect to Vietnam and to discover, if possible, where and why we had gone wrong. He hoped such a study would help to avoid future mistakes and asked me to assign some able people to help. It was a typical McNamara gesture, knowing that the study was likely to be critical of him as well as others but putting the public interest first. I assigned Dick Holbrooke and two or three others to the job. Of course there was no intention that the study should become public while the war was still going on. I do not remember ever considering the possibility that it would be leaked to the press. But that is what happened early in the Nixon administration, when Dan Ellsberg gave a copy to the *New York Times*. The Nixon administration, unaware that the so-called Pentagon Papers even existed, scrambled to get a copy and then unsuccessfully tried to stop its publication.

Just before Christmas, the president asked me to go to Europe between Christmas and New Year's to assure governments there that our balance of payments, which for the first time in years was negative, would soon be corrected. With one eye on Vietnam and the other on his Great Society program, LBJ was always concerned about any development that looked as though the war was weakening our dominant, robust financial position. The secretary of the treasury, Henry Fowler, had suggested an import tax, which State opposed, and LBJ thought the proposal should be discussed with our European friends. I was to be accompanied by William Roth, who headed our trade negotiations, and Fred Deming, undersecretary of the treasury for monetary affairs. I got the impression that neither thought the balance-of-payments deficit was as serious as it was being made out to be, but both were very capable experts on trade and foreign exchange who could explain the steps we contemplated taking to restore a positive balance. I was confident that they would understand what this trip (which made little sense to me) was all about and explain our policy to LBJ's satisfaction. I thought there were a lot of bigger fish to fry in our relations with Europe.

We did the trip at what seemed to me lightning speed, dealing with at least two countries a day and carefully explaining our position. The commanding general of our forces in Germany provided a plane and crew, and except for the good company of my companions, there was nothing particularly memorable. I do remember the Swiss volunteering to help us promote tourism in the United States, and the French quite correctly telling us that the problem would disappear once we left Vietnam. In general we met with senior officials who dealt with finance and trade, and Bill and Fred did most of the talking. For some reason, LBJ was insistent that we meet with the British prime minister, Harold Wilson. Mr. Wilson had no desire to meet with us, apparently sharing my lack of interest in balance-of-payments problems. However, out of respect for our distinguished ambassador, David Bruce, he agreed to meet with us at eight p.m. on a Saturday evening at the prime minister's country residence, Chequers, provided that we stayed no more than fifteen minutes. We met Saturday morning with the British officials, and when I returned to the ambassador's residence David Bruce told me that the BBC wanted to interview me on Vietnam. He said it was a good idea, but warned me that the prime minister might not like it. I agreed to an interview that afternoon. At least I felt I knew something about the subject and hoped that a quiet and thoughtful session might help calm British criticism. The interview went quite well, I thought, and David agreed.

That evening the ambassador and the three of us set out in the embassy limousine for Chequers, carefully timing our arrival for about two minutes before eight. It was snowing lightly as we arrived. Knowing that we were limited to fifteen minutes, I had planned a late dinner, since after our short meeting with Wilson we expected to be back in London by about nine-thirty. The prime minister and his colleagues greeted us warmly, and we proceeded to brief him on the balance of payments, honing our presentations to about ten minutes. We said we were prepared to answer any questions. Wilson, a former Oxford don who had taught economics, had none, so we rose to leave.

"No," said the prime minister. "Don't go yet. I listened to your talk on BBC. I thought it went very well, but I have some questions on Vietnam."

There followed some questions on Vietnam, but it soon became obvious that his real interest was not Vietnam but what kind of a man President Johnson was. The questions kept coming and the time kept passing. Thinking not only of his fifteen-minute limitation but my dinner, I rose several times to leave. But Wilson was insistent there was no rush, and one hour and then part of another passed.

"Why do you suppose it is," he asked, "that throughout history the names of the evil men behind the throne have so often started with 'R'—Richelieu, Robespierre, Rasputin, and now in your country . . ." He paused. "Ah, to say more would be indiscreet." At the time I wondered whether he was thinking of Rostow or Rusk, or both. In any event, I have never forgotten the observation, which has its present-day parallel in Donald Rumsfeld.

Finally, just before ten, he asked if we had ever visited Chequers before. When I said we had not, he volunteered to be a tour guide through the beautiful old estate with its priceless art and antiques. What I recall most vividly was a Titian painting of the La Fontaine fable about the elephant and the mouse. Both animals were quite visible in the painting, and Wilson explained that this had not always been so. When Winston Churchill was prime minister, he was frustrated not to be able to find the mouse in the old painting. So he simply painted the mouse back on the canvas where he thought it should be. Having any other artist add to a Titian might have lessened its value, but Churchill's addition undoubtedly enhanced it.

We got back to London well before midnight but too late for dinner. The ambasssador's staff had all retired for the night, but David's charming wife, Evangeline, made us sandwiches. Missing dinner did not matter. The evening was far more interesting than balance of payments. But despite Churchill and Titian, the "R's" showed again how Vietnam permeated everything, even outside Washington, and how everyone was curious about our tall Texan president.

Hanoi celebrated Clifford's confirmation as secretary of defense on

January 30, 1968, by launching its Tet offensive—ironically, during the president's weekly Tuesday luncheon to discuss Vietnam policy and initiatives with his principal advisers. There had been a great deal of intelligence, none of it made public, that Hanoi might launch some kind of major offensive during the Tet religious holidays. LBJ was convinced it would be at Khe Sanh, the large U.S. Marine base. But it began with an audacious attack on the U.S. embassy in Saigon and continued with fierce attacks in five of Vietnam's six major cities and most of its provincial capitals. American forces, though not anticipating such a broad-scale offensive, fought back efficiently and inflicted huge losses on the enemy. The American public, informed only by a steady diet of reports of progress in the war, was stunned and angry.

One can argue quite persuasively that the huge losses suffered by the Vietcong and Hanoi amounted to a United States military victory. Supporters of the war did their best to paint such a picture in the days and weeks following Tet. But even if true, it was irrelevant. The massive attacks on the heels of upbeat progress reports effectively destroyed the public's confidence in the administration and the president's leadership. It also caused the incoming secretary of defense to question the assumptions he had previously held, and he spent most of February and March examining for himself conflicting views on Vietnam.

Tet had the effect of further separating hawks and doves within the administration. The president ordered expanded bombing of North Vietnam, which seemed to doves somewhat inconsistent with claims of a major defeat for the Communists. Westmoreland hinted at the need for 205,000 additional troops, although it was not clear why a victory at Tet caused a need for more soldiers. Rusk and Rostow generally joined the military in arguing for increased pressure on Hanoi, and the president was anxious to take advantage of our claimed success to make a major speech. Wheeler went to Saigon to talk to Westmoreland about the need for more troops, and Philip Habib, now Bill Bundy's deputy, accompanied him. Habib had been the deputy chief of mission in Saigon and was not only familiar with the problems but honest and blunt in his assessment. I was in a meeting with Rusk, Rostow, Clifford, McNamara, and others when he called from Hawaii to give me his report orally. He expressed grave concern over the stability of the government in the south and said that embassy civilians who were aware of Westmoreland's request were divided over its wisdom or necessity. Like most assessments, it changed no views within the group, though I was hopeful that Clifford, who was careful not to express his own position, took note.

It is fair to say that the administration's loss of credibility on Vietnam after Tet meant that no amount of positive spin on that event—even though much of what was said was accurate—succeeded in convincing the public that Tet was really a victory for our side. Clifford, whose vast experience made him sensitive to public attitudes, was painfully aware of this fact. In March he continued his education, and I attended a number of meetings in the Pentagon on the subject as a member of his informal task force. Oddly, Rusk usually declined and sent me, I believe, because he did not think the secretary of state should go to the Pentagon to a meeting called by the secretary of defense. The laboring oar was taken by Paul Warnke, with support from Paul Nitze, and their views, often expressed in the Non-Group, came as no surprise. One most persuasive advocate for a dovish position was Townsend Hoopes, the secretary of the air force, who wrote some excellent memos analyzing the problems. While Clifford kept his conclusions to himself and for LBJ alone, it was increasingly clear that his doubts were mounting and that he was search- ing for some plan that he could sell the president. The split, epitomized by the Pentagon civilians versus the Pentagon military, grew more and more pronounced. It centered on Westmoreland's request for 205,000 more men, which eventually was leaked to the press just two days before the New Hampshire primary.

Eugene McCarthy did far better in New Hampshire than had been expected, as his "end the war" message got a big boost from Tet. The effect of his showing on LBJ seemed to be to toughen his stance on the war. He planned a major speech, and the task force preparing it was divided, as usual, between those who wanted to step up our military action and those who wanted to halt bombing as a hopeful prelude to negotiation. The military and Rostow, strongly supported by Fortas, were leading the first group; Arthur Goldberg, now ambassador to the UN, argued strongly for the second; Rusk and Clifford were somewhere in between. While LBJ was reluctant to increase the military force or take off the restraints on actions in Laos and Cambodia, he was, if anything, even more reluctant to stop the bombing.

What turned out to be a genuine turning point was another meet- ing of the Wise Men late in March. I met briefly with Dean Acheson, McGeorge Bundy, George Ball, and Cyrus Vance before a dinner in the State Department dining room. It was obvious that Acheson, the leader of the group (if such a distinguished group can be said to have a leader), was having serious second thoughts, and I could not help wondering if he had been talking to his son-in-law, Bill Bundy, or Bill's deputy, Phil Habib. All had read background papers prepared by State and Defense. LBJ stopped by to shake hands but did not remain. At dinner there was lively discussion, Rusk and Clifford were questioned closely, and Helms, Bundy, and I chipped in from time to time.

After dinner we all went to the State Department Operations Center for detailed briefings by George Carver of the CIA, General William DePuy, a special assistant to the joint chiefs who had commanded troops in Vietnam, and Habib. Carver's presentation was somewhat more pessimistic than previously, in that he saw a longer time frame before real pacification, though it was still fundamentally upbeat. General DePuy saw Tet as a serious defeat for Hanoi, but his credibility was seriously damaged on that issue by a vigorous cross-examination by Arthur Goldberg, who manipulated the death and casualty figures to demonstrate that there could now be no Vietnamese Communists left in shape to fight. Phil Habib gave a candid and somewhat alarming picture of the fragility of the South Vietnamese government. His intelligent analysis and blunt Brooklyn honesty came through in spades. Asked by Clifford if he thought military victory possible, he did not fudge in his reply: "Not under present circumstances." In response to a further question on what he would do, he said he would stop the bombing and negotiate.

The Wise Men reported to the president the next day at lunch in the White House. I was not there and only heard about it secondhand. The upshot was that their unanimity was shattered and they too, like the administration itself, were divided. It was a blow to LBJ, and to some extent to Rusk and Rostow as well. When a statesman like Acheson, with his vast experience, is no longer supportive, it is a serious matter. It was not a unanimous turnaround, but it did not have to be to matter.

Others continued to work on the president's major address for Sunday, March 31. While I felt certain that Clark Clifford no longer supported a military solution, I fully expected a strong speech in support of a hawkish position. I felt that the division of the Wise Men, rather than causing LBJ to reconsider his whole Vietnam policy, was more likely to harden his position. Presidents do not like to be told they are wrong, even by old friends.

On Saturday, March 30, Dean Rusk left for the annual meeting of ANZUS, the foreign ministers of Australia, New Zealand, and the United States, so I attended a long and somewhat contentious meeting in the Cabinet Room with the president and his principal advisers with respect to his Sunday speech. The speech was far more conciliatory than I expected, but still a mixture of hawk and dove. The president looked exhausted and lacked his usual sparkle.

My contribution was to change the language that we would not bomb above the 20th parallel to a more generalized statement that we would bomb only "in the area north of the Demilitarized Zone, where the continued enemy buildup directly threatens allied forward positions." That was the rationale for the 20th parallel. I vividly recall the change, which all agreed to, because it led to public and congressional misunderstandings almost immediately after the speech, when the first U.S. attacks were just south of the 20th parallel (which was permitted but certainly not expected) and over 200 miles north of the DMZ. I should have left well enough alone.

I was at home with my family on Sunday evening when the president spoke. While most of the speech was familiar, the ending sentences—LBJ's decision not to run again for the presidency—were not. They came as a total shock to all of us, except my wife, Lydia. Unknown to me, she had made three or four fifty-cent bets that he would announce just that.

"Why," I asked her, "did you think he would refuse to run?"

"I've suspected it for months. The burdens and disappointments were just too great—and it showed."

XXVI

Nineteen sixty-eight was my eighth consecutive year in government, and it was by far the most frustrating and depressing year for me—and I think for many others as well. Perhaps that is often the case in the final year of an administration, when people are tired and thinking of returning to private life. But I think 1968 was more so, even if one puts aside the constant bickering about Vietnam and the failure of the peace talks we eventually got started.

The year began with the capture in January of the U.S. communication ship *Pueblo* and its entire naval crew by the North Koreans. The *Pueblo*, equipped much as the *Liberty* had been, was not damaged in an attack. It was simply forced into the North Korean port of Wonsan by ships from North Korea while cruising in international waters. Unfortunately, and inexcusably, the navy had no ships or planes in the area capable of providing protection. Captain Lloyd Butcher and his crew were unable to destroy the vast amount of classified information on board, and the capture was a serious loss from that viewpoint, and it was exploited by the Koreans for propaganda purposes. There really was not anything very effective one could do about it.

The Security Council, augmented by naval officers, met with the president in the White House Situation Room and discussed possible actions. The navy was confident the ship had been in international waters, but, not surprisingly, the North Koreans claimed otherwise. We could and did strongly protest its seizure and demand return of the ship and its crew, knowing that the protests were futile, as were our complaints to North Korea's allies, China and the Soviet Union. Military action would accomplish nothing. By the time we located the *Pueblo* in Wonsan harbor, it had been ransacked, and sinking it would have been pointless and further endangered the crew. As it was, we knew they were suffering from coercive treatment designed to get confessions for propaganda use. A very small number "confessed" under such torture, but most of the crew did not. Indeed, when the Koreans released a picture of the crew for publicity, most of them unobtrusively extended their middle finger upward, a gesture unfamiliar to the Koreans but greatly appreciated at home and elsewhere in the free world.

We did not abandon Captain Butcher and his crew, and we kept working on ways to secure their release. Their capture was protested vehemently by our military representatives at the Panmunjom meetings in the Demilitarized Zone, to no avail, and the crew was cruelly exploited for Communist propaganda reasons. Finally, in October, a former ambassador to South Korea, Winthrop Brown, came to my office with Jim Leonard, a Foreign Service officer who had been his deputy chief of mission and was now working in the State Department Intelligence and Research Group.

"Jim and I have been talking about the *Pueblo* crew," said the ambassador, "and he has an idea that just might work."

"What's that?" I asked, more wearily than expectantly.

Jim said that he did not think the Koreans would release the crew unless we admitted that they had been unlawfully in North Korea's territorial waters. At the same time, he explained, the Koreans were very literal, and he thought that if we said exactly what they wanted us to say, we could say anything else before and after we said it. For example, we could say that every word we were about to utter was false and was said only to gain the return of the crew, which was unlawfully being held hostage. We would then "confess," as the Koreans wanted, followed by a denial that the "confession" was truthful.

It sounded crazy to me. I asked him if he meant that the Koreans would accept the apology knowing in advance that we were repudiating it immediately before and after it was made. He said he thought they would, and the ambassador agreed.

After they left my office, I thought about the proposal. Obviously our "confession" could be used with the denials cropped out in North Korea, but the rest of the world would hear our version. That seemed to me a reasonable price to pay, since the North Koreans were already brainwashed into accepting their government's view.

I started at the top. There was no point in going forward if LBJ was not on board. As in every phone conversation I was to have with others on the subject, he was incredulous that the North Koreans might agree. He said it was okay with him if the navy agreed. There was no problem with the civilians in the Pentagon, Paul Warnke and Paul Nitze. So I talked to the admiral, who, by the luck of the draw, was our representative at the Panmunjom talks (the services rotated).

"You mean I can say all that and they'll still agree?" Like me, he had difficulty understanding the Korean mind.

"You can say whatever you want before and after, as long as you make precisely the apology they insist upon," I said.

"Okay," said the admiral. "Let's see if it will fly."

It did, but it took us some weeks to work out the details of the exchange. On December 23, I sat anxiously in the State Department Operations Room with Jim Leonard as the exchange came off exactly as planned and Captain Butcher and his crew were turned over to us. I felt a little as I had felt six years earlier at Christmas, when the Cuban prisoners were released by Castro.

The Communist attacks of Tet occurred less than a week after North Korea captured the *Pueblo,* and LBJ was convinced it was a coordinated Communist plot designed to embarrass him. But he remained cool, and Soviet experts convinced him that the USSR was probably not involved. With the administration badly divided, talk turned to the possibility of a bombing cessation in return for peace talks—all in the context of the president's major Vietnam address of March 31. In that speech the president had announced that if peace talks occurred, Averell Harriman would lead the U.S. negotiating team, an announcement designed in part to conciliate doves.

Just three days after the president's speech, with Senator Fulbright and much of the press attacking LBJ for the bombing almost 200 miles north of the DMZ, Hanoi radio announced that the North Vietnamese were willing to sit down with United States representatives and negotiate—not peace, but an end to the bombing. Still, it was more than we had seen before, and Clifford, Harriman, and I were anxious to flesh out its meaning. As might be expected, the announcement continued the controversy between hawks and doves—a controversy that was repeated countless times over the remaining months of the administration and, in my view, impeded the negotiations once they got started in Paris.

On this occasion the president again sided with the doves, rejecting Rostow's advice to step up military action as a means of encouraging negotiations. I think my prior suggestion had raised such a storm that LBJ did not want to be accused of missing an opportunity, if opportunity it was. I was pleasantly surprised when he asked Clifford and me to draft a response. He did not want to get public hopes too high, but in typical LBJ fashion, he wanted a response to be on the evening news. Our response was short but direct, saying that the president would send representatives to any forum at any time to discuss with the North Vietnamese the means for ending the war.

Before there was any response from Hanoi, another tragedy occurred. The next day, April 4, Martin Luther King was assassinated in Memphis, and all hell broke out around the country as blacks, angry at the loss of their great leader, took to the streets. Riots occurred in over a hundred cities, and the National Guard was called out in Washington and a number of other major metropolitan centers. Bobby Kennedy, now a candidate for the Democratic presidential nomination, was on his way to speak to a predominantly black audience in Indianapolis. Ignoring the warnings of the police chief and his own staff, Bobby gave one of his great speeches, mostly extemporaneous, decrying violence and praising King for his love of humanity and peace. In a day and night of violence and despair, his words were the only bright spot.

King's funeral service was scheduled for April 7 in Atlanta. LBJ called me at home on the evening of the fifth and told me that he would not be going but that Hubert Humphrey would lead the official delegation. He thought it important that I go and had made arrangements with Humphrey for me to be in the delegation. I assumed his own absence was at the insistence of the Secret Service and was flattered at his request that I go, even though I suspected it was a counterbalance to Bobby and an effort to strengthen Humphrey's candidacy for the Democratic nomination. Later Humphrey's staff confirmed the arrangements.

I do not know what happened next, but in the morning Humphrey's people called again. Sorry, there was no room on the plane. A lot of important people had to be accommodated. I was stunned and angry. Hubert Humphrey always had difficulty saying no to anyone, and I guessed he had just said yes too many times to politicians who wanted the publicity. I still wanted to go, though I knew any commercial flight would be hopeless. With some hesitation, I called Bobby's office.

My hesitation was founded not in his candidacy but on an incident some months before. A young Foreign Service officer had come to my office and told me that Bobby was relying in his talks on Vietnam on an unreliable source, and the officer felt Bobby should be warned. I had written Bobby a letter to that effect, thinking that I was being helpful. As it turned out, Bobby was right and the Foreign Service officer wrong. The source turned out to be reliable, and Bobby had interpreted my letter as an effort to moot his criticism of the war rather than be helpful.

He wrote me a quite nasty, sarcastic letter. I responded with an explanation and took exception to his tone, stating that I strongly resented the thought that I would do what apparently he thought I had attempted to do. I had not seen or talked to him in the weeks since.

Bobby's office called back and said that if I could get to Kennedy Airport, I could go to Atlanta with Jackie and return to Washington with Bobby. I did so, but when I got to Kennedy, Jackie had already departed, earlier than scheduled. She had left me a note saying that I had a ticket on a commercial flight from Newark. I took a limousine to Newark and went on to Atlanta.

The area surrounding the Ebenezer Baptist Church was packed with thousands of people, and there was no possibility that I would attend the funeral itself. It was a hot and humid day, and after the service, which was broadcast on loudspeakers, a long procession began walking through the streets of Atlanta, some five miles, in honor of King. I joined the march and saw many familiar figures as we straggled along. After a while I was joined by Ivan Allen, Jr., the mayor of Atlanta, whom I knew to be dedicated to racial equality. We chatted awhile, and he described the small, crowded church. He also told me that he had been the person who had had the sad task of informing King's wife, Coretta, of the assassination. I was tired, hot, disappointed, and out of sorts when he suggested we stop in his office for a cold Coke. We did, and he got me a car to go to the airport.

I left for the airport early so as to be sure not to keep Bobby waiting— or to be left waiting myself. He arrived in his shirtsleeves, a familiar sight, with a couple of staff members. When we got on the small jet, he made it a point to sit next to me. We were barely airborne when he put his hand on my knee and told me to forget about our dispute, it was over, finished, and forgotten. I am not sure whether he was forgiving me or apologizing for his own conduct. Nor did it matter. Our friendship was restored, and I was tremendously relieved.

We talked about a variety of things. Bobby was convinced that LBJ remained a hawk on Vietnam, and it was hard to say he was wrong. But I did tell him I was enormously encouraged by Clifford's attitude and thought his long friendship with the president might be a turning point. At least, I hoped so. Where Rusk stood, I really had no idea, despite our daily contact and our frequent evening conversations over a friendly drink. I liked the secretary (Bobby did not), but I never was able to penetrate his public personality and get to know the man behind the facade.

On my return to Washington, the city was still recovering from the riot, and LBJ was at Camp David with Rusk and Clifford. Westmoreland had returned to Washington, along with Ambassador Ellsworth Bunker. Neither was very pleased about the possibility of negotiations, for somewhat different reasons. Westmoreland was unhappy about any restrictions on bombing; Bunker was very concerned about the stability of the South Vietnamese government if negotiations got under way. President Johnson spent time selecting Harriman's team. He was concerned that Harriman would not be tough enough and would compromise too quickly. Finally he persuaded Cyrus Vance to join as coleader, an arrangement I thought excellent. Vance was close to LBJ; he had worked with him in the Senate in the early 1950s as well as in the administration with McNamara, and Averell Harriman welcomed him. I believe our Non-Group discussions had something to do with their mutual regard. LBJ thought he was appointing a tough negotiator to keep Harriman from giving the house away, and Harriman knew Vance's real concerns about our continuing to fight in Vietnam. I was also able to persuade Harriman to take as a junior member my assistant, Dick Holbrooke. While I knew I would miss Dick's knowledge and experience, I also knew that he was most anxious to be a member of the delegation and that his knowledge would be helpful. If nothing more, he would give me an objective source of advice on the negotiations once they started. Again, Dick's presence at and contributions to the Non-Group meetings made him acceptable to both Harriman and Vance.

The next month was spent looking for agreement on a location for the talks. Finally the North Vietnamese suggested Paris, as we had hoped they might, and at long last we had a place for the meetings. We were not really well prepared for the talks; it is difficult to give guidance to negotiators when the government itself is still divided. To make it a good deal more difficult, the South Vietnamese government under President Nguyen Van Thieu remained weak and wary.

Ambassador Bunker was very concerned that the meetings in Paris would themselves threaten the existence of the South Vietnamese government and cause its collapse. Bunker was experienced and able, and his concerns had to be taken seriously. They were, I am sure, a major factor in Rusk's taking a hard line with respect to the negotiations, joining Rostow and the military in wanting to step up the amount of bombing below the 20th parallel. The thought was that stepped-up military pressure would bolster South Vietnamese confidence and convince the north we were serious about remaining. Secretary Clifford was concerned that such action would sabotage the peace talks and we would be back to square one. The president was hesitant, as always, to disagree with the military, but he continued to give his old friend very cautious and conditional support. There was agreement between hawks and doves that the Communists were likely, as usual, to take a tough negotiating position, but there really was not a lot of agreement on how we should respond. For a long time it made little difference, since Hanoi came forward with nothing of substance and a lot that was demonstrably silly, such as its insistence that it had no troops in the south.

Once the Paris talks got started, I had relatively little to do with instructions to the negotiating team. Their instructions, such as they were, came out of the White House Tuesday luncheons, which I only rarely attended when Rusk was away. Rusk took an active role and a very tough one in attempting to guide the negotiations—he was much more active than he had been before they commenced. Clifford had his work cut out for him, but he had some help from Vance, who returned from time to time.

I have always felt that in government or business or law, the only way to negotiate is to select the best people you can find, be sure they have all the information they need, and trust their judgment in the negotiations. If what they come up with is not good enough, so be it. But trying to tell people on the spot what to do and not do is in my view counterproductive. They know the situation better than you do. Both Vance and Harriman were skilled professionals. I recalled that a year or so earlier there had been a flare-up of relations on the island of Cyprus and a real danger of war breaking out between Greece and Turkey. With LBJ's approval, I had asked Vance, on a few hours' notice, to fly to Cyprus and see if he could bring the Greeks and Turks together. I provided him with a plane, translators, and two or three of our best experts on Greece and Turkey.

"What," he asked, "are my instructions?"

"Prevent a war," I responded. And he did.

I felt much the same way about Paris. If the negotiators had questions or wanted advice on particular proposals, we should try to respond helpfully. Otherwise, it would be most productive to stay out of their way. Unfortunately, we did not.

ABOUT THREE A.M. ON JUNE 5, I WAS AWAKENED BY THE BEDSIDE phone. It was a voice I knew from Bobby Kennedy's staff.

"Bobby has been shot!"

I could not believe it. It was just too much. First Medgar Evers. Then

JFK. Then Martin Luther King. Now Bobby. The world was crumbling all around me.

"Is he alive?" I asked.

"Yes," came the reply, "but there is no way he can survive."

Lydia and I got up and dressed. I wanted to do something but could not think of anything useful to do. I would call Ethel Kennedy later, but this did not seem the time to do it. I just felt helpless, powerless, and angry at a world where this could happen. I thought of our plane ride from Atlanta and the vibrant, energetic idealist I had known and worked for in the Department of Justice. I was sad now not to have been a part of his campaign to be president. I felt so out of it—out of everything that mattered.

Later I heard not only about his death but about the funeral arrangements. He would be flown back to New York and would lie in Saint Patrick's Cathedral all day Friday and Friday night. The service was scheduled for Saturday morning, and at its conclusion the body would be carried by a special train to Washington for burial next to his brother at Arlington Cemetery. Someone on his staff had thoughtfully reserved a room for Lydia and me at a hotel near the cathedral. Along with many others, I was scheduled to be one of a shifting honor guard standing by his coffin, and I was given times for my duty. It was all very efficiently run, which simply increased my feeling of total despair.

I did get slightly involved in the planning, with Bob McNamara's help. When the train arrived Saturday in Washington, a motorcade would follow the hearse from Union Station past the Justice Department, where it would pause a moment in memory of Bobby's service, and Attorney General Ramsey Clark would leave the mass of loyal employees present to pay their respects to join the motorcade as it went on to Arlington. When Bobby had been AG, his favorite driver had been Clyde Herndon, who had become mine as well. When I moved to State, I made arrangements for Clyde to get a raise and come with me. I thought it appropriate to have Clyde meet Ethel and the children he knew so well and follow the hearse on this last trip.

That weekend Lydia had been planning to join our children at her parents' summer camp in the Adirondacks while I attended my twenty-fifth reunion at Princeton. Instead, we both went to New York. I have never seen, before or since, lines as long as those that wound through the streets of the city, with people of all races and ethnic backgrounds waiting to view Bobby. Many were unabashedly in tears as they patiently stood and waited hours for their turn. Well before my appointed time, I approached Saint Patrick's and its cordon of police officers. I identified myself and was immediately escorted into the huge cathedral. I sat for a few minutes and then was taken up to my place, with three others, to stand at a corner of the coffin. Tears were streaming down my face, but the tears made me feel at one with the others in the church. Bobby had that effect on people, and I think the country suffered a loss the magnitude of which may never be fully appreciated.

The next morning Lydia and I went to the funeral mass and listened to Teddy Kennedy give a moving eulogy. The church was packed, with hundreds outside as well. At the conclusion I joined the many honorary pallbearers and followed Bobby's casket to the hearse that would take him to the special train at Pennsylvania Station. There was a long line of cars waiting to transport us there as well.

The train was late in starting its long, sad journey. Bobby's casket was in the last car, a glass observation car with seats for Ethel, the family, and very close friends. How Ethel survived is a miracle to me, but she never broke down for a minute. As at the cathedral, Bobby's friends took turns standing by the casket in silent mourning.

All the way to Washington the tracks were lined with thousands of people paying tribute to this young leader. They were silent; many knelt, many crossed themselves. The train was often forced to slow down to a crawl because so many people had crowded onto the tracks to get a final glimpse of Bobby. As we went through Princeton Junction, the nearest station to the university where I had been planning to celebrate my major reunion, I was pleased to see many alumni in their orange-and-black outfits lining the tracks on both sides in silent tribute.

The train was crowded with Bobby's friends. As so often happens at funerals, one sees many friends whom one has not seen in months or even years, and despite the sadness of the occasion, there is pleasure in talking to old colleagues. Many were civil rights leaders and activists, many were from Bobby's campaign staff, many were from the press, many were his colleagues in the Department of Justice and the Senate. Averell Harriman was back from Paris, a tribute to a young man he had much loved and admired. I remember talking to the Reverend Ralph Abernathy, whom I had not seen in years. Indeed, I was chatting with him when I got word that Ethel, who, realizing it would be dark by the time we got to Arlington because of the slowness of the trip, wanted candles. Candles seemed much more fitting than flashlights or spotlights to illuminate the gravesite and prevent the many spectators from stumbling around in the night. There was only one place I could think of to find a couple of thousand candles. I used the telephone on the train to call the Catholic diocese in Washington. They were so obliging that it occurred to me that they had already thought of it, or that someone else had called as well.

When the train arrived at Union Station, we waited while Bobby was taken to the waiting hearse. Waiting for Ethel and the family was Clyde, his tall, thin figure clearly recognizable above the heads of the crowd. We made the slow drive to Arlington, and there, to my delight, were hundreds of people with candles lighting up the cemetery as we proceeded to the gravesite. It was a sad but beautiful picture. The president and Mrs. Johnson were there, along with every dignitary Washington was capable of producing. Finally, in the candlelight and with a faint moon in the sky, Bobby was put to rest beside the grave of his brother.

———————— • ◆ • ————————

I HAD MADE UP MY MIND BEFORE BOBBY'S DEATH TO LEAVE government at the end of President Johnson's term, irrespective of the election results. The last two years had been terribly frustrating, I was tired, and I could not support a family with four children, two of college age, even on a cabinet salary of $25,000, let alone the $20,000 I received as undersecretary. Doing an honest job in a high governmental position is exhausting, with long days at the office, including Saturdays and often part of Sundays, and little vacation time—a week, if you are lucky. Further, I think government benefits from the new energy and new ideas of incoming officials even of the same political party. The routine seems less so when seen with the fresh excitement of new people taking over.

Much of the last six months I felt as if I were treading water, even though some interesting and even important things were still taking place. I spent quite some time working with Assistant Secretary Joe Sisco on possible scenarios for settling matters in the Middle East, with the thought that the work would be useful if talks ever did get started. Our thoughts were enriched by the new Israeli ambassador, Yitzhak Rabin, who in my opinion was the most thoughtful and most candid of a succession of able ambassadors. As the general in charge during the Six-Day War, he could speak with authority about Israel's security needs and was surprisingly flexible as to what was truly essential. I liked him tremendously.

I flew down to Nicaragua to celebrate some anniversary of the Somoza family rule. Anastasio ("Pachito") Somoza, a West Point graduate, had succeeded his brother Luis as president after heading up the armed forces. I remember the trip not for its substantive importance but for two amusing events. I decided to give my speech in Spanish, which was carried to the country on television, and had the department prepare a Spanish version, if indeed my nerve did not fail me. I had taken a couple of years of Spanish in college, could read it pretty well, had a good accent, but could not speak it with any fluency at all. My speech in Spanish was a great success, so much so that the press was all over me at the end, with questions shouted in Spanish that I was totally unable to answer, and my denials that I spoke the language fell on deaf ears. It does not always pay to show off. The second memory that I have is a late afternoon reception and conversation with Pachito Somoza. I forget the conversation, but I was impressed with his consumption of seven scotch and sodas while I gulped down one.

As I have said, I had little to do with instructions to our negotiators in Paris, although I kept in touch with Harriman and Vance throughout and received cables from Dick Holbrooke assessing progress, or the lack of it. Vance and Harriman had established quite good relations with their North Vietnamese counterparts in informal discussions away from the negotiating table, but progress was often frustrated by tough instructions from Washington. The problem was not simply the expected rigid position of Hanoi and the Vietcong, but the difficulty of getting the South Vietnamese to agree to anything. So long as the United States was in Vietnam in force, they saw little to be gained and much to be lost in the talks if they led to our withdrawal. Nothing was happening, and LBJ was convinced that President Thieu was dragging his feet because Nixon, through Anna Chennault, an old China hand, was urging him to await the election results and agree to nothing. If so, probably nothing of substance would happen, since, paradoxically, the weak position of the South Vietnamese government increased the strength of its bargaining position. Rusk and Bunker—and therefore LBJ—were constantly worried that the government would collapse and we would be held responsible.

Rusk had agreed with the Indian government that there would be a three-day meeting in New Delhi to exchange views on various international matters, such as the cold war, economic assistance programs, and other matters of common interest. I was named to lead the U.S. team to the midsummer meeting. With Luke Battle, the assistant secretary for Near East affairs, Larry Eagleburger put together an agenda and a list of participants. Lydia and I, Luke and his wife, Betty, and a group of State Department professionals took off for the heat of summer in New Delhi. There Lydia and I stayed with our ambassador, Chester Bowles, and his wife, Steb, a couple I had always liked. We had known both slightly when he was governor of Connecticut and I was teaching at Yale Law School. My affection increased when he told me to get out of my coat and tie and ordered me some loose white cotton short-sleeved shirts to wear to our meetings although not to our courtesy call on the prime minister, Indira Gandhi. I had expected to be impressed with Mrs. Gandhi, but I was not. Perhaps I caught her on a bad day.

The meetings, accompanied as usual by too much food and drink and too many speeches, went off extremely well. Larry had done a superb job of preparation, staying up all night to refine and hone the presentations of others. The Indians were pleased and very complimentary. Chet Bowles was pleased. For the most part I was just hot.

On the way home to Washington we stopped in Paris and I met with Harriman and Vance. It was a long flight from New Delhi, and with the time change, Lydia and I were quite tired. Nonetheless, Averell insisted he take us to dinner at Le Grand Vefour, a centuries-old Parisian restaurant with a three-star Michelin cuisine and my favorite Paris menu. We were really too tired to enjoy the great cuisine and too depressed by the lack of progress in the talks to enjoy ourselves. I cannot remember what I ordered, but I will never forget my shock and amazement when Marie Harriman ordered two boiled eggs.

The next morning Dick Holbrooke drove us to the airport and gave me a thorough briefing on what was, or was not, happening. The negotiating team was increasingly frustrated by instructions from Washington that they felt were totally unresponsive to North Vietnamese proposals. I felt powerless to be much help now that Rusk was becoming more and more active in controlling instructions. I could and did try to help Clifford, but that was about the limit of my ability. Dick was disappointed in my lack of any real thoughts as to how to help the negotiators. But it was clear that this able young man was not wasting his time. I was greatly impressed with how quickly he had learned to drive with the nonchalance of the French as he cut in and out of traffic, talking the whole time.

It was an election year, and that fact was bound to affect much of what was going on in Washington, as it was affecting the negotiations in Vietnam. Harriman was convinced that the election of Nixon would be a far greater tragedy than the loss of Vietnam, and often said so. He felt strongly, whether or not correctly, that achieving a settlement through negotiation would help elect Humphrey and free him of the taint that attached to what the left and many others perceived as LBJ's failed war in Vietnam. I have handwritten notes from him asking if LBJ really wanted Humphrey to get elected, and if so, why the instructions he and Vance received were so inflexible.

When I got back to Washington, the election had given me a new assignment. One of the jobs of an election year is to brief the candidates of both parties on various foreign affairs. It fell to me to brief Richard Nixon; Rusk was out of town. I had never met Nixon, but together with some experts, I spent an afternoon briefing him and answering his questions. He was clearly well informed and asked good questions, not easy to answer. We spent a lot of time on the cold war, and particularly the situation in Czechoslovakia, which was enjoying what has become known as Prague Spring. Alexander Dubcek, a new brand of reform Communist, had become head of the party and was liberalizing both political and economic activity in small ways. Every time he gave a little, the Czechs took more, and it was exciting to see the iron grip of the party losing a measure of control. The burning question was how much liberalization the Soviets would tolerate.

There were many, including Nixon, who felt that the Soviets had been weakened so much since the death of Stalin that they would not interfere. As I told Nixon, however, that was not the dominant view of our intelligence experts, who felt that if things continued to unravel, the Warsaw Pact countries, under Soviet leadership, would have to intervene. I am not sure that the intelligence officials and I convinced Nixon, but thereafter he took a very cautious public stance. On August 20 and 21, thousands of Soviet tanks crossed into Czechoslovakia, removed Dubcek from power, and put an end to the Prague Spring. Given the cold war atomic bomb standoff, there was really nothing we or our NATO allies could do apart from issuing strong verbal protests and denunciations of the invasion. We did not repeat the unfortunate fiasco of 1957, when, incredibly, the CIA encouraged a Hungarian uprising that caused the deaths of hundreds of brave freedom fighters and we were able to do nothing to help.

The invasion did have a small dividend for me. The president wanted to reassure Yugoslavian president Marshal Tito of our support without making any commitment to that effect, so he sent me to Belgrade, where I met with President Tito and members of his government. Averell Harriman knew Tito personally—they were roughly the same age—and I conveyed Averell's personal greetings as well as those of LBJ. Like many dictators, Tito was quite charming when meeting with an official from another country, and we got on quite well. He was not really concerned about the Soviet Union, which he had defied for years, and he thought the Soviets had bitten off a lot more than they could easily digest in Czechoslovakia. My visit was scarcely necessary to reassure him, but perhaps it served to annoy the Soviets a little.

Even though we had thought the invasion likely, coming as it did during our election period, it could not help being something of a blow to LBJ and to Hubert Humphrey as well. The president was hoping to have a final summit with Kosygin that would jump-start disarmament talks, and that was now impossible in the short time remaining. With the Vietnam talks stalled in Paris, Humphrey desperately needed some good initiative to inspire Democratic Party liberals, and what he was getting was anything but. The disadvantage of running for president when you are vice president is the difficulty of establishing your own persona and not simply being seen as the president's person. You have to defend the administration and can scarcely attack the president. So anything that hurt LBJ hurt Humphrey, and Humphrey could not bring himself to demonstrate a measure of independence until it was too late.

The election was a disappointment, not because I wanted to stay in government, but because I felt that the last eight years deserved better treatment from the public. There had been major accomplishments, but our failure to achieve peace in Vietnam and the residue of white racial resentment topped LBJ's Great Society accomplishments. George Wallace took the South away and revealed by his large third-party vote how much racial prejudice remained—and not only in the South. Perhaps the American public did not fully understand that the commitment to racial equality for African Americans, like all political commitments, required adjustments in our way of living.

Apart from bringing the *Pueblo* crew home for Christmas, I can recall only two events of interest. We had worked hard to devise some small but positive steps toward restoring relations with China and finally had come up with some plans that seemed to me and my staff useful and imaginative. LBJ, however, had been firm that we should take no new initiatives after the election. I told him the Republicans might welcome our doing so. If it did not work, they could blame us; if it worked, they had something to build on. He told me to take it up with Nixon's people. I sent the papers we had prepared to Henry Kissinger for his opinion, confident that he would see their merit. I was disappointed when, after several days, he came back to me and requested that we do nothing. It seemed unlike Henry not to appreciate the approach.

In fact, I had not underestimated him. Not long after Nixon was sworn in as president and Kissinger as national security adviser, the new administration made its first overture to China. I was pleased that it was virtually verbatim the approach we had proposed.

The other initiative was one that pleased me, and it came as a result of something Dean Rusk said to me. One day shortly after the election he said that he wished something could be done to restore the security clearance of John Paton Davies, Jr., a China expert who, along with others, had been a victim of the McCarthy attacks on the "Communists" in the department in the Eisenhower regime. Davies's sin was to predict that Mao would be successful in defeating Chiang Kai-shek. Despite repeated clearances of Davies in security hearings in the department, Secretary John Foster Dulles, albeit reluctantly, had succumbed to right-wing pressure and fired him. Rusk said he would like to see it put right, but for reasons he did not disclose, he could not be involved. Would I look into it.

I got in touch with Davies, who was in Washington, and then with his lawyer. There were all kinds of technical complexities and very little time. What I wanted to accomplish was a top-secret security clearance for Davies. The fastest way to do it seemed to be to have him hired as a consultant whose employer could request the clearance. The Arms Control and Disarmament Agency (ACDA) had a lot of outside contractors, and the head of the agency was more than willing to join our secret conspiracy. The contractor he selected was MIT, which was also an enthusiastic participant. It did not really make any difference if Davies ever actually did any work. The important thing was that he would be cleared to do so. This meant that the department would have to review the enormous files accumulated during his service and prior hearings and forward them with a recommendation to the Arms Control and Disarmament Agency, which would do its own review and make a decision Despite the paperwork, I saw no problem. The department, I felt sure, would want to see justice done to one of its own.

But I found out that the fear so carelessly paraded by Senator McCarthy was not yet dead. The administrative people kept dragging their feet, and January arrived without a transmittal to ACDA. I kept pushing and eventually lost my temper with the delays. Finally the information got to ACDA, with State's positive recommendation. I talked with ACDA, and officials there saw no problem in arriving at the same conclusion, although they had not yet done so. I decided that was enough. Since ACDA could not yet issue a press release (but would back me up), and after consulting with Davies's lawyer, I decided for the second time in my government career to leak a story intentionally to the press.

I wanted a reporter unfamiliar with Davies and the problems of the China hands in the department, and I wanted the story removed from the Washington scene. I selected Hedrick Smith of the *New York Times* and invited him to my office. I told him simply that the department had cleared John Davies to do top-secret work on an ACDA contract with MIT and that the story was exclusively his for twenty-four hours. I think he was somewhat baffled, but he also knew he must have something important. He did not let me down. Within the deadline, a front-page story appeared that laid out the whole sorry history and featured Davies's vindication more than a decade after he was fired.

I felt it was one of the few concrete things I got done in the department. Dean Rusk was pleased too.

Apart from that leak, the final days were boring and inactive. Kissinger asked for a list of a dozen or so outstanding Foreign Service officers, and I prepared one for him. Since I thought it unfair to give Henry all the best talent, I sent the same list to the incoming secretary of state, William Rogers. I knew Rogers slightly from conversations I had had with him on Justice Department matters, going back to his days as deputy AG and attorney general. I also asked him to use Clyde Herndon as his principal driver—an easy sell, since he knew Clyde from the Justice Department. I spent a little time with my successor, Elliott Richardson, whom I was delighted to see take over as undersecretary. I attended a big reception honoring Dean Rusk. On the morning of January 20, I headed for Armonk, New York, to take over my duties as IBM's general counsel.

I had enjoyed my eight years in the Kennedy and Johnson administrations. There had been successes and there had been failures, victories and defeats, joys and sadness. The country had changed—mostly, I thought, for the better, but only time would tell. All my life I had thought of government as the most interesting and exciting profession one could pursue. In a democracy, government requires political skills as well as governmental ones, but it is important to keep in mind the relationship. You use politics and public relations to promote governmental policies, not government to promote political success. Polls are important in informing officials of the difficulties a policy may encounter and the need for leadership and persuasion. They do not tell you what is right or wise or just.

Even today I take satisfaction from the progress we made on race and feel disappointment and sadness from the failure to end the venture in Vietnam, with so many unnecessary deaths long before it eventually collapsed. All of it, failure as well as success, was hard work.

But some of it was fun.

Epilogue

ALMOST FORTY YEARS HAVE PASSED SINCE I SERVED IN GOVERNMENT. Unlike some officials, I did not exit through a revolving door, did not remain in Washington, did not lobby. I have testified a few times before congressional committees at their request but have not otherwise been directly involved. My interest in government has not diminished, though obviously my information has. I cannot even assume that insider swagger which seems to attach to those who live inside the Beltway.

In November 2001 I was invited to attend the naming of the Justice Department building after Bobby. I was hesitant about accepting, because it seemed to me so incongruous for the Bush administration to be honoring RFK, although I had a vague impression that Senator Kennedy had been seeking such recognition for his brother. Further, I was in Martha's Vineyard for the Thanksgiving holidays, and getting from there to Washington was not easy. I talked to Burke Marshall, and while he shared my hesitation, we knew how much our presence would mean to Ethel, and so we decided to go. Early on November 20, which would have been Bobby's seventy-fifth birthday, I chartered a small plane for the trip. I picked up Burke and Bobby Kennedy, Jr., in Connecticut and headed for Dulles International Airport.

Attorney General John Ashcroft had invited a number of us to lunch in his office, which had been Bobby's and mine, so after clearing the elaborate security arrangements at the building's entrance, we headed for the fifth floor. In the hall outside the AG's office—inside they were preparing for the luncheon—were a few senators and congressmen, including Ted Kennedy and some of Bobby's former assistants: Lou Oberdorfer,

John Douglas, Joe Dolan, John Nolan, Jack Miller, Bill Geoghegan, and others. It should have felt like Old Home Week, but it did not.

The luncheon was pleasant. Ashcroft welcomed everyone warmly, and Teddy made a quite witty response while thanking the AG for his hospitality. We were then escorted to a conference room, where Teddy brought in the president and introduced us all, one by one, to Mr. Bush. After he had shaken our hands, we went to the Great Hall for the dedication ceremony. On the podium were President Bush, Ethel Kennedy, the attorney general, Joe Kennedy (Bobby's oldest son), Senator Kennedy, and the administrator of the General Services Administration. The statue of Justice was still there, unfamiliarly draped to avoid exposure of her aluminum breasts to prying eyes. I found a seat in the middle of the audience, next to the Oberdorfers and directly behind Joe Dolan. In the middle of the front row was former attorney general Edwin Meese, which, given his views on civil rights, struck me as somewhat insensitive.

Ashcroft spoke briefly, praising Bobby for his fight against organized crime, which he compared with the war on terror. Joe Kennedy warmly—too warmly for my taste—praised as well as thanked President Bush. The president then made a short speech praising Bobby for his many contributions to government and to his brother's administration. He referred positively to civil rights by mentioning the 1964 Act and the Freedom Riders, and then he formally named the building for Robert F. Kennedy. Shortly after three o'clock we were on our way home.

I have described the simple ceremony in some detail because nothing was said or done that in any way was inconsistent with honoring Bobby in a manner that we all appreciated. Yet for some time thereafter I was depressed by the whole affair. I think it was because at no point did anyone, even briefly, describe the Bobby I knew and the department he headed. The speakers—I am sure inadvertently—made it appear routine, business as usual, with a little humor but with none of the energy, the excitement, the hope that permeated the building in the early sixties. What, I wondered, is government if it cannot seek to realize the hopes and aspirations of the governed? It may not succeed, but it must try.

When I read about the sixties, I find them described as tumultuous, with violence, riots, demonstrations, sit-ins, arrests, political assassinations, student unrest over Vietnam, and so forth. All true, but that is not how I remember them. More important, they were a time of hope, of shared aspirations for a better America. I think of Dr. King leading hundreds of black citizens, tired of racial discrimination and of being treated as second-class citizens, to assert their rights in the certain knowledge of arrests, beatings, and police brutality. I think of the Freedom Riders, blacks and whites riding integrated buses with knowledge of the dangers they were courting from southern authorities. I think of the young people going south to help blacks register to vote, the murders of Goodman, Cheney, and Schwerner for trying to help others exercise constitutional rights to which all of us are entitled. I think of the dignity of both whites and blacks in the March on Washington, proclaiming the need for this country to live up to its great democratic tradition. I think of students protesting a war they did not understand or approve of. I think of nations all around the globe seeing us vindicate our beliefs about human equality and individual worth in the face of opposition and looking to us for leadership to a better world.

But most of all I think of this nation coming together, finally, to face up to our problems and try to live up to our principles; of Republicans and Democrats working together to attempt to solve a racial problem as old as our democracy; of Congressman William McCulloch of Ohio, with absolutely no political gain for himself but with a conscience and a sense that Congress must represent all the people, leading the way in the House to the passage of the 1964 Civil Rights Act; of the party of Lincoln, with Senator Dirksen from Lincoln's Illinois, acting with determination and courage. Had Republicans left the problem to the administration and Democrats, there would have been no solution, and the rule of law would have been immeasurably damaged.

Those were the thoughts I had during and after the naming of the Justice Department for my friend and leader. I longed for rhetoric about what this country could be, how we could work together, how together we could face up to and solve our problems. I longed for an end to partisan bickering and political confrontation, and for a restoration of leadership that sought to persuade, not unilaterally seek to have its own way and thereby divide. If we had learned anything from the tumultuous sixties, it was that racial problems could not be resolved effectively by a judicial elite but required the voice of the people and the hard work of a bipartisan Congress to put policy into law; and that a president, however sincere and determined, could not conduct a war without the support and understanding of the Congress and, through it, the people. The leadership of President Kennedy and President Johnson worked when it was open and designed to persuade, as in civil rights, the Cuban missile crisis, and the Great Society programs, and it failed—in the Bay of Pigs and Vietnam—when the Congress and the public were not an essential part of the policy.

Looking back on the 1960s, I take satisfaction in what we, together with so many others, did, and what we attempted to do, with respect to civil rights. I had hoped that in a generation, race would no longer be an issue and there would be genuine equal opportunity for all. Sadly, we have not yet climbed to the top of that mountain. Racial discrimination is far less rampant, far less venal, and rarely overt. To a large extent it has been driven underground, but it still exists to a far greater degree than we like to admit. While we have succeeded in opening doors to a growing black middle class in business, the professions, and the arts, there remains a large black underclass. I take great satisfaction and pride in our political process when I see many African American elected officials, particularly at the state and local level, two Supreme Court justices and two secretaries of state, a few CEOs, many fine actors in the movies and on TV, doctors and lawyers and accounting professionals, engineers and architects, and even a serious candidate for president. But there are also an inordinate number of blacks in prison, on welfare, and among the unemployed. That fact helps prolong our historical racial bias born of slavery and undermines the huge progress toward genuine equality we have made.

In 1968, George Wallace ran for president on a third-party ticket, carried five southern states, and received some 10 million votes. He did not run as a segregationist, but he knew how to appeal to bias without raising race directly. He did so by talking of crime, welfare, and lack of values, in each mention conjuring up a vision of inferior blacks. His success in attracting votes was not lost on other politicians, and those kinds of subtle appeals to bias have been shamefully present in every election since. We all remember the first George Bush and Willie Horton, the black on work-release who committed a crime when he was released, whose race was never mentioned but whose picture was well publicized. Penalties for nonviolent crime such as drug use were increased and sentences made mandatory in a crude attack on crime. It is not lost on most supporters of "get tough on crime" legislation that blacks are disproportionately the victims of long prison sentences; law enforcement pays less attention to the fact that they are also disproportionately the victims of crime.

The Republicans largely took over the Democratic solid South, as expected, and while that gain removed a conservative element from the Democratic Party, it also removed a balance wheel which, except on racial issues, tended to push both parties toward the center. In the 1960s, southerners exercised power in the Democratic Party by virtue of their seniority and committee chairmanships, were a conservative influence on the party, and more often than not voted with Republicans.

Republicans, as part of their southern strategy, put the brakes on affirmative action programs designed to help poorer blacks compete and talked states' rights, the language of segregation. What bothered me most was their use of Dr. King's dream of a color-blind society as though we had achieved that dream, and then its invocation to block programs helping blacks on the ground that somehow a white government and white power establishment was wrongly discriminating against whites whenever it helped blacks. In the 1980s politicians played on bias by suggesting that unqualified blacks were getting jobs and promotions, or being admitted to colleges, in place of far better qualified whites, or were somehow committing fraud, like President Reagan's imaginary welfare queen in her white Cadillac. No one in fact ever urged employing or promoting an unqualified worker because of skin color, but the myth persisted. Even the Supreme Court, which had led the way to desegregation, capitulated to some degree by viewing affirmative action in a negative light. In *University of California Regents v. Bakke*, Justice Powell, joined by a new majority, found that somehow equal protection of the laws, part of the post–Civil War Fourteenth Amendment, protected whites as well as blacks from discrimination—not precisely what that war had been fought about. As a consequence, some programs designed to help blacks were in danger of being found unconstitutionally to hurt whites.

What made all of these arguments acceptable to so many was the fact that they could be entertained without any conscious bias against African Americans. The argument that achievement on the basis of merit was being denied to whites in order to assist less competent blacks can persuade because on its face it appeals to fairness and equal opportunity, not bias. Thus efforts to create a level playing field, which is the essence of equal opportunity, were often defeated simply because it was unthinkingly assumed that we already had one.

Our public schools are still largely segregated, and those that are predominantly or exclusively black often offer inferior educational programs. Unhappily, economic factors continue to divide races with respect to housing, and therefore neighborhood schools remain segregated. Poor black families, often with a single parent, cannot offer the supplemental educational advantages of the well-to-do, and we need much more attention to preschool and after-school programs to close the gap. Our sophisticated economy depends on an educated population, and we are penny wise and pound foolish to starve this obvious priority.

We are nevertheless moving toward Dr. King's dream, and our direction cannot be reversed, however dissatisfied I am with the pace of progress. I am pleased as well by the increasing role of women in government, business, and the professions. Here, I suppose, credit should go to Judge Howard Smith, who led the southern opposition in the House of

Representatives to the 1964 civil rights bill and who introduced equality of women into it, not because women deserved unbiased treatment but in a cynical attempt to defeat the bill. I regret to say that we opposed his amendment in the thought that he might be right in its effect, but happily, we failed, and the amendment became law. Again progress has been slower than it needed to have been, as men have resisted the entry of women into traditionally male jobs. I recall that even when I worked for such an enlightened company as IBM, there was resistance to hiring women to sell typewriters because they would have to carry a heavy demonstration model on their sales calls.

In many ways I think the movement of women into what was thought of as the male marketplace has been of far more significance than we customarily accord it. The nation benefited from a huge infusion of educated talent into the economy (as had happened in World War II on a temporary basis while the men were fighting abroad) at a time when our economy was coming to depend more and more on just such talent. As a consequence, their entry greatly assisted our economic growth. It undoubtedly had unintended side effects as well, which have caused political problems today. The existing pool of educated women entering the workplace may well have caused us to pay less attention to improving education for the poor. Together with our repressed white bias and segregated schools, it may have contributed to keeping the pipeline of educated people inadequate for our growing economic needs. Further stimulated by new technology that required more intelligence than muscle, our society has reaped the benefits of having increasing numbers of women in a service economy, a development that has caused profound changes in our culture and many traditional values. It has changed our views of sexual relations and affected family stability. Surely a significant measure of the growth of conservative ideology has been fueled by the difficulties of adjusting to this rapid and necessary change, which has unavoidably had an impact on long-held convictions about life, marriage, church, and family. Change is never easy to absorb, and most of us have occasionally wished we could turn the clock back to something more familiar. Judge Smith, I am sure, would be most unhappy with the changes that have occurred, not as a consequence of his amendment but as a consequence of shifting values and perspectives in our society, to which the Congress properly reacted at the time and from which all of us, male and female, have benefited enormously.

In our democracy we depend on elected officials to determine policy and executive officials to respect and enforce that policy fairly, even if they would prefer a different policy and a different result. While we depend heavily on an independent judiciary to correct those officials if they fail to enforce the laws as written by Congress, far more important is the role of lawyers, and especially the Department of Justice, in doing so. As the final arbiter within the administration, it cannot be partisan either in its enforcement of the law or in its interpretation of the words of a statute embodying our national policy. Its performance has not always been perfect, and sometimes, especially in recent years, it has been deplorable, but if we do not honestly adhere to the rule of law, we destroy that which underlies the freedom on which democracy depends.

We sometimes forget that our Constitution is largely concerned with process, not results. It is the process that is designed to protect our freedoms, and adherence to law is essential to that process. But if we do not also face our problems and seek to solve them with legislation, public frustration can endanger the process. So much attention is focused today on elections and so much money and organizational time is spent to gain the support of officials for particular viewpoints that those elected to Congress are losing their independent judgment and substituting that of constituents whose money has made their campaign successful. Representing the viewpoint of constituents on matters of policy is, of course, what elections are all about. But adopting a policy perspective because one person or group, often not even voters within a candidate's state or district, makes important campaign contributions comes too close to selling public office. The extent to which money can exert political influence endangers democracy, and it is essential that we find ways of limiting its effect. When financial contributions result in commitment to a viewpoint for reasons of past or future financial support rather than honest conviction, they tend to make rational discussion more difficult, defeat reasonable compromise, and destroy a government "by the people."

Today the most serious problem facing the country is finding the proper role for Congress in determining policy through a rational approach to problems, particularly where national security is involved. Finding a way to engage the Congress and through Congress the public on these important matters is not easy. Since much of our security depends on foreign policy, the executive is bound to have a leading role. That was the case during the cold war's nuclear standoff, but the public understood, at least in general terms, our policy of Communist containment, and both political parties supported measures to that end. Unfortunately, there may have been more delegation of authority to the executive than necessary, and accountability was by no means as stringent as I would find desirable. Too much secrecy has surrounded our activities overseas for many years, mainly as a consequence of the cold war, and continues unabated. During the cold war we at least understood and supported the basic objectives of our foreign policy. With the disintegration of the Soviet Union and the end of the cold war, how to cope with the threat to our security from terrorist organizations and their state sponsors is far less clear. As yet, there is little public understanding of how we plan to attain our foreign policy objectives, or even what they are.

I have no difficulty accepting the need for presidential leadership in foreign affairs. I have no difficulty putting our national security at the top of the list of governmental responsibilities. I understand that preserving the national security depends greatly on the skill with which we conduct our relations with other nations.

What I cannot accept is that this is somehow the sole responsibility of the president or that he or she alone determines and carries out that policy. Leadership in a democracy does not equate with the power to decide but rather with the power to persuade others with rational argument. Responsibility must be shared with Congress and through Congress with the people, and must, like all policy in a democracy, be restrained by law. Today there is far too much totally unnecessary secrecy surrounding our policy and our efforts—and secrecy is the enemy of shared values and the friend of governmental blunders.

We used to say that partisanship stopped at the water's edge—and with good reason. We simply cannot have an effective foreign policy that is not supported by a stable majority of Americans and, in its essentials, by both political parties. There cannot be a flip-flop with a change of leadership or party. Continuity in seeking long-term results is necessary to successful leadership in the international community. The president and the Congress need each other, and the American people need both, acting together if we are to be reasonably secure.

Effective foreign policy really requires not a president with great formal power but a president whose policies are understood and supported by Congress and the public. That requires intelligent leadership. Of equal importance and even greater difficulty, it also requires Congress to get its house in order and have the courage to play a useful role. It cannot act as a rubber stamp for presidential proposals or a mindless critic of them. It must see its role not simply as one of partisan advantage but as promoting bipartisan support and public understanding, and seeing the merits of points made by a thoughtful opposition and accommodating them where possible.

It is vital that Congress play a constructive role, and the president should help it do so. We can be partisan about many things, but we must preserve the constitutional process that permits a democratic society to determine its own policies and its own future and to come together in the process. Differences can be healthy or destructive. That depends on our capacity to listen, to debate, to tolerate differences, to admit mistakes, and to seek compromise where there is merit in dissent. It also depends on honesty and integrity and results determined by rational thought with knowledge and understanding of the facts, not simply the power of money to work one's will.

Today I think the words uttered by President Eisenhower in his first inaugural address have a special force. He said, "We Americans know and we observe the difference between world leadership and imperialism, between firmness and truculence, between a thoughtfully calculated goal and spasmodic reaction to the stimulus of emergencies."

Do we? I hope so.

Acknowledgments

A<small>N INITIAL DRAFT OF THIS MEMOIR WAS READ BY</small> W<small>ILLIAM</small> G. B<small>OWEN</small>, an outsider, and Jack Rosenthal, a participant, and both made comments from their different perspectives. My son John, his wife, Madeleine Blais, and my daughter Maria, all experienced writers, were also helpful. My son Chris and daughter Anne contributed memories and thoughts. Marcia Snowden went over the whole draft, carefully correcting many errors of punctuation, grammar, and obtuse writing. Bruce Oudes, who was a reporter on my trip through Africa, read that chapter and made some useful corrections. My wife, Lydia, who knows most of my bad habits, helped me correct them before they were too embedded in the text and reminded me of incidents I had forgotten or inadvertently omitted. My editor, Drake McFeely, was gentle and encouraging while doing an editor's job to perfection, for which I am most appreciative.

Despite their efforts I am sure some recollections are imperfectly recalled or described, and the responsibility is, of course, mine.

Illustration Credits

Index